BRITISH PAMPHLETEERS
VOLUME TWO

BRITISH PAMPHLETEERS

A peep into the Cave of Jacobinism.__"Magna est Veritas et prævalebit"

BRITISH
Pamphleteers

VOLUME TWO
FROM THE FRENCH REVOLUTION
TO THE NINETEEN-THIRTIES

EDITED BY

Reginald Reynolds
WITH AN INTRODUCTION BY A. J. P. Taylor

LONDON
Allan Wingate
MCMLI

First published 1951 *by*
ALLAN WINGATE (PUBLISHERS) LTD.
12 *Beauchamp Place, London, S.W.*3.

Made and Printed in Great Britain by
Tonbridge Printers Ltd.
Tonbridge

CONTENTS

CONTENTS

LIST OF ILLUSTRATIONS

INTRODUCTION

By A. J. P. Taylor

THE subject of this anthology is British pamphleteers, not British pamphlets. Its aim is to display some remarkable individuals; not to illustrate the development of a particular literary form. Or perhaps it would be truer to say that the pamphlet becomes literature only when it is written by a remarkable individual. The ordinary pamphlet does not merit resurrection. It is designed to be read quickly and to be thrown away. Like the bee, it can only sting once. Yet anyone who recollects the Labour movement in its missionary days thirty or forty years ago must look back with some nostalgia to the 'literature' stall where pamphlets by Lenin, Blatchford, Daniel De Leon, Walton Newbold, and the secretary of the Vegetarian Society were indiscriminately displayed. 'Don't forget the literature, Comrades!' was the last, the parting cry of the chairman; it took the place of the Blessing at more orthodox gatherings. Now the chairman's voice is silent (unless he is presiding over the Board of a nationalised industry); and the 'literature' is forgotten. Nowhere in the world is there a complete collection of the stuff; no one anywhere will ever read it through. Something has survived! the best of it reprinted here. It has survived, by virtue of its literary excellence; preserved, as it were, from destruction by the strong spirits of individualism which soak through these pages. It is agreeable to reflect how enraged the authors of these pamphlets would be if they were ever to know that one day people would read them merely for fun.

Individualism is the essence of the successful pamphlet. It is the most immediate and the most personal of all literary forms; the Hyde Park of the written word. The writer of a pamphlet has a single idea to express and is in a hurry to express it; usually he thinks in terms of addressing a single reader. A pamphlet is argument or it is nothing; and it is not surprising that so many pamphlets are written in the form of dialogue—failing a more satisfactory opponent the pamphleteer has to argue with himself. Even if the pamphlet is written as straight prose, it still proceeds in terms of personal intimacy; and the reader usually finds himself addressed in the second person. You can feel the pamphleteer reaching out of the pages, buttonholing you, prodding home his points with aggressive forefinger. Sometimes you are made to feel foolish; sometimes your vanity is flattered (though the writer clearly despises you all the time); one way or another you are never allowed to forget that you are being argued at. You can be pretty sure when you pick up a pamphlet that at the end you will be expected to agree with something or to protest against something or, most usual of all, to send a subscription. It is, I suppose, true that the first pamphlets were in the nature of reprinted sermons; and the pamphlet has always retained something of the atmosphere of the pulpit, with its mixture of intimacy and exhortation.

All this, and much more, was said by George Orwell in his introduction to the first volume of British pamphleteers. Here we are concerned with something more limited: the pamphleteers of the nineteenth and early twentieth centuries. It would be hard to say whether they are better or worse than their predecessors; it is certain that they are different. Though they say more daring things, they say it in more commonplace language; though they are more individualistic, they have less to be individual about. What has happened to them is that they have won; and the moment of their victory is the French revolution, which quite rightly marks the division between our first volume and our second. Until the time of the French revolution, the individual who was out of step knew that he was threatened; that he had to keep up the attack in order to hold his own at all. Defoe might enter the pay of William III; and Swift might accept a Deanery from Queen Anne. They still belonged to a secret conspiracy, the sect of those who thought for themselves. Samuel Johnson, despite his supposedly orthodox views, was the last of the old school. No one can read Johnson, even when he was justifying Lord North's treatment of America, without realising that here was a man fighting desperately against great odds to hold his own. When Johnson gets a pension from George III, we are not so much shocked as surprised – staggered indeed at the incongruity. No one would be surprised if Carlyle got a pension from Queen Victoria; indeed it would be curious if he did not. All the authors in this book are individualists for whom rebellion has paid big dividends. If they had remained respectable and conformist, no one would ever have heard of them; and their bank balances would have been very much smaller. I observe from Mr Reynold's note that the author of the last pamphlet in this book lost his post as a lecturer at Swansea University College after the action which he describes. This does not prove that individual opinions are dangerous; it only proves that the Welsh are intolerant – more backward than the English, in fact, which it was the argument of the pamphlet to refute. If Mr Saunders Lewis achieved the independent Wales of his dreams, he would undoubtedly be flung into prison, if not burnt alive. As it is, his martyrdom (thanks to English protection) has been gentle in the extreme; after all no one can regard the position of a lecturer at Swansea University College as something of which one is deprived with regret.

It is worth considering why individualism did the trick at the time of the French revolution, and what the trick is that it has done. The secret I believe to be this. The earlier pamphleteers praised by George Orwell, though individualistic, did not extol individualism as a good in itself; they extolled it for the rewards it would bring. The Protestant, however extreme, did not say: 'It is desirable that every single person should have a religion different from that of everyone else.' He said: 'The judgment of the individual will lead him to a religion which will be finer, purer, truer – which will be, in fact, remarkably like mine'. The Protestants of the seventeenth century used to puzzle a good deal what they should do if the individual's judgment led him to believe in the Devil, or even in no religion at all. The 'inner light' was recognised as an admirable illumination only so long as my voltage was the same as yours. Even now Quakers who take to drink or divorce or even to an enthusiasm for the Mass are not easily accommodated within the Society of Friends. The French revolution changed all that. Liberty was demanded for its own sake, not for what it would produce. This is really the only argument by which liberty can be justified. It is humbug, for instance, to suppose that scientists produce better results if they are allowed to ramble over the Universe on their own than if they are organised in high-grade concentration camps. Both Russian and American scientists are chained by the leg, the one to the secret police, the other to their dollar-balances; but they are doing very well as scientists all the same. They can keep up the bidding indefinitely until between them they bring civilised life to an end. The English scientist, in comparison, is quite a harmless creature.

The argument is just as true of literature, thought, or the arts. Spain produced great art at the height of the Inquisition; French civilisation flourished under the absolutism of Louis XIV; Mozart and Beethoven managed to compose great music under the dead hand of the Habsburgs. Freedom is not justified of its fruits. Why should it be? It is justified of itself. This was the great achievement of the French revolution. It launched the irresistible doctrine of human Rights. The Established order does very well so long as it can keep up an air of superiority and can make rebels appear tiresome, insignificant people. Even the greatest rebels were weighed down by their fault. For instance, it never occurred to Milton or to any of his contemporaries that Satan was the hero of his poem; to us it is so obvious as hardly to be worth saying. The English rebels of the seventeenth century had to devise all sorts of imaginary crimes in order to justify their execution of Charles I. By the nineteenth century a rebel could propose as a matter of course his admirable objective 'to strangle the last King with the bowels of the last priest'. And once he had coined the phrase he did not need to put his precept into action – no kings were in fact strangled in Europe in the nineteenth century or even executed. A Tsar was assassinated in Russia; that only proves its remoteness from Europe. After the French revolution the bottom fell out of the Establishment. It had to go over to the defensive, and a very half-hearted defensive at that. France, for instance, became divided into the party of movement and the party of resistance; a very revealing distinction. Who would be against movement for its own sake? Genuine conservatism disappeared. What has called itself conservatism in the last hundred years has merely consisted in putting a brake on 'the march of progress'; at best conservatism has defended the liberal achievements of the previous generation.

It is very nice to feel yourself on the winning side; and the individual has been very much on the winning side for the last century and a half in our European civilisation. John Stuart Mill or Victor Hugo or Mazzini said daring things; but nothing could stop them becoming the most respected citizens of their countries. In our own day Bernard Shaw spent an inordinately long lifetime trying to shock public opinion on every conceivable subject. He left the largest fortune of any contemporary writer; and his tasteless suburban house has become a national shrine. George Orwell, who wrote the admirable introduction to the first volume of this work, wanted to be a rebel all his life; when he died, tragically young, he was a best-seller in two continents. Long ago David really marched out to challenge Goliath. Nowadays Goliath welcomes David to the field; picks up the pebbles for him; and then falls down flat before the sling is discharged. Talk about 'dare to be a Daniel; dare to stand alone!' It is impossible to be alone, if you are a Daniel. The lion's den is close crammed; except, of course, for the lion. He is out hunting food for the Daniels.

Agreeable as is the life of a Daniel under such circumstances, it has its disadvantages. The Daniels of to-day are no more conformist in spirit than their predecessors; it is the age which has conformed to them. The desire to be out of step remains; and the agility of foot required for this becomes greater and greater. It is difficult to be both advanced and unpopular in an age which has seen such oddities as the voluntary recognition by this country of the Irish and Indian republics; a Labour government with a large majority; the hanging of the principal Nazi leaders; Bertrand Russell an O.M. and the principal sage of British broadcasting. As a result the adventurous individual has to get increasingly odd and queer in his views. You can see the process at work in this volume – the chase for eccentricity getting ever more difficult, as the rewards for eccentricity mount ever higher. One solution of this problem, the most paradoxical of all, is to astonish everyone by remaining upright instead of standing on your head. This is why our gayest and most irresponsible characters are to be found writing leaders for respectable Conservative papers or producing novels in favour of the Roman Catholic Church. Mr Betjeman, most daring of all, actually patronises the Church of England. This is a good line, and has been spotted as such by acute intellects for some time. It is curious that even Mr Reynolds has been taken in by it. He is himself something of a connoisseur in the individual and daring; yet when it comes to the really adventurous pamphlets in this volume, he is shocked by them and dismisses them as nonsense. Though, for my part, I do not care much for Carlyle's style, I find his pamphlet on 'the Nigger Question' a thousand times more sensible than Edward Carpenter's soft-headed ramblings. Carpenter, it seems to me, was individualism at its worst. He really thought that if he let his beard grow, wore homespun tweeds, lived on grated carrots and preached (though without much practice) free love, he became a remarkable man. No one can share this belief who has tried to struggle through his prose.

Now Carlyle was a remarkable man, though in many ways a detestable one. With Scottish clarity and cynicism he realised, almost the first, that the game of straight individualism was played out; and so turned himself into the champion of intolerance, despotism, and obscurantism. All the same he was too great a man not to be sensible occasionally; and his pamphlet here stands like an oasis of profundity among the sands of the Quaker Pease and the muscular curate Kingsley. It needed penetration as well as daring to understand, in the age of individualism and emancipation, that little would be achieved for the negroes of the West Indies merely by abolishing slavery; the history of the West Indies in the hundred odd years since then has proved Carlyle right and the abolitionists wrong. Or rather the abolitionists were too high-minded even to be wrong: though they detested slavery, they did not care for the slaves, and, once slavery was abolished, they were indifferent to what happened afterwards. Mr Reynolds, I suspect, dislikes Carlyle's pamphlet from its relevance to our own day. Carlyle's 'Quashee' is no longer confined to a few West Indian islands; and, much as our hearts glow at the destruction of the British Raj, they will glow less as the vast Indian continent gradually sinks back into the anarchy and violence from which it was preserved by a century and a half of British rule.

Take another example from this volume. Brougham on reform is all very well; and it brought him a good life into the bargain. But is Sydney Smith on the ballot, or rather against it, such rubbish as Mr Reynolds makes out? Would Hitler have succeeded without the ballot-box? At least it did nothing to stop him. Probably Sydney Smith attached too much importance to the ballot; probably Gresham's Law will operate in politics and the bad defeat the good with the ballot or without. But at least Sydney Smith did not think that everything would be perfect if only we had a system of universal suffrage, combined with secret voting. The fresh air of common sense blows through his admirable prose. Or again, William Hone on George IV is highly entertaining; it was well worth doing at the time. But who now cares for George IV's infidelities, or even for those of Queen Caroline? On the other hand, George IV was the only King of England who did anything to make his capital beautiful; and, looking at the work of John Nash which George IV inspired, there can be no two answers to the question – which King of England did most good and deserves to be remembered with most gratitude? It was the elderly lecher, once a figure of fun, now a king without a rival.

It is the nature of pamphlets to provoke disagreement. Mr Reynolds and I seem to have managed between us to have disagreed with every one of them. Our pleasure in them is no whit the less. But every man has his boiling point, the moment at which eccentricity ceases to be funny or even engaging and becomes merely malicious and irresponsible. I have, I fear, sometimes provoked this reaction in others; and therefore it is deserved that it should be here provoked in me. For my conscience would be offended were I not to make it clear, in all seriousness, that – to my mind – Mr Brailsford's pamphlet on the origins of World War I is an example of British complacency at its worst, as well as being bad history. It is easy to understand how British pamphleteers, with a century and a half of wrongheadedness behind them, were tempted to keep out of step even when their country became involved in war with Germany. This was admirable so long as their criticism was confined to the reputation of their own rulers. After all the government which trod down the Easter rebellion in Ireland was not the most perfect champion of Belgian independence. Still, this independence was being championed; and even the most contrary hesitated to argue that Belgium would be better off under German rule (though Mr Brailsford seems to have done his best in a pamphlet not reprinted here). Instead British complacency took it out on the Serbs. How enlightened and how daring to argue that the Serbs were really much better off under Austrian rule, representing 'an older and maturer civilisation'! How challenging (though untrue) to state that the Serbs in Austria-Hungary had Home Rule! It is not surprising that most of the leading members of the Union of Democratic Control, which sponsored this pamphlet, ended up as cabinet ministers. To use a phrase of Johnson's in another connexion, this British cleverness at the expense of others is mighty offensive. Mr Brailford has often criticised British Imperialism in India; more recently he has criticised American Imperialism in Korea. But when it comes to German-Austrian Imperialism in the Balkans, he can only find it 'alien, but relatively civilised'. It is one thing to say: 'the government of my country is always wrong'. It is quite another to say: 'the enemies of my country are always right'. It is more likely that all governments are pretty bad, and that our government, exposed as it is to the constant harrying of the eccentrics, is rather better than the others. At any rate, it is certain that no one who values intellectual freedom would choose any other country to live in.

There are, of course, some limitations on that complacent judgment. It may be true, as George Orwell suggested in his introduction, that the expression of unpopular or unusual views is becoming more difficult. I should doubt it; though I would admit that unpopular or unusual views are becoming more difficult to find. On the other hand, the practice of intellectual freedom may sink into a game and one which no one takes seriously; even this introduction may have given some excuse for doing so. In fact I care for intellectual freedom very deeply; and can think of nothing else which can make existence tolerable. The danger is not that we should abuse it; but rather that it should seem irrelevant. The greatest error of the nineteenth century, of which we are reaping the fruits, was to try to make out that freedom was good for something – usually that it would make you better off. If you had democracy and national self-determination, it was suggested that you would have more to eat. When this did not happen, the intellectuals at once began to cry out: What is the good of freedom if it does not fill your belly? The answer is simple: You are still free. I wish that Mr Reynolds had found room for a Chartist pamphlet or two, in order to remind us that not only educated and relatively well-to-do men cared for freedom. The Chartists were the one truly independent working class movement in our history; yet they cared as much for freedom as though they had been journalists, dons, or lawyers all their lives. It was middle-class writers, from Marx onwards, who told the workers that they wanted more food and better houses, not more freedom. It was the middle-class Trotsky, and the country-gentleman Lenin, who told the Russian workers that they would not mind losing their new freedom if they got Communism instead; and now it is the former theological student Stalin who tells them that they don't mind losing their freedom even if they don't get Communism. William Morris said: 'No one is good enough to be another man's master'. And I'd add: 'No one is good enough to take away another man's freedom'.

That brings us to the spook in the cupboard at any discussion of intellectual freedom – the spook at which, incidentally, George Orwell took fright towards the end of his life. The most monstrous tyranny is on the march, and not only in countries which have never known freedom; it seeks to capture the minds of the most enlightened Europeans, and often does so. In face of Communism, dare we risk intellectual freedom any more? Ought we not instead to organise anti-Communism and merely call it a Congress of Intellectual Liberty (as the Communists call their war-propaganda World Peace)? There are reasons to be frightened. For a hundred and fifty years authority, as I remarked earlier, has been on the defensive. It has had to apologise for itself; it has even had to pretend that really it was on the side of freedom, though of course in an orderly fashion. Communism is the first serious counter-offensive by the forces of authority and tyranny. Instead of apologising it claims that oppression is actually better. It either waves freedom aside as unimportant or else makes out that it does not exist. The temptation to drop every trivial difference in face of Communism is very strong; there has been no peril like it since the days of militant Islam.

All the same, it is a temptation to be shunned. So far as Communism depends simply on material power, it can be resisted only by superior power; no one in his senses would dispute that proposition. But Communism is not solely a movement of power; it is much more a disease of the mind, a perversion of the liberal world. Though you cannot argue people out of Communism, you can shake their faith in it by the general atmosphere of argument which it is still possible to breathe in the western world. I hope we shall never see anti-Communist pamphlets; and, if we do, they are not likely to merit a place in an anthology. But every pamphlet which expresses an individual opinion forcibly is, in its way, a stroke against the march of uniformity. A great deal of humbug is talked about 'the British way of life', as though it were synonymous with respectability and good taste. The British way of life, at its best, has meant a great deal that was disreputable, irresponsible, and explosive; in fact the outstanding merit of the British way of life is that there is no British way of life. There is solely the practice of intellectual freedom, which is common to all humanity. The only way to defend freedom is to assert it; and no one has asserted it better than the British pamphleteers of the last century and a half. He who cares for freedom will do well to remember the chairman's cry: 'Don't forget the literature, Comrades!' Hence this volume is presented not only as a collection of literature in the stricter sense. It is presented also as a display of freedom, and a justification for it.

ACKNOWLEDGMENTS

We gratefully acknowledge the help of many in compiling this second volume. Kind permission was given for the use of copyright material by Mr Gilbert Beith and his fellow Executors, in the case of the pamphlet by Edward Carpenter; and we are indebted to Mr Laurence Housman for our use of his pamphlet, *The Bawling Brotherhood*, to Mr H. N. Brailsford and the Union of Democratic Control for permission to reprint the *Origins of the Great War*, and to Mr Saunders Lewis who has allowed us to republish *Why We Burnt the Bombing School*.

Valuable criticisms of the notes attached to the two pamphlets by William Hone were supplied by Mrs Anne Renier from her extensive knowledge of Hone and his period. In connection with James Connolly's pamphlet we had the kind co-operation of Connolly's daughter, Mrs Nora Connolly O'Brien, of Mr William O'Brien and of Mr Desmond Ryan. Finally, in the reading of the proofs, we had the ever-willing and valuable assistance of Mr Gilbert Turner and Miss Anne Chilton

The complete disagreement between the views expressed by Mr. Taylor in his Introduction and Mr. Reynolds in his notes to the individual pamphlets will be obvious. It needs no apology and is, indeed, appropriate to a volume dealing with controversial literature. But it should be emphasised that neither writer is in any way responsible for the opinions of his collaborater.

EQUALITY

THE repercussions of the French Revolution on the political life of England were rapid and extensive. Though some of the Whigs at first welcomed the Revolution, interpreting it in terms of their own 'Glorious Revolution' of 1688, the greater number of them shared with the Tories a real terror of the popular movement in France, compared with which (as they knew very well) the events of 1688 were a mere palace intrigue.

The French Revolution differed, in fact, from all previous revolts in two important particulars. Firstly, although the democratic principles upon which it was founded gave way to the Jacobin dictatorship and eventually to the despotism of Bonaparte, the right of the people to revolt was proclaimed to the world, and the possibility of such a revolt established as a fact. Secondly, where all previous political revolutions had been purely national in character, having little traceable effect beyond the frontiers of a single country, this upheaval stirred the whole of Europe. With the exception of the Protestant revolt against the Papacy, there had been no such international movement before; and Protestantism had left the political structure of society monarchic and aristocratic. The French Revolution, which paradoxically gave birth to the modern nationalism and imperialism of France, was originally international in its principles—indeed, the history of Russia since 1917 affords a close parallel for those who are interested in such comparisons. It was not the rights of Frenchmen, as such, which the revolutionaries originally asserted, but the RIGHTS OF MAN; and it was mainly foreign intervention which perverted this initial principle into a form of patriotism (at first defensive and later aggressive) just as foreign intervention created the excuse for dictatorship and terrorism.

As these uglier aspects of the Revolution developed, those who defended the older order concentrated increasingly upon them. They either could not distinguish, or did not desire to distinguish, between revolutionary principles and their perversions. In our own time a great deal is written about 'Socialism' which may be sound criticism of Stalin, of the British Labour Government or even of Hitler (who, after all, called himself a 'National Socialist'); but it happens to be entirely irrelevant to the real issue of socialism versus capitalism. And in the time of the French Revolution the same irrelevance is to be observed—it is, in fact, the subject of our second pamphlet.

With a surer instinct, a large number of the lower middle class and the artisan class in England was stirred by the events in France. The failures and the blunders and the crimes were, after all, less important than the central fact: that the people had the right, and had demonstrated their power, to depose their rulers and change the constitution of their country. England was still governed by a small minority of the well-to-do; and the rest, a landless people in their own land, many of them living in such poverty as the present generation cannot imagine, had no voice in the government of the country. The lesson of France was therefore clear enough for all to read: political power could be achieved; and once achieved it could be used to rectify economic injustice.

How widely this view was shared it is impossible to say, except that the literature which expresses it, though extensive, is an inadequate gauge. Thousands of those who were influenced by the French Revolution must have been illiterate. Others could read a pamphlet or a newspaper, but were quite incapable of putting their own views in writing. Of those who could express themselves in this way, few had the means to do so. In view of these facts the number who wrote on this side is, in fact, surprising. History is generally written by the 'top dog', whether he is the courtly historian of the Middle Ages, the middle-class mirror of the nineteenth century plutocracy, or the Party-line pandit of the Dritte Reich and the U.S.S.R. But these impeccably orthodox writers often give us a glimpse of the movements which they seek to suppress by their vigour in denouncing them; and the amount of literature from 1789 onwards which is concerned with persuading the poor not to be misled by talk of liberty is indeed surprising. It cannot have been without some pressing sense of danger to the established order that so many members of the upper and middle classes spent so much of their time and money exhorting the labourer to be content with the social set-up.

The anonymous pamphlet which follows has been selected for its naïvety in expressing this standpoint. It is difficult to imagine a working man today being deeply impressed with the arguments used by this persuasive employer; and even perhaps in 1793, when this pamphlet was published, the 'labouring poor' suspected some catch in the sudden solicitude for their welfare which was so often shown by their employers in a similar manner. For this pamphlet is only one of hundreds

which were published between 1789 and about 1820, in which gentlemen who themselves enjoyed a good deal of liberty assured their
employees that liberty was useless if not positively harmful; while
landlords explained to their tenants how much better off they were by
not owning their own farms or houses. The intentions of the upper
classes were, it appeared, entirely philanthropic; and all that remained
unexplained was how it came about that those who worked hardest
remained poor while others remained rich without any noticeable
effort. . . . On reflection perhaps we shall find that this pamphleteer is
no more a stuffed owl than many present day writers, in spite of his
Sunday School manner.

This pamphlet was printed and sold by George Gower at Kidder-
minster (1793).

EQUALITY, AS CONSISTENT WITH THE BRITISH CONSTITUTION, IN A DIALOGUE BETWEEN A MASTER-MANUFACTURER AND ONE OF HIS WORKMEN

Anon.

Workman. Good morning, master; I am come to tell you I cannot work today.

Master. Why, John, what is the matter, are you ill?

W. No, thank God! but I have made an engagement, which I want to go to.

M. Consider, John, you have a wife and four children, who entirely depend upon you for support; and, if you remain idle but one day in the week, you lose one-sixth part of what is to subsist you and them, and you wrong your family!

W. Ah, master! what signifies a wife and children, when compared to liberty! It is to meet the friends of liberty that I am going and, when I think of the rights of man, I never think of the wrongs of my family.

M. I find then, John, you are for the new system?

W. Yes, Master? and so would you, had you read Tom Paine: he makes it quite clear that we are all born equal, and that we ought to have remained so; and that it is a shame to have kings and lords amongst a people who ought to live like brethren.

M. Indeed, John, I seldom read, except in my Bible and Ledger; it is sufficient for me to mind my shop, post my books, and take care of my affairs. On Sunday, which is a day of leisure, I go to church, and am content, without perplexing myself with different doctrines, to listen to the parson of my parish, who recommends me to live in peace, and to do as I would be done by. Yet, I own, Mr Paine's book made so much noise, that, from curiosity, I have read it, and I find nothing in it to make me alter my conduct.

W. What, master! are you an enemy to the rights of man?

M. No, John! but I am a friend to the happiness of man, and I would prevent him from exercising rights which are injurious to himself. Mr Paine has said, that every age and generation are free; but it is not the question, whether they *may*, but whether they *ought*, in prudence to use that freedom; and whether by using it they will better themselves; and, that I may be able to judge, let me know, John! of what you and your party complain.

W. Lord, master! why you know well enough we complain that some are too rich, that others are too poor, that the people are taxed to support the expenses of the king, and that the money we labour for is taken from us, and squandered in places and pensions. We dislike lords: Why should a man be a lord because his father was?—We dislike kings: Why should one man be master of so many millions, who are as good as himself?—We dislike the mode of elections: Why should not every man be entitled to a vote?—In short, provisions are too high, liberty is too low, and we would be free and equal, as they are in France.

M. Ah! John, these are numerous complaints and great grievances to be sure; but, that we may perfectly understand them, let us examine them separately. Your first complaint is, that some are too rich, and others too poor.

W. Why don't you think so, master?

M. Indeed, John, I do not: and, though there may be some exceptions, which under no government can be prevented, I believe people in general may choose whether they will be rich or poor.

W. Why, master, I choose to be rich.

M. How, John, you choose to be rich, when you are this very day going to make holiday! You earn, John, a guinea a week, which, excluding Sundays, is three shillings and sixpence a day, and, if in every week you lose a day, you lose nine pounds two shillings a year; this, in fourteen years, would make the sum of one hundred and ninety-two pounds. I believe you will confess, that, every day you make holiday, you spend on yourself as much as you miss getting: and thus, in fourteen years, you might have saved three hundred and eighty-four pounds.

W. Ah, master! every body has not the same head for these reckonings that you have.

M. Every body, John, has nearly the same head, but every body has not the same inclinations to make use of it. The idle man, who prefers pleasure to gain, says, it is but one day, and but three shillings and six-pence lost. The frugal man, who prefers gain to pleasure, says, it is an hour, and that is threepence farthing got. The first clamours against government because he remains poor through his own indolence and extravagance; the last is contented with it, because it secures to him the fruits of his industry and economy.

W. To be sure, master, there is some truth in that.

M. I began the world, John, just as you did. I was the son of a small farmer, whose condition was little better than that of a common labourer. I had learned to read and write at a charity-school. I was first porter, then clerk, and afterwards partner in the house I entered into. I am now fifty years of age, and am worth thirty thousand pounds. The laws of my country secure me in the possession of it; the king dare not touch a farthing of it: I pay taxes, it is true, and they are considerable; but I pay them as a contribution for the protection of the rest of my property: heavy as they are, they are certainly not beyond the strength of the nation, since it flourishes under them; nor is my own situation singular, since the rise and conditions of my neighbours have been and are nearly the same.

W. But certainly, master, you would pay less taxes if you were not to allow the king a million a year.

M. A great deal has been said about this million a year; but, though the sum sounds great, when examined it will not be found much: he pays out of it the judges, the foreign ambassadors, the secretaries of state, and other ministers. Without these no government ever attempted to stand, not even the new one of France: and, when these deductions are made, the sum will not be so enormous as you suppose.

Instead of a king, I will suppose a national assembly, as in France: the members I will fix at seven hundred and forty-five, as there, and the salaries of each at five hundred pounds per annum, a sum in proportion to what is allowed in France: thus, John, when we had got rid of monarchy, we should still have near four hundred thousand pounds to pay, besides supporting our judges and our ministers.

W. But then, master, if you could strike off the pensions!

M. The pensions, John, are chiefly paid out of the same million; and how far, John, do you think it would be justice or policy to reduce every man to want, who has served his country bravely and faithfully. You got drunk, I remember, John, when Rodney beat the French; you then thought he and his family deserved every thing; you now wish to make his children beggars.

W. However, master, taking away the titles would do no harm!

M. It might, John; and I am sure it would do no good. In this country, industry and frugality are the sources of everything, and their rewards cannot be too numerous; and why should I be deprived of any distinction which accompanies those qualities?

W. You, master! why you are merry, surely: you do not expect to be made a lord?

M. Certainly I do not, John; but it is not at all improbable that my children should. I have four sons; my eldest I have bred up to my own business, and I bless God that he is diligent, sober, and frugal; my second is at the Temple, and studies the law; my third is in the army; and my fourth is in the navy. It is from such as these that lords are made: the first pursues trade, purchases lands, his son becomes an esquire, is returned to parliament and, if he has abilities, may justly pretend to a peerage. The road of the others is more immediate; eloquence, skill, and valour, conduct them to eminence in their professions, and they are made lords by the same means that have promoted the whole house of peers; such has been the condition of all; and what has happened to them may happen to my children, and might to yours, if, instead of attending levelling meetings, you would work every day in the week.

W. Well, master; but, though your children may come to be lords, they can never come to be kings; and I do not see why a particular man, whether he is wise or foolish, should be made the master of so many millions?

M. I understand you, John: you do not see any reason why the crown should be hereditary. I have already told you I do not study politics much, and I fancy that is one of the reasons that I have succeeded so well in business; for two of my neighbours, who were thought to understand as much of the affairs of Europe as most men, understood, I find, so little of their own, that they have become bankrupts, and I am told will not pay three shillings in the pound. Yet, though I do not study politics, those who do are so very industrious in communicating their knowledge, that I daily hear something: when any of these come to buy at my shop, they generally turn the discourse that way; and I have learned from them that there is but one crown in Europe elective, and that is the crown of Poland; and I find that the very people, who have appeared most zealous for abolishing hereditary distinctions here, have attempted to render the crown hereditary there. You see, John, how one part of their conduct contradicts another; and hence, I conclude, that their principal object is to talk themselves, or to hear others talk of them.

Nor is the king either your master or mine, he can neither make us go here or there, to do this or that: he cannot take from us a farthing, neither he nor his minister can encroach upon the liberty of the meanest Briton; and, if they do, they are subject to damages in a court of law.

W. All this, master, is very well but why should I not vote for a member of parliament as well as you?

M. I have already told you, John, that industry and economy are in this country the source of everything: it is by the first alone that a fortune can be made, and it is by the last alone that it can be kept. Instead of working only five days in the week, work six; and, in six years, you will have gained money enough to purchase a vote, if you please: this privilege the meanest man may soon acquire by persevering in his labours, and the richest will lose it should he be idle and spend his property. I set out without anything, and have got a vote; and, should my son be an idle fellow and a spendthrift, in selling what I leave him, he loses his vote.

W. Then, master, from all this, I suppose you do not approve of the French revolution?

M. How often, John, must I tell you, that I seldom trouble my head about these matters; yet, if you wish to know my sentiments, I will tell you them. In the first place, I do not think there is any comparison between France and England: there were certainly great grievances in France; the king could seize the property and person of every man; he could reduce him to beggary, could confine him to prison, and take away his life. Can the king of England do any such thing? I believe, John, that you would be glad that he were to take you up without your offending against the laws; it would be a good fortune to you.

W. Why, to be sure, master, I would make him pay sauce for it.

M. Then, John, if you would make him pay sauce for it, and he can do you no injury without your having the same redress against him as you could have against any of your fellow-subjects, are you not in the eye of the law equal to the king?

W. True, master, we are so in England, but you own it was not the case in France, and therefore they were certainly right in what they did.

M. That is a different thing, John: it does not follow, that, if government acted wrong, the people have acted right; I only know this, John, that it appears to me there never was a time when there was less right in France; and I will give you two instances of it in what has happened to myself. You remember that shopkeeper in Paris, who refused to pay me, about seven years ago, for a quantity of hardware that I sent out to him: I went to Paris, you also remember, applied to one of their courts of justice, and got my money.

W. To be sure, master, it would be very hard if every man were not paid his own.

M. Yes, John: but what has happened since?—I sent out another parcel of hardware last year, to a person at Marseilles, who also refused to pay me; I went there to oblige him, I found there were no longer any courts of justice; I found that he was become a great patriot, a captain, John, in the national guards, and he only laughed at me, and told me, if I teazed him about money, he would *denounce* me, as he called it, and have me put in prison.

W. What, put you in prison when he owed you money! Why master he must be a great rascal indeed!

M. This was not all, John:—to appear a little smart, I had carried with me a new coat, with handsome steel buttons; in this I walked the streets, and was followed by some boys, who began to call out, 'Aristocrat! Aristocrat!' (a word which means an enemy to their constitution) a mob immediately surrounded me, dragged me through the street, and would have hung me on one of the ropes on which they hang their lanterns, if luckily, my banker had not come by, rescued me from their hands, by assuring them that I was in England a great patriot, or what he called a Jacobin.

W. Lord, master, were not you frightened terribly?

M. Certainly I was, John; and I'll take care how I venture there again.

W. But, master, the common people in France, such as myself, live surely better than they did.

M. How so, John! manufacturers are at end; and, when the master can no longer sell his commodities, he can no longer pay the journeymen.

W. Why, what becomes of them?

M. They, John, as well as all of similar description, such as servants, labourers, and the lower class of manufacturers, are obliged to enter into the armies for bread; they are paid fifteen pence a day, but they are paid in paper; that paper they are forced to exchange for little more than half of the commodities that could formerly be purchased with money of the same amount; they march without shoes or stockings, and their necessities oblige them to plunder, or exact contributions from every country they enter.

W. Why, I thought, master, they carried liberty everywhere?

M. It don't appear so, John, from the event that has lately taken place at Frankfort, where the inhabitants have driven out these friends to equality; and from the account that the inhabitants of Nice have presented to the national assembly, in which they complain that the French have ravished their wives and daughters, and stole their goods:—how should you like that, John?

W. Faith, master, not at all!

M. Nor is this the only thing to be dreaded; the farmer and labourer have left their ploughs, to preach or fight for reform; the consequence is, that the ground has been uncultivated, a famine begins to appear, and all provisions are double the price of what they were before the revolution:—how should you like this, John, who complain of the price of things, when bread is no dearer than it was ten or twenty years ago? In short, John, if the French and their doctrines come here, I shall shut up my shop, and have done with business; I shall place my money where I can most safely, and even bury it under ground, sooner than lend it to a constitution that subsists, as their's does, by violence, and where every person, who is suspected or accused of being an aristocrat, is dragged to prison without any evidence, and is afterwards massacred by the populace. The French have always been our enemies; and if they once enter England, they will not forget to revenge themselves for the many times we have beaten them by sea and land; nor do I desire any of their equality, since, as this country now stands, I can become by industry and economy equally rich as a lord, and, while I behave myself with propriety, am equally independent as the king.

W. Right, master! and I thank you for explaining all this to me; and, instead of going to the liberty-club, I will begin my work; for, I should not like to see a Frenchman lie with my wife, or take the bread out of my children's mouths; and I now see, that, if I go on as you do, and mind my business, I may in time be as rich and as happy as you.

SOBER REFLECTIONS

BURKE'S *Reflections on the Revolution in France*, published in 1790, produced a number of forcible replies, including Paine's *Rights of Man*. The work of Thomas Paine has already been discussed in our previous volume, with an example of his style; so we have decided to reprint, as typical of the same 'school' in the seventeen-nineties, the following pages from a pamphlet by John Thelwall. It was written as a reply to another of Burke's outbursts—the *Letter to a Noble Lord*. As our next extracts are from Burke himself, the reader is referred to the note which precedes them for an account of the circumstances in which this *Letter to a Noble Lord* was written. For the rest, Thelwall's words are self-explanatory. He is concerned with analysing the common tendency to confuse democratic principles with those Jacobin methods which were, in fact, a negation and a betrayal of democracy. This tendency, already mentioned in our note to the preceding pamphlet, had its best example in the writings of Edmund Burke, whose rhetorical pleading was summed up in Paine's immortal phrase: 'He pities the plumage, but forgets the dying bird'.

It has been suggested by Raymond Postgate (*Revolution from 1789 to 1906*) that the English revolutionary movement was non-existent or negligible—indeed, he dismisses it in a footnote with a half-contemptuous reference to Thelwall, and another to Paine, as being to the 'right' of the Jacobins. The matter is, of course, one of definition. Paine, who was a humane man, opposed the execution of Louis XVI on grounds which would appeal today to every progressive penal reformer—he said, in effect, that to chop off the king's head was merely vindictive, and that nobody brought up in the corrupt atmosphere of Versailles, could be expected to behave much better. This did not make Paine any less adamant in his opposition to monarchy; in fact he remained true to his democratic convictions when France drifted first into dictatorship and then (inevitably) into imperialism. If this stubborn opposition to 'The March of History' made Paine 'right' as distinct from the 'left' (which shed so much innocent blood to so little purpose), then we must concede that Paine was a reactionary who stood by the principles of the revolution when it had become fashionable to betray them, and anticipated a humanitarianism for which the world is still not ready.

As to the extent of the revolutionary movement in England, we have already indicated the difficulty of assessing it. Postgate suggests that Pitt deliberately exaggerated its importance. In that case, the Government was not alone in its exaggerations, for countless pamphleteers (especially in and about the year 1803) were at great pains to counter what they evidently believed to be a revolutionary and Francophil movement. Their task, by 1803, must have been easier, as Bonaparte had not exactly the reputation of a liberator. And yet, judging by the nature of numerous appeals to the patriotism of the poor, there seems to have been great uneasiness regarding them. 'Valerius' (William Combe) in a broadside of 1803 stated frankly that he was 'not addressing persons of rank and property; for those who have a large and obvious stake in the country are sufficiently convinced of their danger' (i.e. from a French invasion). He therefore addressed 'those who live by their daily labour', and expressed the fear that there were people who would betray them, insinuating 'that your lot is poverty; you exist by your labour from day to day; that you can but work hard and gain little in whatever hands the Government of this country is vested'.

It is certainly remarkable that so many patriots were anxious to answer this argument if, in fact, it was not being effectively put forward. War is the strongest test of a revolutionary movement, especially if it is of an international character. In the heat of war, especially when invasion is threatened, such movements normally lose heavily, and only regain support in the event of defeat. Yet the evidence, at the very height of the war with France, points to the existence of a revolutionary party in England which was appealing with some success to working men on a 'defeatist' programme; for William Combe's summary of this argument will be found in numerous broadsheets and pamphlets, written with the same object, of refuting this dangerous doctrine. If one accepts the view that the revolutionary movement was mainly imaginary, one is driven to the opinion that the Government and the patriotic pamphleteers were doing their best to create such a movement by suggesting that it existed, and even outlining its case in the course of 'replying' to fictitious opponents.

What is beyond question is the fact that the leading British republicans and democrats at this time were not enthusiastic with regard to the course actually followed by the Revolution in France. They were, of course, inevitably denounced as 'Jacobins', just as Socialists were called 'Bolshies' in the nineteen-twenties. (On the same principle, critics of the Soviet policy were later to be called 'Social-fascists' or 'Trotsky-fascists', showing how misleading all such names can be; for the same man could be a 'Bolshie' to one person and a 'Trotsky-fascist' to another.) The publication of *The Anti-Jacobin*, of course, helped to make the 'Jacobin' label stick, but not to determine the contents of the bottle. John Thelwall, as may be seen from the following pages, was as anti-Jacobin and as democratic or—if you prefer—as 'right-wing' as Paine and he admirably reflects what intelligent Englishmen of liberal sentiments thought about the Revolution and about emotional critics such as Burke.

Thelwall's distinction between the principle of liberty and the historical course of the Revoltuion is a vital one which his own words will elucidate. Of the man himself, it is enough to say here that Thelwall was a widely read man, and at one time well known and popular both for his writings and for his speeches. Postgate's 'insignificant academic person' was, in fact, a leading member of the 'Society of the Friends of the People' and of the 'Corresponding Society'—the latter being an organisation which covered under its innocuous title one of the democratic movements of his time. Thelwall's integrity and high principles do not appear to have been queried in an age when accusations of corruption were common, because the vice was even commoner. As a teacher of elocution he was a successful pioneer in the cure of stammering, his methods being described by himself in an interesting account published in 1814.

The *Sober Reflections* were published in 1796.

SOBER REFLECTIONS ON THE SEDITIOUS AND INFLAMMATORY LETTER OF THE RIGHT HON. EDMUND BURKE TO A NOBLE LORD

By John Thelwall

THESE principles, I repeat it, in themselves are good. If our antagonists are seriously of a different opinion, why do they not examine them, without misrepresentation or abuse, on the simple foundation of their own merits or defects? Why confound them with other things? Why pretend to discuss principles, and talk of nothing, in reality, but the actions of unprincipled men? Is time unsteady, because my watch goes wrong? Is it not noon when the sun is in the meridian, because the parish dial is out of repair? Can *principles*, which are the sun of the intellectual universe, be changed in their nature or their course by the vile actions of a few ruffians? Prove to me, by dispassionate argument, that the *principles* of the French revolution are false and pernicious, and I will relinquish them at once, and thank you for delivering me from my errors. But while my reason tells me that they are consonant *in themselves* with truth and justice, it is not calling them *French* principles—it is not calling them *new lights*—it is not *the hoary prejudice of six thousand years*—it is not calling me *Jacobin*, nor calling others *cannibal philosophers*—it is not talking of the 'ignorant flippancy'[1] of a man whom the learned solidity of colleges and consistories have never been able to answer—it is not all the declamatory bitterness of *Burke*, the metaphysical frenzy of *Windham*, the sanguinary rage of *Pitt*, nor the long-winded sophistry of *Scott* and *Mitford*, shall compel me to relinquish these important truths:—no; not though it

[1] Letter, &c., p. 77. [This and several later references are to the two works by Burke mentioned in the preface. Ed.]

could be proved that the crimes of *Marat* and *Robespierre* surpassed the savage wickedness of the fiend *Zuwarrow*, and the ferocity of Croats and Hulans.

Marat and *Robespierre* were no more to be regarded as integral parts of *the new principles of France*, than *Pitt* and *Dundas* as parts of *the old principles of England*; or than the *fire of London* as having been a part of the river Thames, because its waves were blackened by the rubbish of falling houses, and the blazing rafters floated along the stream. The rafters and the rubbish were swept into the sea, and the Thames regained its wonted clearness: *Marat* and *Robespierre* are swallowed up in the ocean of eternity, and the new principles of France remain; and if *Pitt* and *Dundas* were to die of a surfeit, after a *Wimbledon* dinner, I do not believe, for my own part, that our liberties would be less secure.

As men are not principles, so neither are particular actions. Mr *Burke* might as well contend that barracks and subsidised mercenaries, and the short memory of a minister on a trial of life and death, are the British constitution, as that the tyranny of *Robespierre* was the new French system of philosophy and politics. To come still closer to the point, it were as rational to affirm, that the massacres of Glencoe were the principles of *our* Glorious Revolution, as that the massacres of September were the principles of the Revolution of France!

That the revolution has had its 'harpies',[1] as detestable as either *Virgil* or Mr *Burke* has described, who feasted on the general wreck, and were for leaving 'nothing unrent, unrifled, unravaged, or unpolluted',[1] there can be no doubt: nor is it necessary, to account for the generation of 'these foul and ravenous birds of prey',[1] to descend with the poet to the regions which superstition has peopled with more than mortal wickedness; or to mount with the political declaimer to the regions of philosophy and metaphysics.

What sort of figure *Fouquier Tinnanville* (*sic*) would have made by the side of the metaphysical Sir *John Scott*, I do not pretend to say; but who ever suspected either *Marat*, *Robespierre*, *Le Bon*, or any of that sanguinary party, of visionary subtilties and metaphysical abstraction? Which of those fine-spun metaphysical theories, whose abstract perfection is so abhorrent to Mr *Burke's* 'instincts',—which of those breviaries of fundamental principles which commanded the assent, and excited the admiration of the philosophical world, is attributed to either of these men? *Robespierre*, it is true, was a member of the Constituent Assembly; and we find him, at an early period, in possession of considerable popularity: but his popularity was not of a description to class him

[1] Letter, &c., p. 21.

with those *speculative literati* against whom the politicians of the *old sect* have conceived such an inveterate abhorrence.

However this country may be disposed to indulge its vanity in comparisons, they are not always to our advantage. The *French* Robespierre was no *apostate*. There was a certain steadiness and consistency in his conduct and character, which, (together with some grand traits of simplicity and disinterestedness) even in the midst of abhorrence, compel us to respect him. Again, I repeat it, comparisons are not always in our favour: in the character of the *French* Robespierre there was nothing to excite our contempt. He had vices—demons of desolation! bear witness, he had vices: but they were not the vices of corruption! He neither maintained himself in riotous luxury, nor enriched lethargic brothers, and imbecile relations with the plunder of his country, dignified under the specious names of places and pensions. He had cruelty too, the thought of which makes one's flesh creep: but though he issued a decree to give no quarter to *Britons* or *Hanoverians*, found in arms, he never entered into a conspiracy to *starve* twenty-four millions of men, women, and children!—He had virtues too—grand magnificent virtues! for 'pure unmixed, dephlegmated, defoecated evil', exists no where but in the inflamed imagination of Mr *Burke*. He was superior to all the sordid temptations that debauch the little mind—the allurements of luxury, ostentation, and rapacity. Surrounded by all the temptations of unlimited power, he lived like a private citizen, and he died a pauper.

Robespierre was, however, from the first a man of blood. He was for giving every thing to the people, it is true; but he was for giving it them not by the cultivation and expansion of intellect, but by commotion, and violence, and sanguinary revenge: and therefore it was that the revolutionary movements of *Robespierre*, perhaps, in despite of himself, hurried him into the most insufferable of all tyrannies, instead of conducting the people to freedom. There can be no freedom in the world but that which has its foundations in the encreased knowledge and liberality of mankind. Tyranny comes by violence, or by corruption: but Liberty is the gift of Reason.

Of this important truth the Revolutionary Tyrant seems to have been entirely ignorant: and from this defect, and the want of personal courage, proceeded, I believe, all the errors and all the horrors of his administration. Nay, so far was he from that metaphysical abstraction, which places its confidence in fine spun theories and bird's-eye speculations, that his conduct has given birth to a report, that he cherished almost as inveterate an abhorrence against philosophers and literati, as Mr *Burke* and his new friends.—So far was he from upholding the dangerous heresy of illimitable inquiry, that he would have roasted an atheist at the stake with as much satisfaction as the most pious bishop of the church.

During the reign of his desolating tyranny, philosophy was silenced, science was proscribed and daring speculation soared no more. France was threatened with midnight ignorance; and in the *Club of the Cordeliers*, at that time one of the instruments of his tyranny, a motion was even made to consume the public libraries.

Away, then, with these shallow pretences for degrading the noblest exercise of human intellect. Away with this idle jargon of cannibal philosophers and literary banditti! So unnatural an alliance never yet was formed; nor ever will. The assassins and ruffians of every clime, whether in the pay of *regular* or *revolutionary* tyrannies, have a sort of universal instinct whispering to them, that knowledge and oppression cannot thrive together.

'If we do not silence the press,' says *Woolsey*, 'the press will silence us': and *Robespierre* (a little wiser in this respect than *Edmund Burke*) prohibited, in the Jacobin Club, the publication of his own speeches; lest his intemperance should provoke discussions which his tyranny could not afterwards controul.

But though the pretences of Mr *Burke* for confounding together the *philosophy* and the *crimes of France* are thus completely refuted, I do not expect that the ground will be abandoned. It is too important a part of the permanent conspiracy against the liberties of mankind to be readily given up. Remove but this delusion from the eyes of the people, and the reign of Corruption could not last—'no, not for a twelvemonth'. The principles of liberty are so consonant to the general good—the cause of the rotten borough-mongers is so destitute of all rational support, and the miseries produced by that system are so numerous, that nothing but the groundless terrors so artfully excited—nothing but the prejudices inspired against all speculation and enquiry, by confounding together things that have no connection, could possibly prevent the people of Britain shouting from every village, town, and street, with one unanimous and omnipotent voice—

'REFORM! REFORM! REFORM!!!'

Of this the faction in power are sufficiently aware, and therefore it is, that their hatred and persecution are principally directed, not against the furious and the violent, but against the enlightened and humane. Therefore it is, that they endeavour to confound together, by chains of connection slighter than the spider's web, every sanguinary expression, every intemperate action of the obscurest individual whose mind has become distempered by the calamities of the times, not with the oppressions and miseries that provoke them, but with the honest and virtuous labours of those *true sons of moderation and good order* who wish to render their fellow citizens firm and manly, that they may have no occasion to be tumultuous and savage; to spread the solar light of reason, that they may extinguish the grosser fires of vengeance; and to produce a timely and temperate reform, as the only means of averting an ultimate revolution. These are the men against whom the bitterest malice of persecution is directed. These are the men against whom every engine of abuse and misrepresentation is employed; to calumniate whom their 'Briton', and their 'Times', and their dirty Grub-street pamphletteers, are pensioned out of the public plunder—and against whom grave senators from their benches, and *pensioned Cicero's* from their literary retreats, are not ashamed to pour forth their meretricious eloquence, in torrents of defamation, and to exhaust all the fury of inventive (or *deluded*) malice. These are the men for whose blood they thirst; and whom they endeavour to destroy by new doctrines, not only of accumulative and constructive treason, but of *treason by second sight:* making them accountable for actions they were never consulted upon, books they never read, and sentiments they never heard. These, in short, are the men for whose destruction laws are perverted, spies are employed, and perjurers are pensioned: and when all these artifices prove inadequate to the end, these are the men to stop whose mouths bills have been proposed, in parliament, subversive of every principle of the constitution, lest the nation at large should be in time convinced that they are not what they have been represented: but that *the friends of Liberty and Reform, are the true friends of Humanity and Order!*

This would be, indeed, a terrible discovery for those who are supported by corruption: and in this point of view one cannot blame them for the selection they have made of the objects of their persecuting hatred. To let their vengeance fall at once upon the really violent, would be an act of impolicy, that would shew them 'to be foolish, even above the weight of privilege allowed to wealth'[1] and power. Were these suppressed (arguing upon their own supposition, that persecution can suppress) what would become of those pretences by which, alone, they have rendered the advocates of reform obnoxious to the fears, and consequently to the hatred, of the alarmists? But if they could destroy the real reformers, the men of reason, of humanity, of intellect, they would destroy the magnets (if I may so express myself) around which,

[1] Letter, &c., p. 55.

whenever their influence shall become sufficiently diffused through the intelligent atmosphere, the good sense, the spirit, the virtue of the country, must be attracted; and when it is so attracted, and when the parts shall firmly and peacefully cohere, and, thus brought under the influence of the true laws of nature, shall press together, with the united force of attraction and gravitation, to one common centre of truth, the seven days work of creation is complete—the system is restored to order. . . .

*   *   *   *

That popular commotions call all the vices, as well as the virtues of the community into action, cannot be denied. That when 'the cauldron of civil contention' is boiling over, the foulest ingredients will sometimes be at the top; and that, in the general fermentation, combinations the most deleterious will sometimes be formed, no reflecting man has ever yet denied. It is an additional argument why the rulers of the earth should take care not to render such commotions necessary and inevitable.

Happy, thrice happy shall it be for those princes and governments, who derive a useful lesson from the events that have passed before us! Happy, thrice happy, shall it be for those wise and moderate rulers, who, in this busy, changeful, and enquiring age, put not their trust in *janissaries* or *Swiss Guards;* but, adopting the salutary advice of the great Lord *Verulam*, shall illustrate by their conduct that profound and salutary maxim, that 'the surest way to prevent sedition is not by suppressing complaints with too much severity, but to take away the matter of them'.[1] In other words, the best way to manage the distemper is not to amputate the limb but to remove the cause.

But whatever vices and dispositions the heat of popular commotion may call into action, must have been generated by former circumstances. Extraordinary exigencies place men in strong lights, and shew them such as they are: but they do not create characters of a sudden; nor manufacture mankind anew. Revolutions are touchstones for the real dispositions; but they do not, like the whisp of a harlequin's sword, change the dove into a tyger, or the tyger into a dove. If, therefore, we were to admit that all the revolutionists—the whole body of the French people, were indiscriminately involved in the guilt of those excesses so exultingly quoted, and so wickedly exaggerated by the foes of liberty—what would be the conclusion? Where would the blame in

[1] Essays, Civil and Moral, p. 77 and 80. *edition* 1725. Title—*Of Seditions and Troubles.* Query, Why has Mr. *Burke* overlooked this essay!

reality fall, but upon that old system of despotism, for the restoration of which Mr *Burke* 'would animate Europe to eternal battle'.

The revolution in France, or more properly speaking, the philosophers and patriots who first set the *new order of things* in motion, did not create their agents. They did not sow the earth (like *Cadmus*) with dragon's teeth, and reap a harvest of men to carry on their projects. They were obliged to make use of the instruments already made to their hands; and when the game was on foot, the bad as well as the good would have their share of the play. If, to resume the allusion, a race of contentious homicides did burst from the ground, and alternately destroy each other, the seed was sown by the *old despotism*, not by the *new philosophy*.

Mr *Burke*, indeed, himself seems conscious, that the wild and ferocious characters he declaims against, could not have been formed by the revolution—he knew that *the men whom he stigmatises for projecting and forming the Republic, could not have been formed and educated by the Republic.* Unwilling, therefore, to assign, in plain terms, the generation of the monsters he describes to the right cause, he calls in the aid of poetry, and tells us, that these 'revolution harpies, sprung from night and hell, and from chaotic anarchy, which generates equivocally all monstrous, all prodigious things'.—True, Mr *Burke*, I thank you for the allusion. The revolution *harpies* did spring, most assuredly, from what with classical precision of metaphor you have called *hell*, and *night*, and *chaotic anarchy*. They sprung, indeed, from that hell of despotism, into the very abyss of which *France* had for whole centuries been plunged.—They sprung, indeed, from that night of ignorance in which the best faculties of the human mind had been so long enveloped and extinguished.—They sprung, indeed, from that chaotic anarchy of vice, licentiousness, profligate luxury, and unprincipled debauchery, into which the morals of the country had been thrown by the influence and example of the court, and which, it is rightly said, *generates equivocally all monstrous, all prodigious things!* These were, indeed, the infernal sources of all the evil: and but for that 'night, that hell, that chaotic anarchy', of the old despotic system, such 'obscene harpies',—such 'foul and ravenous birds of prey', never could have been in existence, to 'hover over the heads, and souse down upon the tables', of the revolutionists, and 'rend, and rifle, and ravage, and pollute, with the slime of their filthy offal', the wholesome banquet, which the philosophers of the revolution had occasioned to be spread for the social enjoyment and sustenance of mankind.

Such *were* the monsters generated in the infernal region of the old tyranny and in such regions such monsters always *must be* generated, till effects shall cease to be commensurate to their causes, and nature's self shall change. Was it not time then, think you, that this 'great deep' were broken up—that the chaotic mass of tyranny and corruption might be thrown into new motion, by the addition of some fresh principle, or stimulus, by means of which (through whatever noise and uproar) a more wholesome arrangement might be produced. . . .

'And from confusion bring forth beauteous order?'

It is in vain to tell me, that these harpies were no harpies to mankind till they shewed themselves as such. Despotism had always its harpies: and they were always well banqueted. They banqueted in silence, indeed, under the *old system;* they were not garrulous, as under the *new order;* nor did the press trumpet forth their attrocities. But they rent, and ravaged, and rifled, and polluted, and devoured, and acted all their horrors and abominations, with avidity and diligence enough, for centuries before the revolutionary system was set in motion. Of this Mr *Burke,* and every man who is travelled, either in climes or books, is well informed. They had their public theatres, in which they tore the quivering limbs of their prey, for the amusement of courtly spectators; and they had their cages—their cells—their Bastiles, or, as Mr *Burke,* more delicately calls them, 'king's castles',[1] where they might banquet in silence, and riot undisturbed in all the horrid luxuries of cruelty. The revolution gave them nothing but a voice: and this attribute was ultimately beneficial: for their hideous shrieks and yells, and the audacious publicity of their cruel ravages, concentrated, at last, the general hatred of the country they infested. They were hunted to their caverns; and the race has become extinct.

I do not, however, mean to affirm that the harpies of the new system were the same individuals as would have been the harpies of the old: though, in many instances, it was probably the case. Cruelty is cruelty, under whatever system it acts; and an inquisitor, a Fermier General, and the president of the revolutionary tribunal, in the *reel* of political mutation, might join hands, turn round, and change positions *ad infinitum,* without ever appearing out of place.

But this is not all. Inhuman oppression generates inhuman revenge. All strong impressions produce strong effects. That which we passionately detest, we are sometimes in as much danger of imitating, as that which we passionately admire. How often does the hatred of cruelty degenerate into the very thing we abhor? How often does the hatred of

[1] Reflections, &c.

37

THE CONTRAST
1792

RELIGION.   MORALITY.
LOYALTY OBEDIENCE TO THE LAWS
INDEPENDANCE PERSONAL SECURITY
JUSTICE INHERITANCE PROTECTION
PROPERTY. INDUSTRY NATIONAL PROSPERITY
          HAPPINESS

ATHEISM   PERJURY.
REBELLION. TREASON. ANARCHY MURDER
EQUALITY. MADNESS. CRUELTY INJUSTICE
TREACHERY INGRATITUDE IDLENESS
FAMINE NATIONAL & PRIVATE RUIN.
MISERY

WHICH IS BEST

(Typical Cartoon of the Period)

tyranny render men most tyrannical?—for the hatred of tyranny is one
thing—the love of liberty is another. The former is a common instinct;
the latter is the noblest attainment of reason. Add to which, that *lex
talionis* is, with the generality of mankind, the law of moral action. 'Eye
for eye, and tooth for tooth,' is inculcated as the mandate of Deity. But
the nobility and clergy of France, had not eyes and teeth enough to
answer this account. Can we wonder at what ensued?

It would have been well for France, if the influence of the old tyranny
upon the moral character of the people, had terminated with the evils
here enumerated. If the cruelty of long-established oppression had only
made the irritable ferocious, and the ignorant revengeful, these destructive passions might have been controuled by the energy of more
cultivated minds, till they had been softened and humanised by the
influence of more favourable circumstances. But tyranny had not left
to the revolution the possibility of the crime with which Mr *Burke* has
charged it in a former pamphlet. It had 'slain the mind[1] of the country'
long before that revolution took place. Literature, it is true, had been
highly cultivated. Science had been liberally patronised, in the upper
circles; and even that republican talent, *eloquence*, had been cherished

[1] Reflections, &c.

with a diligence most important, in its ultimate consequences, to mankind. But the jealous nature of the government—the terrors of the Bastile—the shackles of an imprimatur—the homage exacted by birth and fortune, and, above all, the frivolity and effeminacy of character imposed on the nation by a profligate, thoughtless, and luxurious court, which, having nothing manly in itself, could not be expected to tolerate manhood in its dependants, 'dwarfed the growth' of that mental energy which these tastes and studies could not otherwise have failed of producing. Hence originated the circumstance of which the female citizen *Roland* complains, that the revolution produced no *men*. The course of study had been perverted by the influence of the government. The closet of the philosopher was infected by the contagion of the court. Solidity was sacrificed to ornament—the virtues to the graces. In acuteness, subtility, penetration, and even profundity, their literati were not deficient: but they wanted that boldness—that active energy—that collected, unembarrassed, firmness and presence of mind, which nothing but the actual enjoyment of liberty, and an unrestrained intercourse with a bold, resolute, bustling and disputatious race of men can possibly confer. This energy of mind, without which it is impossible, in any useful and important sense of the word, to be a man of business, must be sought among 'thronged and promiscuous audiences', 'in theatres and halls of assembly;' for there only it is to be found. The philosophers of France, however, from the necessities under which they were placed by the government and institutions of the country, either mingled with the gay circles of the dissolute and great, and became infected with servile effeminacy, or indulged their speculations in a sort of sullen retirement, where the masculine boldness of the true philosophic character was chilled by solitary abstraction.

Thus did the genius of the old despotism destroy, alike, the humanity of the bold, and the energy of the humane and enlightened. And thus it was that, the philosophers being feeble, and the men of intrepidity being ferocious, the republic was torn and distracted by the crimes which the despotism had prepared.

If it were necessary to strengthen this argument with historical evidence—if it were necessary to prove by particular records, that the disposition to these inhuman crimes did not originate in the nature and influences of *republican government*, we might appeal to the *massacres of St Bartholomew:* to the barbarous oppressions and wanton cruelties described by *Arthur Young*, in the first edition of his travels, as spreading misery and desolation through the lordships and seigniories of what

Mr *Burke* calls 'the *virtuous* nobility of France';[1] and, above all, to the inhuman punishments—the savage protraction of lingering, but exquisite tortures, with which inventive cruelty, in some notorious instances, gratified the appetite of royal vengeance. Nay, whatever might be the conduct of particular leaders, rendered cruel at first by their intolerant zeal, and afterwards, still more so by their dread of retribution, it would not be difficult to prove, that *the character of the people* was *humanized* and *improved*, instead of being rendered more ferocious by the influence of the revolution. I appeal, in particular, even to the dry circumstance of the decree, that no quarter should be given to the *British* or *Hanoverians*. What was the consequence of that decree? The brave soldiers of the republic refused to execute it, even in an individual instance; and the dictator was obliged to recal a mandate which he found himself unable to enforce. Would the soldiers of the old despotism, who perpetrated the horrors of the night of St Bartholomew, have so refused? Did the military slaves of our good ally, the Empress, display the same obstinate repugnance to a still more inhuman order? Let the ghosts of murdered babes and sucking mothers, that still hover unappeased over the captive towers of *Ismael* and *Warsaw*, answer the solemn question!

*   *   *   *

The only novelty in this event, as far as relates to causation, consists in the circumstance of the nobility and the monarchy being overthrown together. But this very circumstance shews the profundity of *Machiavel*, and the accuracy of his reasoning; and exposes the 'flippancy' of Mr *Burke*. It is novelty of combination in the history of facts; but not novelty of combination in the history of cause and effect. It is an additional argument in support of the assertion, that popular revolutions are consequences of the revolutions of tyranny and oppression. In *France*, two[2] revolutions took place at the same time; because two[2] kinds of tyranny domineered together, and therefore two[2] revolutions were necessary. The nobility, by 'their natural ignorance, their indolence, and contempt of all civil government';[3] and still more by their unbounded rapacity, their wanton insolence, their barbarous exactions, and all-desolating pride—or, in the language of my quotation, by *the rapine, oppression, ambition, and adulteries*, which they indulged *without*

---

[1] Letter, &c., p. 49.

[2] I might say three. But I omit the ecclesiastical tyranny, because it does not fall immediately in the way of my argument; and because the same reasoning will evidently apply in this instance as in the others.

[3] Montesq. Spir. Laws, b. ii. c. 4.

respect or consideration of justice or civility, had brought themselves into general abhorrence and detestation, even before any *conjurations and conspiracies against the prince* had arisen. They had made themselves partners in the guilt, and were therefore partners in the punishment of the tyranny. Instead of being a bulwark between the prince and the people, to preserve the latter from the oppression of the former, they were indeed the chief battery from which the destructive engines of Gallic tyranny spread ruin and desolation through the land.

And are these the persons whom Mr *Burke* pretends 'are so like the nobility of this country, that nothing but the latter, probably not speaking quite such good French, could enable us to find out any difference?'[1] I would not for the whole pension of this 'defender of the order', that this comparison should be true: for if it were—if the titled great of Britain were what those of France have been, then should I exclaim, in the bitterness of my soul, that their crimes and their oppressions ought no longer to be endured—no longer protected by the laws and institutions of the land; but that they, also, in their turn, ought to be driven into ignominious banishment.

Never—never (let us hope) will our nobility and great proprietors realize the simile Mr *Burke* has so imprudently made! Never—never (let us hope) will the vices, the profligacy, the insolent oppression, and immeasureable rapacity of the French aristocracy, ravage and depopulate this country: for if they should, not all the rhapsodies of pensioned eloquence—not all the treason and sedition bills of *Pitt* and *Grenville*, can avert the terrible catastrophe.

But the danger to this country comes from another quarter. It is not from the aristocracy, properly so called, that we have most to dread. It is not even from the prerogatives of the executive power. It is from the oligarchy of the rotten borough-mongers. It is from the corruption of that which ought to be the representative branch of the legislature. This it is that is undermining (I must not say has undermined) the constitution and liberties of Britain. This it is that is realising, with with fatal rapidity, the prophesy of *Montesquieu*—'As all human beings have an end, the state we are speaking of will lose its liberty. It will perish. Have not *Rome*, *Sparta*, and *Carthage* perished? It will perish, when the legislative power shall be more corrupted than the executive!'[2]

[1] Letter, &c., p. 59. Mr. *B.* it is true, applies the comparison only to the Duke of *Bedford;* but it applies either to all or none.
[2] Sp. Laws, book xi. c. 6.

Such, at least, are the apprehensions that have crowded upon my mind. Such are the dangers which, during the last five years, I have endeavoured, with the most laborious diligence, to avert, by the only means through which they can be averted—by provoking popular enquiry; by rousing, as far as I had power to rouse, the energies of peaceful but determined intellect; and by endeavouring, with all the little persuasion I could muster, to wean my fellow citizens from the prejudices and delusions of party—from all idolatrous attachment to names and individuals, and to fix their hearts and affections upon principle alone—the great principle of philanthropy—the principle of universal good—the source and fountain of all just government—of *equal rights, equal laws, reciprocal respect, and reciprocal protection.*

These are the principles I have endeavoured to inculcate, in political societies, at public meetings; in my pamphlets, in my conversations, and in that lecture-room, (that school of vice, as Mr *Burke* is pleased to call it) at which he is so anxious to dissuade the '*grown* gentlemen and noblemen of our time from thinking of finishing whatever may have been left incomplete at the old universities in this country'.[1]

If to have inculcated these principles with a diligence and perseverance which no difficulties could check, no threats nor persecutions controul—if to have been equally anxious to preserve the spirit of the people, and the tranquillity of society—to disseminate the information that might conduct to reform, and to check the intemperance that might lead to tumult—if these are crimes dangerous to the existence of the state, the minister did right to place me at the bar of the Old Bailey: and, if perseverance in these principles is perseverance in crime, it may be necessary once more to place me in the same situation of disgrace and peril. If to assemble my fellow citizens for the purpose of political discussion—if to strip off the mask from state hypocrisy and usurpation—if to expose apostacy, confute the sophisms of court jugglers and ministerial hirelings, and drag forth to public notice the facts that demonstrate the enormity and rapid progress of that corruption under which we groan, and by means of which *the rich are tottering on the verge of bankruptcy, and the poor are sinking into the abyss of famine* . . . if this is to keep a public *school of vice and licentiousness,*[2] then was it right in ministers to *endeavour* to seal up the doors of that school with an act of parliament; then was it right that I should be held up to public odium and public terror, by the inflammatory declamations of the *Powises* and *Windhams,* the tedious sophistries of the *Scotts* and *Mitfords,* the virulent pamphlets of the *Burkes* and *Reeveses,* and the *conjectural*

[1] Letter, &c., p. 35. [2] Letter, &c., p. 36.

defamations of *Godwin*.[1] But upon what sort of pretence, even the inflamed and prejudiced mind of Mr *Burke*, can regard me as 'a wicked pander to avarice and ambition',[2] I am totally at a loss to conjecture. I have attached myself to no party. I have entered into none of the little paltry squabbles of placemen and oppositionists, by which, alone, profit or promotion can be expected. My heart and soul, it is true, and I believe the heart and soul of every man who entertains one grain of respect for the rights and liberties of mankind, was with the *Whigs* in their conduct and sentiments relative to two bills, to which, as they are now passed into laws, I shall give no *epithet*. I trust they have an epithet, sufficiently descriptive, engraved upon the heart of every *Briton*. I thought, and I still think, that the man must be extravagant, indeed, in his expectations, who was not satisfied with their behaviour in this respect; and particularly with the firm and manly opposition of *Fox*, *Erskine*, and *Lauderdale;* from the first of whom, I confess, I did not expect a conduct so bold and *unequivocal*. If any thing can preserve the party from that perdition into which, by its *cold, half measures*, it has so long been falling, it is persevering in the temper, spirit, and sentiments of *that* opposition. So long as they do persevere in that temper and spirit, I hope, and trust, that the hearts and souls of Britons will continue to be with them. So long as they do so persevere, my heart and soul, for one, will be with them, most undoubtedly: . . . not as a *partisan*, for that I abhor . . . but as one who, coinciding with them in a particular principle, is anxious to neglect no opportunity by which that principle can be promoted. But if ever, which, I trust, will not be the case, they should be again weighed down by the pondrous millstone of that sort of aristocracy already described,[3] which so long hung round their necks, and prevented them from soaring to the heights of consistent principle, INNS and OUTS, WHIGS and TORIES, will become once more objects alike of indifference . . . of contempt!

[*Extracts*]

[1] It is painful to see such a name, in such a list. But if men of great powers, however sincerely attached to liberty, voluntarily, by cold abstraction and retirement, cherish *a feebleness of spirit*, which shrinks from the creations of its own fancy, and a solitary vanity, which regards every thing as vice, and mischief, and inflammation, but what accords with its own most singular speculations, and if, under these impressions, and regardless of the consequences to an isolated individual, assailed already by all the malice and persecutions of powerful corruption, they will send such bitter defamations into the world, as are contained in the first 22 pages of 'Considerations on Lord *Grenville's* and Mr. *Pitt's* Bills,' they must expect to be classed with other calumniators. The bitterest of my enemies has never used me so ill as this *friend* has done. But nothing on earth renders a man so uncandid as the extreme *affectation* of candour.

[2] Letter, &c., p. 47.   [3] P. 24 to 27.

THOUGHTS AND DETAILS ON SCARCITY

THERE are those who profess to find complete consistency in the career of Edmund Burke; but to most people he is likely to remain an enigma.

Burke attacked 'the poor rotten constitution' of Britain, and particularly the existence of 'rotten boroughs', whilst himself representing one of those boroughs, the property of a political patron. He attacked oppression in India and in Ireland, he defended the American colonists in their struggle against the British Crown; and yet his zeal against the French Revolution was so intense that he could see no fault in the tyranny and oppression which had preceded and caused it, except that the 'noble monarchy' of France showed 'a restless desire of governing too much'. His bitterness against the French Revolution was based partly upon a dislike of abstract principles; yet no one in his time voiced more abstract principles in the form of dogmatic assertions relating to monarchy and aristocracy. Not only so, but when revolution was no longer a matter of abstract principles, but a solid fact, with every hope of permanency, Burke continued to incite his countrymen to a crusade against it, denying thereby his own peculiar maxim that 'there is a sacred veil to be drawn over the beginnings of all government'. (Apparently this merciful provision was only intended to apply to the exceedingly doubtful origins of monarchies and aristocracies.)

In the same way the callous discussion, in the pages that follow, of the sufferings of the poor, as though some law of the universe made them inevitable, may be contrasted with the passion shown by the same writer when discussing the tragedy of Marie Antoinette. He could preach thrift to the country, and especially to the poor, but himself ran into debt on an income of four figures, which was at one time £4,000 a year, and often very near it. (£4,000 a year was, of course, a much greater income in the eighteenth century, and should be contrasted with the low cost of living, or the wages paid to, say, a farm labourer, in order to appreciate Burke's affluence.) Economic law, as he understood it, allowed for no provision against old age in the case of 'the people'; yet he was kind enough to admit that Governments were maintained by the people and not (as one might suppose) *vice versa*, and might have added that he was maintained by them himself when writing this pamphlet. Apparently the laws of economics raised no objections to pensioning politicians.

Burke's pensions—amounting to £3,700 a year altogether—were the cause of some criticism by a gentleman somewhat vulnerable to attack, the Duke of Bedford. One might have expected Burke to have left to others the task of defending the allocation and the merit of its recipient, but in his *Letter to a Noble Lord* the outraged pensioner saw fit to reply himself, urging his own great services to the nation. Out of this pathetic and somewhat embarassing incident there emerged yet another of the contradictions in Burke's views, for he threw some glaring light on the origin of the vast wealth owned by the Bedford family. It was hardly tactful for such a strong advocate of aristocracy to dig this up, for there was not a nobleman in the country whose title-deeds would have looked any brighter under such scrutiny. Not without reason many who replied to this injudicious outburst taunted Burke with the 'Jacobinism' which he had been so fiercely denouncing; and the old gentleman was made to look rather silly.

In the main, Burke's life can be divided into two periods. Before the French Revolution he served, on the whole, the cause of justice, particularly in the case of India and that of the American colonies. After the Revolution his principal writings were concerned with fomenting war, interspersed with this special pleading on his own behalf and the *Letters to Sir Hercules Langrishe*—an appeal, more in the old liberal vein, for admitting Irish Catholics to the franchise. We shall make no attempt to analyse Burke's motives during either phase of his life. The extracts which follow are typical of the second period and are from a pamphlet posthumously published in the year 1800, Burke having died in 1797.

THOUGHTS AND DETAILS ON SCARCITY

By Edmund Burke

To provide for us in our necessities is not in the power of Government. It would be a vain presumption in statesmen to think they can do it. The people maintain them, and not they the people. It is in the power of Government to prevent much evil; it can do very little positive good in this, or perhaps in any thing else. It is not only so of the state and statesmen, but of all the classes and descriptions of the Rich—they are the pensioners of the poor, and are maintained by their superfluity. They are under an absolute, hereditary, and indefeasible dependance on those who labour, and are miscalled the Poor.

The labouring people are only poor, because they are numerous. Numbers in their nature imply poverty. In a fair distribution among a vast multitude, none can have much. That class of dependant pensioners called the rich, is so extremely small, that if all their throats were cut, and a distribution made of all they consume in a year, it would not give a bit of bread and cheese for one night's supper to those who labour, and who in reality feed both the pensioners and themselves.

But the throats of the rich ought not to be cut, nor their magazines plundered; because, in their persons they are trustees for those who labour, and their hoards are the banking-houses of these latter. Whether they mean it or not, they do, in effect, execute their trust— some with more, some with less fidelity and judgment. But on the whole, the duty is performed, and every thing returns, deducting some very trifling commission and discount, to the place from whence it arose. When the poor rise to destroy the rich, they act as wisely for their own purposes as when they burn mills, and throw corn into the river, to make bread cheap.

When I say, that we of the people ought to be informed, inclusively

46

I say, we ought not to be flattered: flattery is the reverse of instruction. The *poor* in that case would be rendered as improvident as the rich, which would not be at all good for them.

Nothing can be so base and so wicked as the political canting language, 'The Labouring *Poor*'. Let compassion be shewn in action, the more the better, according to every man's ability, but let there be no lamentation of their condition. It is no relief to their miserable circumstances; it is only an insult to their miserable understandings. It arises from a total want of charity, or a total want of thought. Want of one kind was never relieved by want of any other kind. Patience, labour, sobriety, frugality, and religion, should be recommended to them; all the rest is downright *fraud*. It is horrible to call them 'The *once happy* labourer'.

Whether what may be called moral or philosophical happiness of the laborious classes is increased or not, I cannot say. The seat of that species of happiness is in the mind; and there are few data to ascertain the comparative state of the mind at any two periods. Philosophical happiness is to want little. Civil or vulgar happiness is to want much, and to enjoy much.

If the happiness of the animal man (which certainly goes somewhere towards the happiness of the rational man) be the object of our estimate, then I assert, without the least hesitation, that the condition of those who labour (in all descriptions of labour, and in all gradations of labour, from the highest to the lowest inclusively) is on the whole extremely meliorated, if more and better food is any standard of melioration. They work more, it is certain; but they have the advantage of their augmented labour; yet whether that increase of labour be on the whole a *good* or an *evil*, is a consideration that would lead us a great way, and is not for my present purpose. But as to the fact of the melioration of their diet, I shall enter into the detail of proof whenever I am called upon: in the meantime, the known difficulty of contenting them with any thing but bread made of the finest flour, and meat of the first quality, is proof sufficient.

I further assert, that even under all the hardships of the last year, the labouring people did, either out of their direct gains, or from charity, (which it seems is now an insult to them) in fact, fare better than they did, in seasons of common plenty, 50 or 60 years ago; or even at the period of my English observation, which is about 44 years. I even assert, that full as many in that class, as ever were known to do it before, continued to save money; and this I can prove, so far as my own information and experience extend.

* * * *

EDMUND BURKE

I shall be told by the zealots of the sect of regulation, that this may be true, and may be safely committed to the convention of the farmer and the labourer, when the latter is in the prime of his youth, and at the time of his health and vigour, and in ordinary times of abundance. But in calamitous seasons, under accidental illness, in declining life, and with the pressure of a numerous offspring, the future nourishers of the community but the present drains and blood-suckers of those who produce them, what is to be done? When a man cannot live and maintain his family by the natural hire of his labour, ought it not to be raised by authority?

On this head I must be allowed to submit, what my opinions have ever been; and somewhat at large.

And, first, I premise that labour is, as I have already intimated, a commodity, and as such, an article of trade. If I am right in this notion, then labour must be subject to all the laws and principles of trade, and not to regulations foreign to them, and that may be totally inconsistent with those principles and those laws. When any commodity is carried to market, it is not the necessity of the vender, but the necessity of the purchaser that raises the price. The extreme want of the seller has rather (by the nature of things with which we shall in vain contend) the direct contrary operation. If the goods at market are beyond the demand, they fall in their value; if below it, they rise. The impossibility of the subsistence of a man, who carries his labour to a market, is totally beside the question in this way of viewing it. The only question is, what is it worth to the buyer?

But if authority comes in and forces the buyer to a price, what is this in the case (say) of a farmer, who buys the labour of ten or twelve labouring men, and three or four handycrafts, what is it, but to make an arbitrary division of his property among them?

The whole of his gains, I say it with the most certain conviction, never do amount any thing like in value to what he pays to his labourers and artificers; so that a very small advance upon what *one* man pays to *many*, may absorb the whole of what he possesses, and amount to an actual partition of all his substance among them. A perfect equality will indeed be produced;—that is to say, equal want, equal wretchedness, equal beggary, and on the part of the partitioners, a woeful, helpless, and desperate disappointment. Such is the event of all compulsory equalizations. They pull down what is above. They never raise what is below: and they depress high and low together beneath the level of what was originally the lowest.

If a commodity is raised by authority above what it will yield with a

48

profit to the buyer, that commodity will be the less dealt in. If a second blundering interposition be used to correct the blunder of the first, and an attempt is made to force the purchase of the commodity (of labour for instance), the one of these two things must happen, either that the forced buyer is ruined, or the price of the product of the labour, in that proportion, is raised. Then the wheel turns round, and the evil complained of falls with aggravated weight on the complainant. The price of corn, which is the result of the expence of all the operations of husbandry, taken together, and for some time continued, will rise on the labourer, considered as a consumer. The very best will be, that he remains where he was. But if the price of the corn should not compensate the price of labour, what is far more to be feared, the most serious evil, the very destruction of agriculture itself, is to be apprehended.

Nothing is such an enemy to accuracy of judgment as a coarse discrimination; a want of such classification and distribution as the subject admits of. Encrease the rate of wages to the labourer, say the regulators—as if labour was but one thing and of one value. But this very broad generic term, *labour*, admits, at least, of two or three specific descriptions: and these will suffice, at least, to let gentlemen discern a little the necessity of proceeding with caution in their coercive guidance of those whose existence depends upon the observance of still nicer distinctions and sub-divisions, than commonly they resort to in forming their judgments on this very enlarged part of economy.

The labourers in husbandry may be divided: 1st. into those who are able to perform the full work of a man; that is, what can be done by a person from twenty-one years of age to fifty. I know no husbandry work (mowing hardly excepted) that is not equally within the power of all persons within those ages, the more advanced fully compensating by knack and habit what they lose in activity. Unquestionably, there is a good deal of difference between the value of one man's labour and that of another, from strength, dexterity, and honest application. But I am quite sure, from my best observation, that any given five men will, in their total, afford a proportion of labour equal to any other five within the periods of life I have stated; that is, that among such five men there will be one possessing all the qualifications of a good workman, one bad, and the other three middling, and approximating to the first and the last. So that in so small a platoon as that of even five, you will find the full complement of all that five men *can* earn. Taking five and five throughout the kingdom, they are equal: therefore, an error with regard to the equalization of their wages by those who employ five, as farmers do at the very least, cannot be considerable.

2dly. Those who are able to work, but not the complete task of a day-labourer. This class is infinitely diversified, but will aptly enough fall into principal divisions. *Men*, from the decline, which after fifty becomes every year more sensible, to the period of debility and decrepitude, and the maladies that precede a final dissolution. *Women*, whose employment on husbandry is but occasional, and who differ more in effective labour one from another than men do, on account of gestation, nursing, and domestic management, over and above the difference they have in common with men in advancing, in stationary, and in declining life. *Children*, who proceed on the reverse order, growing from less to greater utility, but with a still greater disproportion of nutriment to labour than is found in the second of these sub-divisions; as is visible to those who will give themselves the trouble of examining into the interior economy of a poor-house.

This interior classification is introduced to shew, that laws prescribing, or magistrates exercising, a very stiff, and often inapplicable rule, or a blind and rash discretion, never can provide the just proportions between earning and salary on the one hand, and nutriment on the other: whereas interest, habit, and the tacit convention, that arise from a thousand nameless circumstances, produce a *tact* that regulates without difficulty, what laws and magistrates cannot regulate at all. The first class of labour wants nothing to equalize it; it equalizes itself. The second and third are not capable of any equalization.

But what if the rate of hire to the labourer comes far short of his necessary subsistence, and the calamity of the time is so great as to threaten actual famine? Is the poor labourer to be abandoned to the flinty heart and griping hand of base self-interest, supported by the sword of law, especially when there is reason to suppose that the very avarice of farmers themselves has concurred with the errors of Government to bring famine on the land.

In that case, my opinion is this. Whenever it happens that a man can claim nothing according to the rules of commerce, and the principles of justice, he passes out of that department, and comes within the jurisdiction of mercy. In that province the magistrate has nothing at all to do: his interference is a violation of the property which it is his office to protect. Without all doubt, charity to the poor is a direct and obligatory duty upon all Christians, next in order after the payment of debts, full as strong, and by nature made infinitely more delightful to us. Puffendorf, and other casuists do not, I think, denominate it quite properly, when they call it a duty of imperfect obligation. But the manner, mode, time, choice of objects, and proportion, are left to private discretion; and perhaps, for that very reason it is performed with the greatest satisfaction, because the discharge of it has more the appearance of freedom; recommending us besides very specially to the divine favour, as the exercise of a virtue most suitable to a being sensible of it's own infirmity.

The cry of the people in cities and towns, though unfortunately (from a fear of their multitude and combination) the most regarded, ought, in *fact*, to be the *least* attended to upon this subject; for citizens are in a state of utter ignorance of the means by which they are to be fed, and they contribute little or nothing, except in an infinitely circuitous manner, to their own maintenance. They are truly '*Fruges consumere nati*'. They are to be heard with great respect and attention upon matters within their province, that is, on trades and manufactures; but on any thing that relates to agriculture, they are to be listened to with the same *reverence* which we pay to the dogmas of other ignorant and presumptuous men.

If any one were to tell them, that they were to give in an account of all the stock in their shops; that attempts would be made to limit their profits, or raise the price of the labouring manufacturers upon them, or recommend to Government, out of a capital from the publick revenues, to set up a shop of the same commodities, in order to rival them, and keep them to reasonable dealing, they would very soon see the impudence, injustice, and oppression of such a course. They would not be mistaken; but they are of opinion, that agriculture is to be subject to other laws, and to be governed by other principles.

A greater and more ruinous mistake cannot be fallen into, than that the trades of agriculture and grazing can be conducted upon any other than the common principles of commerce; namely, that the producer should be permitted, and even expected, to look to all possible profit which, without fraud or violence, he can make; to turn plenty or scarcity to the best advantage he can; to keep back or to bring forward his commodities at his pleasure; to account to no one for his flock or for his gain. On any other terms he is the slave of the consumer; and that he should be so is of no benefit to the consumer. No slave was ever so beneficial to the master as a freeman that deals with him on an equal footing by convention, formed on the rules and principles of contending interests and compromised advantages. The consumer, if he were suffered, would in the end always be the dupe of his own tyranny and injustice. The landed gentleman is never to forget, that the farmer is his representative.

It is a perilous thing to try experiments on the farmer. The farmer's capital (except in a few persons, and in a very few places) is far more feeble than is commonly imagined. The trade is a very poor trade; it is subject to great risks and losses. The capital, such as it is, is turned but once in the year; in some branches it requires three years before the money is paid. I believe never less than three in the turnip and grass-land course, which is the prevalent course on the more or less fertile, sandy and gravelly loams, and these compose the soil in the south and south-east of England, the best adapted, and perhaps the only ones that are adapted, to the turnip husbandry.

It is very rare that the most prosperous farmer, counting the value of his quick and dead stock, the interest of the money he turns, together with his own wages as a bailiff or overseer, ever does make twelve or fifteen *per centum* by the year on his capital. I speak of the prosperous. In most of the parts of England which have fallen within my observation, I have rarely known a farmer, who to his own trade has not added some other employment or traffic, that, after a course of the most unremitting parsimony and labour (such for the greater part is theirs), and persevering in his business for a long course of years, died worth more than paid his debts, leaving his posterity to continue in nearly the same equal conflict between industry and want, in which the last predecessor, and a long line of predecessors before him, lived and died.

* * * *

After all, have we not reason to be thankful to the giver of all good? In our history, and when 'The labourer of England is said to have been once happy,' we find constantly, after certain intervals, a period of real famine; by which, a melancholy havock was made among the human race. The price of provisions fluctuated dreadfully, demonstrating a deficiency very different from the worst failures of the present moment. Never since I have known England, have I known more than a comparative scarcity. The price of wheat, taking a number of years together, has had no very considerable fluctuation, nor has it risen exceedingly until within this twelvemonth. Even now, I do not know of one man, woman, or child, that has perished from famine; fewer, if any, I believe, than in years of plenty, when such a thing may happen by accident. This is owing to a care and superintendance of the poor, far greater than any I remember.

The consideration of this ought to bind us all, rich and poor together, against those wicked writers of the newspapers, who would inflame the poor against their friends, guardians, patrons, and protectors. Not only very few (I have observed, that I know of none, though I live in a place as poor as most) have actually died of want, but we have seen no traces of those dreadful exterminating epidemics, which, in consequence of scanty and unwholesome food, in former times, not unfrequently, wasted whole nations. Let us be saved from too much wisdom of our own, and we shall do tolerably well.

It is one of the finest problems in legislation, and what has often engaged my thoughts whilst I followed that profession, 'What the State ought to take upon itself to direct by the public wisdom, and what it ought to leave, with as little interference as possible, to individual discretion'. Nothing, certainly, can be laid down on the subject that will not admit of exceptions, many permanent, some occasional. But the clearest line of distinction which I could draw, whilst I had my chalk to draw any line, was this: That the State ought to confine itself to what regards the State, or the creatures of the State, namely, the exterior establishment of its religion; its magistracy; its revenue; its military force by sea and land; the corporations that owe their existence to its fiat; in a word, to every thing that is *truly and properly* public, to the public peace, to the public safety, to the public order, to the public prosperity. In its preventive police it ought to be sparing of its efforts, and to employ means, rather few, unfrequent, and strong, than many, and frequent, and, of course, as they multiply their puny politic race, and dwindle, small and feeble. Statesmen who know themselves will, with the dignity which belongs to wisdom, proceed only in this the superior orb and first mover of their duty, steadily, vigilantly, severely, courageously: whatever remains will, in a manner, provide for itself. But as they descend from the state to a province, from a province to a parish, and from a parish to a private house, they go on accelerated in their fall. They *cannot* do the lower duty; and, in proportion as they try it, they will certainly fail in the higher. They ought to know the different departments of things; what belongs to laws, and what manners alone can regulate. To these, great politicians may give a leaning, but they cannot give a law.

Our Legislature has fallen into this fault as well as other governments; all have fallen into it more or less. The once mighty State, which was nearest to us locally, nearest to us in every way, and whose ruins threaten to fall upon our heads, is a strong instance of this error. I can never quote France without a foreboding sigh—ΕΣΣΤΑΙ'ΗΜΑΡ! Scipio said it to his recording Greek friend amidst the flames of the great rival of his country. That state has fallen by the hands of the parricides of their country, called the Revolutionists, the Constitutionalists, of

France, a species of traitors, of whose fury and atrocious wickedness nothing in the annals of the phrenzy and depravation of mankind had before furnished an example, and of whom I can never think or speak without a mixed sensation of disgust, of horrour, and of detestation, not easy to be expressed. These nefarious monsters destroyed their country for what was good in it: for much good there was in the constitution of that noble monarchy, which, in all kinds, formed and nourished great men, and great patterns of virtue to the world. But though it's enemies were not enemies to it's faults, it's faults furnished them with means for it's destruction. My dear departed friend, whose loss is even greater to the public than to me, had often remarked, that the leading viee of the French monarchy (which he had well studied) was in good intention ill-directed, and a restless desire of governing too much. The hand of authority was seen in every thing, and in every place. All, therefore, that happened amiss in the course even of domestic affairs, was attributed to the Government.

[Extracts]

AN ADDRESS TO THE GOOD SENSE AND CANDOUR OF THE PEOPLE

BY the time that Burke's *Thoughts and Details* (written, as we have seen, some years previously) appeared in print, food was even more scarce and more costly.

John Ashton, in *The Dawn of the XIXth Century*, describes the food riots in 1800, when Quakers (rather than Jews) appear to have been particularly suspected of contributing to the high cost of living, so that the appearance of a Quaker (easily distinguished in those days by the 'plain dress') made him a special target for the anger of a hungry mob. In London the Lord Mayor was hissed, and a hostile crowd only dispersed when the Riot Act had been read and a charge made by the constables. Indeed, it eventually required the united efforts of the Tower Ward Volunteers, the East India House Volunteers and the Militia to restore order in the city. Similar riots had already taken place in many provincial towns, and a drawing by Cruikshank commemorates the strong-arm methods used by some enthusiasts in discouraging 'forestalling and regrating'. A 'forestaller' is being dragged along with a rope round his neck, and the caption is: 'Hints to forestallers; or, a sure way to reduce the price of grain'. Evidently the principles of Edmund Burke (which so completely anticipated the *laissez-faire* policy of many eminent nineteenth century political economists) aroused no enthusiasm in those whom the economists doomed to starve.

'Forestalling' meant buying up goods in order to re-sell at a higher price—an activity to which some people are always attracted, especially in times of scarcity. 'Regrating' meant much the same thing, the difference being visible only to a lawyer or an economist. Among the celebrated cases at this time was that of Mr John Rusby, who, on July 4, 1800, was convicted at the King's Bench of buying up ninety quarters of oats at 41 shillings a quarter and selling part on the same day in the same market at 44 shillings a quarter—not a very public-spirited action in a time of scarcity. (Students of the Black Market and its history may note, once more, that nobody suggests a non-Aryan origin in the case of Mr Rusby.) Lord Kenyon, who presided, congratulated the Jury on having conferred by their verdict 'almost the greatest benefit on your country that was ever conferred by a jury'.

The City mob, in the riots mentioned above (they took place in the following September) evidently concurred with His Lordship, for they burst into Mr Rusby's house with every intention of hanging him. This he avoided, for being a forestaller he had naturally anticipated the next move, as was his habit, and left by the back door. The visitors appear to have treated Mrs Rusby and her children quite civilly, but left the house with such money as they could find there.

It is this John Rusby whose case is the theme of the following pages, first published in 1800. If hypocrisy is really the tribute which vice pays to virtue, then we may regard it as a slight token of progress in public morality that, although there have been plenty of Black Marketeers in our time, nobody has had the face to write a defence of their activities. Sir Thomas Turton's defence of regrating in general and of Rusby in particular has therefore a fine period flavour—it takes us back to a time when some forms of knavery had less need of a cloak. Indeed, Turton's views were shared by some whose business it was to enforce the law, the more so as the legal position regarding forestalling was none too clear, however simple the moral argument must have appeared to those who saw dealers juggle with the cost of their food. The Chairman of Clerkenwell Sessions stated openly that if he sentenced at all for this offence, the penalties would be the lightest possible.

Of Sir Thomas Turton himself little need be said. He was Sheriff of Surrey in 1795–96. The *Complete Baronetage* cryptically informs us that 'he distinguished himself during the riots of that year, and was consequently created a Baronet'. From 1806–1812 he was Clerk of the Juries in the Court of Common Pleas and M.P. for Southwark. The Black Market was indeed fortunate in having such influential friends as Sir Thomas, and so was the Duke of York, during the Parliamentary investigation of charges made against the Duke's mistress, Mary Anne Clarke, who had been selling commissions in the army, of which the Duke was then Commander-in-Chief. Turton's questions during this enquiry were always directed towards the exculpation of His Royal Highness, who was indeed in all probability stupid enough to have been an innocent tool in very obvious fraud.

AN ADDRESS TO THE GOOD SENSE AND CANDOUR OF THE PEOPLE IN BEHALF OF THE DEALERS IN CORN

By Sir Thomas Turton, Bart.

You have heard that one of this class has been convicted by a jury of his country of the crime of regrating, and though you do not know all the circumstances, yet you feel satisfied his crime must have been of the blackest dye, because the jury were told on that occasion, that a verdict of condemnation 'would carry glad tidings to the people, and particularly to the poor'. Of consequence, he must be considered as one amongst the number of those who are represented as preying on the vitals of the people, and by their avarice contributing to the publick misery. You consider him no longer in the real character he deserves—that of the middle-man, who stands between you and the grower for the mutual advantage of both. You see in him only your bitterest enemy, officiously interposing his offices, where you neither wish them, nor think you can receive ought but deadly injury from them.

What then are the circumstances of this dreadful crime which has so increased your wonted prejudice against this class? What can an individual have done, so as to attach ignominy to *all* those persons who pursue the same branch of trade with himself. If a man has been convicted of the monstrous crime of regrating, let us examine, whether he has been convicted of that, which at the time he did it, he thought wrong—whether he carried to the act, the mind and intention necessary to constitute *crime*—whether he has not been indirectly encouraged by the highest authority in the country, to do what he has done—whether, in legal strictness, he did the act at all; and lastly, whether he has done any thing, which every other man with the same opportunities, not in his business only, but in any of the various branches of trade, to be met with in the kingdom, does not do every day of his life, without the smallest suspicion that he is doing that, which either the laws of his country, or of morality, forbid.

I must premise, that the report of the Trial which I have read, is that printed by Ridgway, and stated to have been taken in short-hand by a Barrister.

This person, Mr John Rusby, was indicted for regrating, or re-selling in the same market, and on the same day, 30 quarters of oats, part of a lot of 90 quarters purchased by him in the morning, and by which re-sale he obtained a profit of 2s. per quarter.—Every man acquainted with the business of the Corn Exchange, or who has taken the trouble to inform himself on this head, will find, that it has been the constant and universal practice, to re-sell any part of a commodity bought, where there was either an advantage on such re-sale—where the quantity originally bought was larger than either party wanted, and of course a mutual accommodation—or where the lot, after it was bought, was repented of by the purchaser either from the price, or quality—Whatever might be his reasons for the re-sale, no one objected to a practice which had existed beyond the memory of the oldest man at the Corn Exchange—which was a general convenience to the trade—which facilitated instead of interrupting the commerce—and from which the public could sustain no possible injury equal in amount to what the restriction on the free agency of the jobber would inevitably occasion.—This was done openly, even when it was known, that there were statutes which prohibited it.—They were generally considered, though in force, as not likely to be acted on, and that which was known to be illegal, was scarcely practised with secresy, or covertly. But when the more enlightened spirit of Commerce began to dawn upon the nation, it was considered possible, that these restraints, though dis-regarded by the bold, might have the effect of restraining the timid (but not less useful) members of the trade, in the free exercise of their industry and capital.—Men of intelligence, and those best acquainted with the true principles of commerce (at that time a science in the mere state of childhood) exerted their influence with the legislature, to pro-cure the abolition of those laws, which they considered (and justly) as tending, if put in force, to the utter destruction of that commerce, and of those very interests they were meant to uphold and protect.—This measure, the result of sound reasoning, was greatly aided in its pro-gress, by the transcendent talents and comprehensive mind of a gentleman[1] who though since dead, has raised for himself a monument 'ære perennius' in the grateful affection of the nation, by the important services which he rendered not only to his country, but to the whole of civilized Europe, in the political writings which employed the few last years of a life, usefully throughout, engaged in the public service. This gentleman considered the freedom of trade as the foundation of national prosperity, and those restrictions and prohibitions, which prejudice and vain fear had engendered in the early periods of its growth, as fungous excrescences exhausting its vital powers, and effectually and most banefully checking its progress to maturity.—The nation felt the sentiment to be just, and instantly repealed the whole of those acts which had remained on the Statute Book, a monument of the poverty of its principles (though nearly as a dead letter) from the time of Edward VI.—The gradual increase of the prosperity of commerce since the year 1772, the period in which this repeal took place, is the best panegyric on the wisdom of the measure. The preamble of the Bill is particularly worthy of attention at this time, when the propriety of restoring them to the statute book, has been suggested from high authority (I think not in the moment of reflection), because it shews the spirit with which it adopted those sound and conclusive principles (and almost the very language) of that great and luminous character Dr Adam Smith, which were afterwards submitted to the world in the able and comprehensive work of that writer. It stated that, 'Whereas it hath been found *by experience* that the restraints laid by several statutes upon the dealing in *Corn, Meal, Flour*, Cattle, and other sundry sort of victuals, by *preventing a free trade* in the said commodities, have a tendency to *discourage the growth and enhance the price* of the same—which statutes if put in execution *would bring great distress* on the inhabitants of many parts of the kingdom, and *particularly on the cities of London and Westminster*, be it therefore enacted', &c. &c.

Now is it possible to conceive a more complete acknowledgement of error—a more candid and manly confession of the imprudent conduct it had hitherto pursued in preventing the benefit of a free trade, and of the effect which had been in consequence produced, in the great distress which the people had suffered throughout the kingdom; but especially in those parts, where the freedom of trade is essentially necessary to the daily regular supply of its inhabitants?

Are these principles then unwise and imprudent to be acted upon in the year 1800, which were deemed not only salutary, but necessary in the year 1772? Does the freedom of trade require less protection or

[1] Mr. Edmund Burke.

encouragement, when the support of ten millions of inhabitants look to it for the supply of their wants and wishes, than when six or seven millions only depended on its aid?—Are its principles to be disputed at this day, when we have witnessed the salutary effects of their operations, in the almost unlimited expansion of that commerce to nearly its acme of perfection since that period? Look to the imports and exports of that year, reflect on the state of the internal trade in 1772, and then say whether the most sanguine could have ventured to form an expectation so vast as that which has been realized in that period. To what is it to be attributed, if not to the enterprising spirit and active industry of the merchants, fostered by the encouraging hand of legislative protection, and by the abolition of those statutes, which had hitherto restrained men from the open employment of their capital and industry in that manner, which, whilst it accords with their views and inclinations, is best calculated to promote the real interest of commerce, and to carry it to its utmost state of prosperity?

From this moment the trade did that openly and extensively, which before they had done covertly and partially. It was not peculiar to an individual or an house, it was the universal practice of the trade. Is it possible to believe that these men imagined they were doing wrong, when the legislature had openly acknowledged the impolicy and mischief of the restraint it had formerly imposed upon them? Could the man who, having bought a parcel of corn, more than his occasion required (or tempted by price if you will) disposed on the instant of part of it, not secretly, but in an open market, in the face of the world, think that he was offending against the laws of his country, when it was written on the highest record of the nation, that his former prohibitions had been found by *experience* an offence against public interest, and such as the nation would no longer encourage, or endure? —Are these dealers then to be told, in answer to this cogent and powerful reasoning? 'It is true, the legislature has repealed the statutes against forestalling, engrossing and regrating (except a little reservation in a parenthesis) but notwithstanding this, if you adopt its sentiments, and act upon the principles which it acknowledges to have caused the abolition of those statutes, the common law will step forwards to punish you.'

Of what advantage then, was it to abolish this act? What benefit could the country derive from this half measure, ushered in with so much solemnity by open undisguised avowal of error and contrition? I know it will be said, that the legislature could not abolish with the statutes, the provisions of the common law—but were there no means it could have taken to protect those who might suffer from its persecutions? If it did not, what a mockery of bounty did it present, what a solemn but contemptible farce was it acting before the public. Of what use was this vaunted privilege, granted in the fulness of its generosity, and which was to protect the trade from *all* 'further prosecutions, informations, indictments, or suits for the *the inflicting of any punishment*, or recovery of any fine, penalty, &c. any *law*, statute or *usage* to the contrary notwithstanding,' except to entrap him into guilt, and to trick him into punishment? In vain can you say, that the repeal of the statutes only was meant to take away the penalty—it says more, it speaks much stronger language; yet if the common law was to have its operations, it would not even protect him so far; for though the exact penalty there inflicted could not be recovered, no one will venture to say, that on a verdict of guilty under an indictment at the common law, the sentence may not be fine and imprisonment. So that you have merely changed the word, and he is still subjected as before to the same actual punishment—indeed to greater.

I declare to God, that since I have read this trial—since I have observed the favoured spirit of persecution stalking abroad, scattering about its venom on the heads of guiltless individuals, and poisoning in its fatal progress the very sources, from which spring all the energies of trade, I have more trembled for my country, I have had greater apprehensions for its safety, than during all that period of political convulsion, when in common with the rest of Europe it was attacked by the absurd but specious philosophy of the Rights of Man, with all the farrago of nonsense imported at that time into the country, in the 'Gipsy Jargon' of the late French School—I have felt my mind more agitated, more worked up into a resentment, which (however warm my mind and temper naturally may be) is not I trust its usual character, when I have reflected on this monstrous and cruel usage of men, who whilst they are contributing to the wealth and prosperity of their country, are subjected to persecutions, the prominent feature of arbitrary government, and forming the strong contrast to those mild, and just principles on which the liberties of Englishmen are founded. Let any man have asked Mr Rusby previous to his trial (God knows the poor man has heard and felt enough of it since) what the common law meant—would he, or nineteen out of twenty of his trade have been able to tell you? Or would he have given you credit, if you had told him, or indeed could he have believed it possible, when the legislature says to him, 'Go on, according to your will and pleasure—henceforth exercise unconstrained liberty in your dealings for the benefit of the public, which has been injured by the former restraints, that in its folly and ignorance of its true interests it imposed upon you,' that some incomprehensible, unknown, undefined, but superior power was lurking in secret to watch his motions, and to punish with the extremest rigour those acts which have the open sanction of legislative approbation, and which have been proclaimed aloud, by the omnipotent voice of Parliament, to be the only genuine and true sources of national prosperity and commercial greatness.

Taking this subject in all its bearings on the character, consistency and justice of the country, and the important consequences connected with it, the ample discussion of it would take a pamphlet of itself—I refrain therefore from further discussion of it, and hasten to the case of Rusby, as the only instance we have lately known of the exercise of this right of the common law, as to the corn trade.

[Extract]

THE LATE

JOHN WILKES'S

CATECHISM

OF A

MINISTERIAL MEMBER.

With Permission.

LONDON:

Printed and Published by R. Carlile, 183, Fleet-Street, and sold by those who are not afraid of incurring the displeasure of his Majesty's Ministers, their Spies or Informers, or Public Plunderers of any denomination, 1817.

Price Two Pence.

THE LATE JOHN WILKES'S CATECHISM

THE *Late John Wilkes's Catechism* owed nothing but its name to Wilkes. William Hone used a well-known name and one chosen for the interest it was calculated to incite, just as his contemporary, Richard Carlile, fathered one of his squibs upon the respectable Greek scholar, Professor Porson.

The *Catechism* was the first of three parodies, published in 1817, and it is perhaps the most biting of all the attacks on the political corruption of the time. This corruption arose partly from the property franchise and the trade in votes and boroughs. (The prices of 'Rotten Boroughs' could be quoted like those of any other stocks; and it was among the complaints of Lord Chesterfield and others that the price of a seat in Parliament had been raised by high bidding on the part of the 'nabobs' who had made their illgotten wealth in India.) But while the votes of electors were sold to candidates, the successful candidate could re-imburse himself for his expenses by selling his own vote in Parliament to the Government. At the disposal of the Government were innumerable jobs and pensions with which the complaisant M.P. could be rewarded. It was to expose these 'Placemen' and Government Pensioners that Hone wrote his *Catechism*.

William Hone was a book-seller of democratic opinions, and a man of considerable learning, as he was soon to demonstrate when tried on a charge of publishing impious and profane libels. There were three separate trials, held consecutively and concerned with the three parodies, which, with Cruikshank's illustrations, had made the Government of Lord Liverpool the laughing stock of the world. Hone himself, alarmed at the success—and possible consequences—of his satires, had withdrawn all three of the parodies soon after their first publication. They were promptly pirated and re-published by Richard Carlile 'and sold by all who are not afraid of incurring the Displeasure of His Majesty's Ministers, their spies and Informers, or Public Plunderers of any denomination'. It is a curious fact that the other two parodies (*The Political Litany* and *The Sinecurist's Creed*) were actually attributed to Carlile by George J. Holyoake, who should have known better—*vide* his article on Carlile in the *Dictionary of*

National Biography (1887). Carlile's edition has been used for the present reprint.

In his trials, of which Hone himself later published a full account, the defendant conducted his own case and insisted upon reading to the court innumerable parodies of the Scriptures and the Liturgy, including many examples by respectable Tory authors whom the Government clearly had no mind to prosecute. The defence consisted, in fact, mainly of an interesting anthology of parodies, blasphemous or bordering on blasphemy (according to the popular conception of blasphemy, which is very vague); and in spite of the mounting indignation of the Chief Justice, Lord Ellenborough, Hone was acquitted on all three charges. The verdict was popularly acclaimed, and Hone was presented with over £3,000, raised by public subscription, which enabled him to move his bookshop to larger and better premises.

This satire is reproduced here as published by Carlile in 1817, with a prefatory note tilting at Hone for his lack of courage, as shown by his withdrawal of his own work.

THE LATE JOHN WILKES'S CATECHISM OF A MINISTERIAL MEMBER

By William Hone

With Permission
LONDON:

Printed and Published by R. CARLILE, 183, Fleet-Street, and sold by those who are not afraid of incurring the displeasure of his Majesty's Ministers, their Spies or Informers, or Public Plunderers of any denomination. 1817.

Price Two Pence.

A CATECHISM

That is to say,

An Instruction, to be learned of every Person before he be brought to be confirmed a Placeman or Pensioner by the Minister.

Question.

WHAT is your Name?
Answer. Lick Spittle.
Q. Who gave you this Name?
A. My Sureties to the Ministry, in my Political Change, wherein I was made a Member of the Majority, the Child of Corruption, and a Locust to devour the good Things of this Kingdom.

Q. What did your Sureties then for you?

A. They did promise and vow three things in my Name. First, that I should renounce the Reformists and all their Works, the pomps and vanity of Popular Favour, and all the sinful lusts of Independence.

Secondly, that I should believe all the Articles of the Court Faith. And thirdly, that I should keep the Minister's sole Will and Commandments, and walk in the same, all the days of my life.

Q. Dost thou not think that thou art bound to believe and to do as they have promised for thee?

A. Yes verily, and for my own sake, so I will; and I heartily thank our heaven-born Ministry, that they have called me to this state of elevation, through my own flattery, cringing, and bribery; and I shall pray to their successors to give me their assistance, that I may continue the same unto my life's end.

Q. Rehearse the Articles of thy Belief.

A. I believe in GEORGE, the Regent Almighty, Maker of New Streets and Knights of the Bath;

And in the present Ministry, his only choice, who were conceived of Toryism, brought forth of WILLIAM PITT, suffered loss of place under CHARLES JAMES FOX, were execrated, dead, and buried. In a few months they rose again from their minority; they re-ascended to the Treasury Benches, and sit at the right hand of a little man in a large wig; from whence they *laugh* at the Petitions of the People, who pray for Reform, and that the sweat of their brow may procure them Bread.

I believe that King James the Second was a legitimate Sovereign, and that King William the Third was not; that the Pretender was of the right line, and that George the Third's Grandfather was not; that the dynasty of Bourbon is immortal; and that the glass in the eye of Lord James Murray, was not Betty Martin. I believe in the immaculate purity of the Committee of Finance, in the independence of the Committee of Secresy, and that the Pitt System is everlasting. Amen.

Q. What dost thou chiefly learn in these Articles of thy Belief?

A. First, I learn to forswear all conscience, which was never meant to trouble me, nor the rest of the tribe of Courtiers. Secondly to swear black is white, or white black, according to the good pleasure of the Ministers. Thirdly, to put on the helmet of impudence, the only armour against the shafts of patriotism.

Q. You said that your Sureties did promise for you, that you should keep the Minister's Commandments: tell me how many there be?

A. Ten.

Q. Which be they?

Answer.

The same to which the Minister for the time being always obliges all his creatures to swear, I the Minister am the Lord thy liege, who brought thee out of Want and Beggary, into the House of Commons.

I. Thou shalt have no other Patron but me.

II. Thou shalt not support any measure but mine, nor shalt thou frame clauses of any bill in its progress to the House above, or in the Committee beneath, or when the Mace is under the table, except it be mine. Thou shalt not bow to Lord COCHRANE, nor shake hands with him, nor any other of my real opponents; for I thy Lord am a jealous Minister, and forbid familiarity of the Majority, with the Friends of the People, unto the third and fourth cousins of them that divide against me; and give Places, and thousands and tens of thousands, to them that divide with me, and keep my commandments.

III. Thou shalt not take the Pension of thy Lord the Minister in vain; for I the minister will force him to accept the Chilterns, that taketh my Pension in vain.

IV. Remember that thou attend the Minister's Levee day; on other days thou shalt speak for him in the House, and fetch and carry, and do all that he commandeth thee to do; but the Levee day is for the glorification of the Minister thy Lord: In it thou shalt do no work in the House, but shall wait upon him, thou, and thy daughter, and thy wife, and the Members that are within his influence; for on other days the minister is inaccessible, but delighteth in the Levee day; wherefore the Minister appointed the Levee day, and chatteth thereon familiarly, and is amused with it.

V. Honor the Regent and the helmets of the Life Guards, that thy stay may be long in the Place, which thy Lord the Minister giveth thee.

VI. Thou shalt not call starving to death, murder.

VII. Thou shalt not call Royal gallivanting adultery.

VIII. Thou shalt not say, that to rob the Public is to steal.

IX. Thou shalt bear false witness against the People.

X. Thou shalt not covet the people's applause, thou shalt not covet the People's praise, nor their good name, nor their esteem, nor their reverence, nor any reward that is theirs.

Q. What dost thou chiefly learn by these Commandments?

A. I learn two things—my duty towards the Minister, and my duty towards myself.

Q. What is thy duty towards the Minister?

A. My duty towards the minister is, to trust him as much as I can; to fear him; to honor him with all my words, with all my bows, with all my scrapes, and all my cringes; to flatter him; to give him thanks to give up my whole Soul to him; to idolize his name, and obey his word; and serve him blindly all the days of his political life.

Q. What is thy duty towards thyself?

A. My duty towards myself is to love nobody but myself and to do unto most men what I would not they should do unto me; to sacrifice to my own interest even my father and mother; to pay little reverence to the King, but to compensate that omission by my servility to all that are put in authority under him; to lick the dust under the feet of my superiors, and to shake a rod of iron over the backs of my inferiors; to spare the people by neither word nor deed; to observe neither truth nor justice in my dealings with them; to bear them malice and hatred in my heart; and where their wives or properties are concerned, to keep my body neither in temperance, soberness, nor chastity, but to give my hands to picking and stealing, and my tongue to evil speaking and lying, and slander of their efforts to defend their liberties and recover their rights; never failing to envy their privileges, and to learn to get the Pensions of myself and my colleagues out of the People's labour, and to do my duty in that department of public plunder unto which it shall please the Minister to call me.

Q. My good Courtier, know this, that thou art not able of thyself to preserve the minister's favour, nor to walk in his Commandments, nor to serve him, without his special protection; which thou must at all times learn to obtain by diligent application. Let me hear therefore, if thou canst rehearse the Minister's Memorial.

Answer.

OUR Lord who art in the Treasury, whatsoever be thy name, thy power be prolonged, thy will be done throughout the empire, as it is in each session. Give us our usual sops, and forgive us our occasional absences on divisions; as we promise not to forgive them that divide against thee. Turn us not out of our Places; but keep us in the House of Commons, the land of Pensions and Plenty; and deliver us from the People. Amen.

Q. What desirest thou of the Minister in this memorial?

A. I desire the minister, our Patron, who is the disposer of the Nation's overstrained Taxation, to give his protection unto me and to all Pensioners and Placemen, that we may vote for him, serve him, and obey him, as far as we find it convenient; and I beseech the minister that he will give us all things that be needful, both for our reputation and appearance in the House and out of it, that he will be favourable to us and forgive us our negligences; that it will please him to save and defend us, in all dangers of life and limb, from the people our natural enemies; and that he will help us in fleecing and grinding them; and this I trust he will do out of care for himself, and our support of him through our corruption and influence; and therefore I say Amen. So be it.

Q. How many tests hath the minister ordained?

A. Two only, as generally necessary to elevation: (that is to say) Passive Obedience and Bribery.

Q. What meanest thou by this word Test?

A. I mean an outward visible sign of an inward intellectual meanness, ordained by the Minister himself as a pledge to assure him thereof.

Q. How many Parts are there in this Test?

A. Two; the outward visible sign, and the inward intellectual meanness.

Q. What is the outward visible sign or Form of passive obedience?

A. Dangling at the Minister's heels, whereby the person is degraded beneath the baseness of a slave, in the character of a Pensioner, Placeman, Expectant, Parasite, Toadeater, or Lord of the bedchamber.

Q. What is the inward and intellectual meanness?

A. A death unto freedom, a subjection unto perpetual Thraldom; for being by nature born free, and the children of Independence, we are hereby made children of slavery.

Q. What is required of persons submitting to the Test of Passive Obedience?

A. Apostacy, whereby they forsake liberty; and faith, whereby they stedfastly believe the promises of the Minister, made to them upon submitting to that Test.

Q. Why was the Test of Bribery ordained?

A. For the continued support of the Minister's influence, and the feeding of us, his needy creatures and sycophants.

Q. What is the outward part or sign in the Test of Bribery?

A. Bank notes, which the minister hath commended to be offered by his dependants.

Q. Why then are beggars submitted to this Test, when by reason of their poverty they are not able to go through the necessary forms?

A. Because they promise them by their Sureties; which promise, when they come to lucrative offices, they themselves are bound to perform.

Q. What is the inward part or thing signified?

A. The industry and wealth of the people, which are verily and indeed taken and had by Pensioners and Sinecurists, in their Corruption.

Q. What are the benefits whereof you are partakers thereby?

A. The weakening and impoverishing the People, through the loss of their Liberty and Property, while our wealth becomes enormous, and our pride intolerable.

Q. What is required of them who submit to the Test of Bribery and corruption?

A. To examine themselves, whether they repent them truly of any signs of former honour and patriotism, stedfastly purposing henceforward to be faithful towards the minister; to draw on and off like his glove; to crouch to him like a Spaniel; to purvey for him like a Jackall; to be as supple to him as Alderman Sir WILLIAM TURTLE; to have the most lively faith in the funds, especially the Sinking Fund; to believe the words of Lord Castlereagh alone; to have remembrance of nothing but what is in the Courier; to hate MATTHEW WOOD, the present Lord Mayor, and his second Mayoralty, with all our heart, with all our mind, with all our soul, and with all our strength; to admire Sir JOHN SILVESTER, the Recorder, and Mr JOHN LANGLEY;[1] and to be in charity with those only who have something to give.

Here endeth the Catechism.

[1] Otherwise Jack Ketch.

A LETTER TO WILLIAM GIFFORD, ESQ.

THE spirit of the pamphleteer is to be found in most of Cobbett's writings, and he even used the word 'pamphlet' to describe one of his periodicals; but unfortunately his best writings do not, strictly speaking, qualify for inclusion here if we are to limit our conception of pamphleteering to the issue of occasional short works, separately published, and exclusive of periodical literature.

There are, however, some *bona fide* pamphlets, in this sense, by William Cobbett, of which we considered including his *Address to the Taxpayers* (1832), and would have done so but for the difficulty of separating the excellent material to be found in it from the somewhat tedious egoism and self-justification of the writer. This pamphlet, nevertheless, offers some very interesting comments, which are worth quoting, respecting the whole art of pamphleteering as it was practised by the hired hacks of the Government; and some of Cobbett's observations on this subject afford an excellent introduction to Hazlitt's onslaught on Gifford. On his return from America in 1800 Cobbett discovered a whole host of scribblers who were paid by the Government to defend its policy. There was John Reeves, a briefless barrister, late chairman of the 'Loyal Association against Republicans and Levellers', who drew £4,000 a year for being 'joint patentee of the office of King's printer'—a meaningless sinecure. Another briefless barrister, John Bowles, was paid under pretext of being a 'Commissioner of Dutch Property'. John Gifford was 'a Police Magistrate, with a pension of 300 l. a year besides'. Sir Frederick Morton Eden, Bart., Cobbett 'found with rent-free apartments in Hampton Court Palace, and with what else I have now forgotten'. Various clergymen were enjoying rich 'livings' of which the Government could dispose, as a reward for their services; and a long list of such instances ends with the name of Nicholas Vansittart, 'who had written a pamphlet *to prove that the war enriched the nation*' and received his reward as 'Commissioner of Scotch Herrings'. (Surely there should be a red herring sinister in the Vansittart arms?) The case of Edmund Burke, to which we have already referred, may be recalled as another instance of pen and pensions.

In this interesting list the name of William Gifford occurs (no relative of John Gifford, mentioned above) with the comment that he shared the profits of 'Canning's Anti-Jacobin newspaper (set up and paid for by the Treasury)', with an additional sinecure of £329 a year. Gifford is mentioned by Cobbett as one of the two men of talent in this bunch of Government hacks; and talent he undoubtedly possessed. Of Gifford Cobbett wrote that 'he despised Pitt and Canning and the whole crew; but he loved ease and was timid . . . all his life he had to endure a conflict between his pecuniary interest and his conscience'. How this conflict was resolved may be realised by the fact that Gifford left over £30,000 at his death in 1826, the sources of this wealth (a useful sum of money even in our own days) having included a 'commissionership of the lottery' and the post of 'Paymaster of the gentlemen-pensioners', the latter worth £1,000 a year. Cobbett's figure of £329 considerably under-estimated the sums paid annually to Gifford in addition to the £900 a year which he received eventually as editor of the *Quarterly Review*.

In return for such substantial rewards Gifford used all his literary powers against the radicals of his time, and the objectives of his malice included not only the new ideas which were upsetting the political world, but those new literary forms which were frequently associated with radical politics. From the French Revolution to the middle of the nineteenth century the Romantic Revival was to be associated with republicanism; and although many of the earlier romantics (Wordsworth, Coleridge, Southey, etc.) changed sides, the tradition was continued by Shelley, Keats, Byron and others, who in varying degrees reflected both the romantic and the revolutionary spirit of their times. Gifford made war on the romantics just in so far as they were also republicans; that he could relax his literary severity is demonstrated by the fact that Sir Walter Scott (an outstanding exception to the rule, as a 'romantic' who lived and died a Tory) contributed to the *Quarterly Review*, as did other 'romantics' who had lived to repent of their radicalism. Even Byron, who belonged in theory to the classical school (witness his criticism of Wordsworth for abandoning eighteenth century poetic diction) managed to escape Gifford's head-on attacks either by his profession of allegiance to 'classical' principles in literature, or perhaps because Byron was at heart a believer in aristocracy who was never really at home among the radicals with whom he so frequently consorted.

But on such as Keats, Gifford poured forth all the spleen of a sick, deformed man who hated people in general, because most of them were stronger and healthier than himself, and hated even an invalid who had not sold himself to the same racket. If ever a man was murdered by the pen, Keats was certainly done to death by an article in the *Quarterly Review*, almost certainly written, and quite certainly sanctioned, by its sour-mouthed editor. Keats died, in Byron's words, 'snuffed out by an article' (Byron himself had not been particularly kind in his references to the young poet's work). But in men like Hazlitt and Leigh Hunt such bullies as Gifford met their match.

Hazlitt, in particular, quarrelled with everybody in turn, and seems to have enjoyed it. Hazlitt was also as incurable an egoist as Cobbett, and equally inconsistent. Indeed, the only reason that it is possible to use the extract which follows, from Hazlitt's *Letter to William Gifford*, is that this portion is fortunately free from the egoism which spoils the rest of the pamphlet.

Gifford's attacks certainly merited such a reply, and the extract which we reproduce here from Hazlitt's pamphlet shows the writer in his best controversial vein. The *Letter* was published in 1819.

A LETTER TO WILLIAM GIFFORD, ESQ.

By William Hazlitt

Sir,

You have an ugly trick of saying what is not true of any one you do not like; and it will be the object of this letter to cure you of it. You say what you please of others: it is time you were told what you are. In doing this, give me leave to borrow the familiarity of your style:—for the fidelity of the picture I shall be answerable.

You are a little person, but a considerable cat's-paw; and so far worthy of notice. Your clandestine connexion with persons high in office constantly influences your opinions, and alone gives importance to them. You are the *Government Critic*, a character nicely differing from that of a government spy—the invisible link, that connects literature with the police. It is your business to keep a strict eye over all writers who differ in opinion with his Majesty's Ministers, and to measure their talents and attainments by the standard of their servility and meanness. For this office you are well qualified. Besides being the Editor of the *Quarterly Review*, you are also paymaster of the band of Gentlemen Pensioners; and when an author comes before you in the one capacity, with whom you are not acquainted in the other, you know how to deal with him. You have your cue beforehand. The distinction between truth and falsehood you make no account of: you mind only the distinction between Whig and Tory. Accustomed to the indulgence of your mercenary virulence and party-spite, you have lost all relish as well as capacity for the unperverted exercises of the understanding, and make up for the obvious want of ability by a bare-faced want of principle. The same set of thread-bare common-places, the same second-hand assortment of abusive nick-names, the same assumption of little magisterial airs of superiority, are regularly repeated; and the ready convenient lie comes in aid of the dearth of other resources, and passes off, with impunity, in the garb of religion and loyalty. If no one finds it out, why then there is no harm done, *snug's the word:* or if it should be detected , it is a good joke, shews spirit and invention in proportion to its grossness and impudence, and it is only a pity that what was so well meant in so good a cause, should miscarry! The end sanctifies the means; and you keep no faith with heretics in religion or government. You are under the protection of the *Court*; and your zeal for your king and country entitles you to say what you chuse of every public writer who does not do all in his power to pamper the one into a tyrant, and to trample the other into a herd of slaves. You derive your weight with the great and powerful from the very circumstance that takes away all real weight from your authority, viz. that it is avowedly, and upon every occasion, exerted for no one purpose but to hold up to hatred and contempt whatever opposes in the slightest degree and in the most flagrant instances of abuse their pride and passions. You dictate your opinions to a party, because not one of your opinions is formed upon an honest conviction of the truth or justice of the case, but by collusion with the prejudices, caprice, interest or vanity of your employers. The mob of well-dressed readers who consult the *Quarterly Review*, know that *there is no offence in it*. They put faith in it because they are aware that it is 'false and hollow, but will please the ear'; that it will tell them nothing but what they would wish to believe. Your reasoning comes under the head of Court-news; your taste is a standard of the prevailing *ton* in certain circles, like Ackerman's dresses for May. When you damn an author, one knows that he is not a favourite at Carlton House. When you say that an author cannot write common sense or English, you mean that he does not believe in the doctrine of *divine right*. Of course, the clergy and gentry will not read such an author. Your praise or blame has nothing to do with the merits of a work, but with the party to which the writer belongs, or is in the inverse *ratio* of its merits. The dingy cover that wraps the pages of the *Quarterly Review* does not contain a concentrated essence of taste and knowledge, but is a receptacle for the scum and sediment of all the prejudice, bigotry, ill-will, ignorance, and rancour, afloat in the kingdom. This the fools and knaves who pin their faith on you know, and it is on this account they pin their faith on you. They come to you for a scale not of literary talent but of political subserviency. They want you to set your mark of approbation on a writer as a thorough-paced tool, or of reprobation as an honest man. Your fashionable readers, Sir, are hypocrites as well as knaves and fools; and the watch-word, the practical intelligence they want, must be conveyed to them without implied offence to their candour and liberality, in the *patois* and gibberish of fraud of which you are a master. When you begin to jabber about common sense and English, they know what to be at, shut up the book, and wonder that any respectable publisher can be found to let it lie on his counter, as much as if it were a Petition for Reform. Do you suppose, Sir, that such persons as the Rev. Gerard Valerian Wellesley and the Rev. Weeden Butler would not be glad to ruin what they would call a Jacobin author as well as a Jacobin stationer?[1] Or that they will not thank you for persuading them that their doing so in the former case is a proof of their taste and good sense, as well as loyalty and religion? You know very well that if a particle of truth or fairness were to find its way into a single number of your publication, another *Quarterly Review* would be set up to-morrow for the express purpose of depriving every author, in prose or verse, of his reputation and livelihood, who is not a regular hack of the vilest cabal that every disgraced this or any other country.

There is something in your nature and habits that fits you for the situation into which your good fortune has thrown you. In the first place, you are in no danger of exciting the jealousy of your patrons by a mortifying display of extraordinary talents, while your sordid devotion to their will and to your own interest at once ensures their gratitude and contempt. To crawl and lick the dust is all they expect of you, and all you can do. Otherwise they might fear your power, for they could have no dependence on your fidelity: but they take you with safety and with fondness to their bosoms; for they know that if you cease to be a tool, you cease to be any thing. If you had an exuberance of wit, the unguarded use of it might sometimes glance at your employers; if you were sincere yourself, you might respect the motives of others; if you had sufficient understanding, you might attempt an argument, and fail in it. But luckily for yourself and your admirers, you are but the dull echo, 'the tenth transmitter' of some hackneyed jest: the want of all manly and candid feeling in yourself only excites your suspicion and antipathy to it in others, as something at which your nature recoils: your slowness to understand makes you quick to misrepresent; and you infallibly make nonsense of what you cannot possibly conceive. What seem your wilful blunders are often the felicity of natural parts, and your want of penetration has all the appearance of an affected petulance!

Again, of an humble origin yourself, you recommend your performances to persons of fashion by always abusing *low people*, with the smartness of a lady's waiting-woman, and the independent spirit of a travelling tutor. Raised from the lowest rank to your present despicable

[1] See the Examiner, Feb. 9.

eminence in the world of letters, you are indignant that any one should attempt to rise into notice, except by the same regular trammels and servile gradations, or should go about to separate the stamp of merit from the badge of sycophancy. The silent listener in select circles, and menial tool of noble families, you have become the oracle of Church and State. The purveyor to the prejudices or passions of a private patron succeeds, by no other title, to regulate the public taste. You have felt the inconveniences of poverty, and look up with base and groveling admiration to the advantages of wealth and power: you have had to contend with the mechanical difficulties of a want of education, and you see nothing in learning but its mechanical uses. A self-taught man naturally becomes a pedant, and mistakes the means of knowledge for the end, unless he is a man of genius; and you, Sir, are not a man of genius. From having known nothing originally, you think it a great acquisition to know any thing now, no matter what or how small it is— nay, the smaller and more insignificant it is, the more curious you seem to think it, as it is farther removed from common sense and human nature. The collating of points and commas is the highest game your literary ambition can reach to, and the squabbles of editors are to you infinitely more important than the meaning of an author. You think more of the letter than the spirit of a passage; and in your eagerness to show your minute superiority over those who have gone before you, generally miss both. In comparing yourself with others, you make a considerable mistake. You suppose the common advantages of a liberal education to be something peculiar to yourself, and calculate your progress beyond the rest of the world from the obscure point at which you first set out. Yet your overweening self-complacency is never easy but in the expression of your contempt for others; like a conceited mechanic in a village ale-house, you would set down every one who differs from you as an ignorant blockhead; and very fairly infer that any one who is beneath yourself must be nothing. You have been well called an Ultra-Crepidarian critic. From the difficulty you yourself have in constructing a sentence of common grammar, and your frequent failures, you instinctively presume that no author who comes under the lash of your pen can understand his mother-tongue: and again, you suspect every one who is not your 'very good friend' of knowing nothing of the Greek or Latin, because you are surprised to think how you came by your own knowledge of them. There is an innate littleness and vulgarity in all you do. In combating an opinion, you never take a broad and liberal ground, state it fairly, allow what there is of truth or an appearance of truth, and then assert your own judgment by exposing what is deficient in it, and giving a more masterly view of the subject. No: this would be committing your powers and pretensions where you dare not trust them. You know yourself better. You deny the meaning altogether, misquote or misapply, and then plume yourself on your own superiority to the absurdity you have created. Your triumph over your antagonists is the triumph of your cunning and mean-spiritedness over some nonentity of your own making; and your wary self-knowledge shrinks from a comparison with any but the most puny pretensions, as the spider retreats from the caterpillar into its web.

There cannot be a greater nuisance than a dull, envious, pragmatical, low-bred man, who is placed as you are in the situation of the Editor of such a work as the *Quarterly Review*. Conscious that his reputation stands on very slender and narrow grounds, he is naturally jealous of that of others. He insults over unsuccessful authors; he hates successful ones. He is angry at the faults of a work; more angry at its excellences. If an opinion is old, he treats it with supercilious indifference; if it is new, it provokes his rage. Every thing beyond his limited range of inquiry, appears to him a paradox and an absurdity: and he resents every suggestion of the kind as an imposition on the public, and an imputation on his own sagacity. He cavils at what he does not comprehend, and misrepresents what he knows to be true. Bound to go through the nauseous task of abusing all those who are not like himself the abject tools of power, his irritation increases with the number of obstacles he encounters, and the number of sacrifices he is obliged to make of common sense and decency to his interest and self-conceit. Every instance of prevarication he wilfully commits makes him more in love with hypocrisy, and every indulgence of his hired malignity makes him more disposed to repeat the insult and the injury. His understanding becomes daily more distorted, and his feelings more and more callous. Grown old in the services of corruption, he drivels on to the last with prostituted impotence and shameless effrontery; salves a meagre reputation for wit, by venting the driblets of his spleen and impertinence on others; answers their arguments by confuting himself; mistakes habitual obtruseness of intellect for a particular acuteness, not to be imposed upon by shallow appearances; unprincipled rancour for zealous loyalty; and the irritable, discontented, vindictive, peevish effusions of bodily pain and mental imbecility for proofs of refinement of taste and strength of understanding.

Such, Sir, is the picture of which you have sat for the outline:—all that remains is to fill up the little, mean, crooked, dirty details.

[Extract]

79

'NON MI RICORDO!'

IN the year 1820 the Prince Regent succeeded to the throne of England as George IV. He had been described by the *Morning Post* as an 'Adonis of Loveliness', but Leigh Hunt gave both the popular opinion and the sober truth when he replied that 'this Adonis of loveliness was a corpulent man of fifty . . . a violator of his word, a libertine over head and ears in disgrace . . . who had just closed over half a century without one single claim on the gratitude of his country or the respect of posterity'. The fact that Leigh Hunt received two years' imprisonment and a heavy fine for these statements did not make the country any more grateful to the Regent, and future king of England, of whom Greville wrote in his diary that 'a more contemptible, cowardly, selfish, unfeeling dog does not exist'. Nor has posterity given the lie to Leigh Hunt's prophesy regarding its lack of respect for this 'Adonis', in spite of attempts to whitewash him.

Apart from the general and well-earned contempt in which the new king was held, the country was heading towards social and political revolution. The 'Peterloo Massacre' of 1819 and the infamous 'Six Acts' of Liverpool's Government (suppressing freedom of speech and of the press by savage penalties) are still remembered as the symbols on which public imagination seized in the widespread hostility which a reactionary régime had evoked. The 'Peterloo Massacre' was not in itself a big affair, and probably the worst aspect of it was the attempt to cover it up by the distortion and suppression of facts. It was not those responsible for the murderous charge of the Yeomanry at St Peter's Fields who were persecuted, but innocent men who had demonstrated there on behalf of Equal Representation who were tried and given vindictive sentences.

General discontent and the unpopularity of George IV found an almost immediate focussing point in the 'Bill of Pains and Penalties' whereby the King attempted to divorce and degrade his wife, on grounds of alleged adultery. In a curious way, and not easily explicable, Queen Caroline's cause and that of the radicals became interwoven. The exclusion of the Queen's name from the Liturgy was very unpopular; and when, in 1820, she arrived in England, after years of exile, she was received with enthusiasm by the populace.

Proceedings in the discussion of the 'Bill of Pains and Penalties' took the outward form of a trial, though in fact it was nothing of the kind. The House of Lords listened to witnesses from Europe, who offered the type of evidence familiar to divorce courts, only (in many cases) to equivocate or retract under cross-examination. One witness, in particular, fell back frequently on the formula 'Non mi ricordo' ('I don't remember') when cross-examined about statements he had made quite categorically on behalf of the 'prosecution'. That the crown witnesses were, in many instances, perjured hirelings, was patent to the world. And the known debauchery of the king, in his long career as Prince of Wales, made the attempt to incriminate the Queen doubly obnoxious, inasmuch as the case against her, at its worst, could only have been relevant on the assumption that the king had been the innocent victim of her infidelity.

Henry Brougham (later Lord Brougham) conducted the Queen's case with great dexterity, the more confidently as he held in reserve evidence relating to the King's previous marriage with Mrs. Fitzherbert—a fact which the Government had every reason to suppress. It was this knowledge to which Brougham alluded in a speech, at once suave and menacing, in which he told the Peers that the evidence against Her Majesty did not now call upon him to utter *one whisper against the conduct of her illustrious consort*. Making it plain that only his conviction of the Queen's demonstrable innocence prevented him from using knowledge which migh 'involve his country in confusion', Brougham left the Government in no doubt that he was prepared to go to such extremes if necessary. In a letter to John Croker, many years later, Brougham explained the nature of this threat: 'Recrimination of adultery was supposed to be the thing threatened. Nothing was more absurd. We had abundant proof of that, but it was of no value; for who ever doubted the adultery? But the other meant a forfeiture of the crown, or at least a disputed succession. . . .' The morganatic marriage had, in fact, infringed the terms of the Act of Settlement, whereby the Heir to the Throne forfeited his claims if he married a Roman Catholic. Mrs. Fitzherbert was a Catholic and Brougham evidently had proof of the marriage, which was not then known to the general public, though rumours spread a generation earlier had drawn an explicit denial of the marriage from Cha les James Fox, at that time a friend of the Prince and completely deceived by him as to the facts.

In the pamphlet which we reprint William Hone assumed the king to be under cross-examination as to his own unedifying life. Though George IV is thinly disguised by the 'Non mi ricordo' (already a popular catch-phrase) of the Crown witness Majocchi, and scraps of pigeon English modelled on the evidence offered in the House of Lords, there is never a doubt as to whom the buffoon in the witness-box is intended to represent. Even if there had been, Cruikshank's diabolical caricatures of the king's familiar figure would have made the target clear enough. The pamphlet appeared in the year of the 'trial' (1820) and had, as may be imagined, a great popular success. The other characters in the 'trial' (and in the mock advertisements at the end) were all easily recognisable—Brougham ('Mr Besom'), Castlereagh, Liverpool and the rest. Even 'more yes than no' was taken direct from the cross-examination of Majocchi—a dramatic episode of which Laurence Housman made excellent use in his play, *Pains and Penalties*.

The Bill of Pains and Penalties was eventually dropped by the Government before it reached its third reading in the Lords. Even among the Peers the Government had been able to muster only a small and diminishing majority. They never had any reasonable hope of pushing the Bill through the House of Commons; and if they had succeeded the rising political temperature outside made it clear that a country already demanding drastic electoral reforms might have found in this strange case the rallying-point of revolution. The exposure of organised tampering with witnesses had proved the final blow to the Government's case; and when Lord Liverpool withdrew the Bill the popular victory was wildly celebrated throughout the country.

This happy ending, which brought Brougham unequalled popularity, probably gave great relief to Liverpool, who had certainly undertaken an odious task with some reluctance. It is a curious fact that, in spite of the daring eloquence of Brougham (in which neither the king's morals nor his repulsive figure were spared), and in spite of the unscrupulous methods used by the Government, both sides had been anxious from the first to arrive at a compromise. Only the obstinacy of the king, on the one hand, and of the Queen, on the other, had prevented Liverpool and Brougham from arriving at the agreement which both desired. The Governmental view was sufficiently well known to achieve immortality in a quatrain:

> Most Gracious Queen, we thee implore
> To go away and sin no more;
> But, if this effort be too great,
> To go away at any rate.

"NON MI RICORDO!"

&c. &c. &c.

" This will witness outwardly, as strongly as the conscience does within."

Cymbeline.

Non mi ricordo!

" Who are you ?"

Seventeenth Edition.

LONDON:

PRINTED BY AND FOR WILLIAM HONE, LUDGATE HILL.

1820.

SIXPENCE,

It was not by his own choice, but to gratify his Sovereign, that Liverpool—like Thomas Cromwell—applied the majesty of the law to such mean ends. He made the Government appear quite exquisitely silly, and echoes of the joke may still be found in such squibs as Hone's pamphlet, or in Leigh Hunt's lines:

> You swear—you swear—'Oh Signor, si'
> That thruogh a double door, eh,
> You've seen her *think* adulterously?
> 'Ver' true, Sir—Si, Signore!'

Another line of attack was that which concerned the morals of the Peers, who were (in effect) the Queen's jury and judges (though they could vote whether they had heard the evidence or not, and decide her guilt by a majority verdict). One such attack was entitled *Fair Play, or Who are the Adulterers?* It was concerned with the popular question: 'How many of the Queen's judges have been convicted of adultery?' Pamphlets and articles of this sort (by Cobbett and other vigorous writers of the period) naturally paved the way for the wholesale onslaught on the House of Lords which we shall consider when introducing a later pamphlet.

'NON MI RICORDO!'

Cross Examined by Mr Besom.

WHO are you? Non mi ricordo.

What countryman are you?—a foreigner or an englishman? Non mi ricordo.

Do you *understand* ENGLISH? No not at all.

Will the Oath you have taken *bind* you to speak the truth, or do you know of any other Oath *more* binding?

The TURNSTILE GENERAL objected to the question, upon which a discussion arose as to the nature of the Oath likely to bind the Witness, who appeared to be playing with a thread. The Witness was accordingly asked, by way of illustration, to what degree he thought the thread was *binding*, and whether he knew of any thing else *more* binding?

The LORD PRECEDENT FURTHERMORE said, if the Witness believed the thread he held was *binding*, that was sufficient.

The LORD PRECEDENT'S opinion gave rise to a long discussion as to whether *more* binding was *binding*, and binding was *more* binding; which ended in a reference to the ERMINIANS, who delivered the following solemn opinion:—If the Witness shall answer that he thinks the bit of thread is *binding*, there is no doubt it *is* binding; but he cannot be asked if a cord is *more* binding, because he in fact, says that the thread itself is *binding*. If the Witness twists the thread round his little finger he is so far bound by it, and it is *binding*; and having done that, it is unnecessary to inquire whether a cord, round another part of his body, would be *more* binding.

Question over-ruled.

Cross Examination resumed.

You are a master tailor, I think? I was cut out for a tailor.

You have been a tailor, then? I only follow tailoring as a mere amusement.

Fond of *Goose* I suppose—but pray Mr Mere-amusement what is your business? I was brought up a *Cabinet* maker.

What can you get at it?—are you a good hand? I can't say I am; I'm badly off; my *tools* are worn out.

What is your place of residence?

(Order. Order.)

The TURNSTILE GENERAL protested against the consequences of this mode of Examination.

Lord JURYMAN—Why does not the Interpreter give the Witness's Answer.

The Lord PRECEDENT FURTHERMORE—Because the Bench objects to the question.

Lord MUDDLEPOOL—Does the Turnstile General object to the question.

The TURNSTILE GENERAL—I do object to it, my Lord. This is perhaps the most important question that ever occurred. By this dealing out, the party is placed in such a situation as he never was placed in before.

Mr BESOM—I ask him where he now lives, and the Turnstile General objects to this, because I do not put all the questions I might put, in a single breath.

The Lord PRECEDENT FURTHERMORE—I feel great difficulty—I doubt.

Lord WHEELBARROW thought there was a *great* deal in what the noble Lord had said; and *he* doubted.

CROSS EXAMINATION RESUMED

How much money has been expended on you since you were born? Non mi ricordo.

What have you done for it in return? More less than more.

How do you get your living? I was waiter for some years at the Hotel *de Grand Bretagne*, and succeeded my father as head waiter at the *Crown* Inn.

What wages have you? Non mi ricordo.

Have you any perquisites? *Veils.*

Are you *head waiter*, or by what other name than head waiter you may be called, at the Crown Inn?

I am after building a new place called the *Wellington Arms*, and trying to be *Barrack-master*: if I dont gain the *Trial* I shall be glad to remain at the old *Crown*.

This answer appeared to excite considerable sensation.

The TWISTER GENERAL thought the meaning was, 'if I don't gain what I attempt to gain'.

[The Short-hand writer was desired to read the answer, and the word *Trial* was retained as the correct translation.]

I do not ask what you are to be hereafter, but whether you are *still* head waiter at the Crown?

The head waiter is dismissed occasionally.

Are you married? More yes than no.

Do you live with your own wife? No.

Is she in this country? Yes.

Why did you marry? To pay my debts.

Then why did you part? Because my debts were paid.

Were you not up to the eyes in debt? Si Signor.

Are you not bound to manifest some gratitude towards those who have paid your debts?

The Interpreter said the witness was a mere *fanfaron*, and that he found it difficult, if not impossible, to explain to the witness's understanding what was meant by *gratitude*.

CROSS EXAMINATION RESUMED

Did not you write to your wife a licentious letter, called a letter of license?—(*Order, order.*)

I ask you again the cause of your separation? She left me.

On what account? I did not like her, and I told her I'd have nothing to do with *her* any more.

After that what did you do? Oh, I rambled about.

Where did you go? To Jersey and elsewhere.

Well, Sir, go on. Non mi ricordo.

Do you mean to say that you never went to Manchester Square? More yes than no.

Were you in the house on the footing of a private friend? No, not as a friend.

You mentioned your father just now:—you did not go in your father's *cart*, I presume; in what sort of carriage did you go? In the old yellow chariot.

How long did it take you to travel from Manchester Square to Richmond? Non mi ricordo.

How many other places did you go to? Non mi ricordo.

Is the Marquis of C. a married man?

(*Order. Order.*)

After you parted from your wife, on what terms did you live? I've been *trying* to get rid of her.

Did you know what Matthew says (c. v. v. 32.)?

Matthew? Matthew? (*trying to recollect*)—what Matthew?—he's no friend of mine.

In what light do you consider your oath at the marriage ceremony? A ceremony.

If your marriage oath has not bound you, can you expect people to believe you if ever you should take a solemn public oath? More yes than no.

By the Roman law, a divorce was granted for Drunkenness, Adultery, and *False Keys;* what is your opinion of that law?

The TWISTER GENERAL said, that it was contrary to common sense to ask the witness's opinion about any *Law*.

How many Wives does *your* Church allow you? Non mi ricordo.

How many have you had since you separated from your own? Non mi ricordo.

Are you a Member of the Society for the Suppression of Vice? Yes (*with great energy*).

The Cross-examining Counsel said that the Interpreter had materially altered the sense of the last question; he had in fact asked, if the Witness was Member of the Society for the suppression of *Wives*, (*a loud laugh*) which Witness had eagerly answered in the affirmative.

The Witness's answer was expunged, and on the question being repeated correctly, he answered that he was told it was his duty to encourage the *Vice* Society, because it professed to diminish the influence of bad example.

Have they ever prosecuted you? Me!—(*with astonishment*)—they like *me* too well!

What do you mean then by *Suppression*—is your Society to prevent little vice from being committed, or great vice from being found out?

More Yes than No.

It was here moved by Lord LE CUISINIER, that 4 o'Clock, the hour of dinner, was arrived.

Another, in a maiden Speech, said, that during his long silence in that Court he had had leisure to observe, that 4 o'Clock in the *morning* was a more usual hour of adjournment.

Another considered that Lord LE CUISINIER's suggestion ought not to be entertained for a moment. We only exist in our formalities. If we suffer ourselves to be put a stop to by the motion, we may find that we

are travelling round again into the obsolete usages of our early ancestors; which will be to describe a circle that must be generally considered
as nothing less than a revolution! I therefore deprecate the least
innovation, and move, as an amendment, that 4 o'Clock is *not* arrived.

The MASTER GENERAL of the *Black* Barracks at Exeter, rose without
his wig, and declaring, upon the memory of his whiskers, that he had
just heard it strike 4, he enquired whether the Clock was in *Order*. (*Loud
and continued* cries of *hear hear*.)

The Home DOCTOR felt his pulse alarmingly quicken one and a
fraction in the minute, and nervously said, that the clock was clearly
guilty of a barefaced libel, and ought to be instantly held to bail for
breach of the peace. The simultaneous action of all the Clocks throughout the nation and their open communication by circulars, was an index
to the existence of an organised correspondence and a systematic
affiliation. He trembled at the 'positive intelligence' he had received,
that millions at that moment held their hands in an attitude ready to
strike; but it was the proudest day of his life that he had so far succeeded by a *circular* movement of his own, as to enable his workmen
to hold them to the peace for an hour together.

Lord BATHOS assured the Black-Barrack Master-General that the
Clock *was* out of Order, and he congratulated the Home Doctor on his
efficiency; but he thought they had not sunk low enough into the
subject; for he had strong doubts whether the striking might not be
construed into an overt act of High Treason, and if he saw any probability of being supported he should conclude with a substantial motion.
Did not the Lord Precedent remember a Clock Case in which, immediately after the chain had been locked up, a principal link suddenly
disappeared? and whether, after the most minute inquiry, there was not
every reason to believe from the best information that could be obtained
at that time, that that link had been *prigged*? (*Hear hear*.) Take even the
very last Clock Case, where the chain was kept together with the
greatest pains, and the utmost care. If the smallest link in that chain
had been *prigged*, it would have been fatal to the works, and yet in that
very case, two days after the chain was locked up, a link was obtained,
which, if sooner discovered, would have lengthened the chain to the
necessary extent, and brought home in the most conclusive manner the
guilt of the Clock. He therefore moved that the Clock be examined, and
the chain kept in their own custody, with liberty to add to the number
of links.

Lord RATSTAIL with his usual animation seconded the Motion.

Marquiz BOUDOIR moved as an Amendment, that the Clock being

in contempt, the *Black stick* be ordered to *walk him* in to-morrow. Seconded.

Upon this Amendment the following Amendment was moved and seconded, that the word 'to-morrow' be expunged, and the word 'yesterday' be inserted in its place. *Ordered.*

CROSS EXAMINATION RESUMED.

Does the Witness recollect whether he was at B—? Non mi recordo.

Who usually closed the Pavilion? I did.

Was it so close as to exclude any person outside from seeing what passed within, or was it partially open? It was quite closed—When I could not close it with C******** entirely, I did it with other pieces.

What do you mean by saying with other pieces? I mean with other pieces of the same quality.

Symptons of impatience were now expressed, with loud cries of *Withdraw, withdraw.*

Do you remember any thing particular occurring one night? No.

Do you not recollect whether a new wing was added during the time you and your mistress were absent? Non mi recordo.

Do you know a certain Colonel Q? Yes, he has *too* little mustachios.

Are you a sober man? More no then yes.

How many bottles a day do you drink? Non mi recordo.

Do you drink six bottles? Non mi ricordo.

Five bottles? Non mi ricordo.

How many nights in the week do you go to bed sober? Non mi ricordo.

Are you sober now? More no than yes.

Where do you spend your mornings? At Curaçao.

Where do you spend your evenings? At the *Cat and Fiddle.*

What is your favorite dish? Trifle.

What is your favorite game? *Bag-at-L—*

What is your favorite amusement? The C.

After Dressing, Drinking, and Dreaming, what time remains for thinking? Non mi ricordo.

I hold in my hand a list of immense sums of money that have been advanced to you, how much have you left? None.

Well, but you have something to show for it? No.

How do you live? I have a *doll*-shop, and a large stable in the country, and some *cow*-houses in different parts.

Are not your favourite friends *horn*-boys and flashmen?—(*Order, order.*)

" *What are you at? what are you after?*"

THE END.

Can you produce a certificate of good character from those who *know* you? Yes, from the *minister*.

Pho! pho! don't trifle; can you from any *respectable* person? More no than yes.

I understand you have the *scarlet* fever, do you not know that it ends here in a *putrid* fever? Non mi ricordo.

You have many companions and advisers, but have you to your knowledge one *real* friend in the world; and if not, why not? Non mi ricordo.

By what acts of your life do you expect you will be remembered hereafter? I shall not answer you any more questions; you put questions to me I never dreamt of.

Suppose every man in society were to do as you do, what would become of society; and what right have you to do so, more than any other man?—(*Witness greatly agitated?*)

The Witness from the *Grillery* asked whether the *Cross* Examination was nearly concluded? (*Cries of* Keep on!)—Supposing that the business would close to-day at 4 o'clock, he had made a private *assignation*, although he was quite ready to *stop* if necessary.

The Lord Precedent Furthermore was in favour of adhering to a square rule; he had not entered the Court till five seconds past ten by his *stop*-watch, in consequence of consulting with his Wife upon a motion-of-course which they had contemplated; and their further deliberation had been postponed until after the adjournment to-day. It was impossible to know what questions might turn out to be doubtful or doubtless; yet adjourning at Five o'clock would gain a delay of six hours in the Week, and the *gaining of any thing* he considered very material in the present case.

An Adjournment then took place, the Witness remaining on

THE GRILLERY.

ADVERTISEMENTS EXTRAORDINARY

CONSPIRACY.

WHEREAS a most abominable GANG, have caused to be published and promulgated throughout the Nation a description of the infirmities and necessities of our nature, of which decorum forbids the mention; and also gross and inflaming allusions to the intercourse between the sexes, and wanton and shocking exposures relating thereto;

to the destruction of youthful innocence, to the shame and disgust of matron modesty, and to the horror of all heads of families: it is therefore proposed to call an immediate MEETING, for the purpose of considering the best mode of preventing an increase of this dreadful contamination, and of securing the ringleaders of the Conspiracy, and bringing them to condign punishment.

NEW VICTUALLING OFFICE.

TO CONTRACTORS.—Persons willing to supply this Establishment with CAST-IRON REPEATERS, having duplex Movements, according to the Working Models now in use as above, may send in Sealed Tenders, stating the number they can instantly supply for immediate use, and the price thereof at   per hundred.

TO NACKERMEN

THE old Hackney, Liverpool, who lately lost his paces, is glandered, gone blind, got cruel vicious, tried to kick his mistress's brains out, shattered himself to nothing, and is expected to go down with the staggers. Any body who thinks it worth while to send a *drag* to the Stable yard may have him for fetching.

TO MANGLERS—JUST LEAVING HIS PLACE.

A STOUT ABLE-BODIED IRISHMAN, for a long time a master hand at mangling; when he begins there is no stopping him, and never tires. Can fold and smooth, and double and iron, all day. Will turn with any body. Was formerly a master in Dublin, where his mangling will never be forgotten. His Character may be had of any body there. Is very smooth spoken, of good address, looks like an upper Valet, and is a perfect devil at his Work. May be heard of at the Triangle in the Bird-cage Walk.

TO LAUNDRESSES, WANTS A PLACE.

AN old Woman accustomed to coarse things; and work, however filthy, never comes amiss. Where she is now they find her in *ruin*, and she finds dishclouts; but is leaving, being almost poisoned by printers' ink. To save trouble, will have nothing to do with cleaning the House. Is used to ironing, and putting by, in any quantities, and never tires at hanging up. Can have an undeniable Character from the Rev. Mr Hay, and the Recorder of London.

STRAYED AND MISSING

AN INFIRM ELDERLY GENTLEMAN in a Public Office, lately left his home, just after dreadfully ill-using his wife about half a Crown, and trying to beat her. He had long complained a great deal of his forehead, and lately had a leech put upon him. He was last seen walking swiftly towards the Horns without a Crown to his hat, accompanied by some evil disposed persons, who tied a great green bag to his tail full of crackers, which he mistook for sweetmeats, and burnt himself dreadfully. Every person he met in this deplorable condition tried to persuade him to go back, but in vain. He is very deaf and very obstinate, and cannot bear to be looked at or spoken to. It is supposed that he has been seduced and carried off by some artful female. He may be easily known by his manners. He fancies himself the politest man in Europe, because he knows how to bow, and to offer a pinch of snuff; and thinks himself the greatest man in Europe, because people have humoured him and let him have his own way. He is so fond of tailoring, that he lately began a suit that will take him his life to complete. He delights in playing at soldiers, supposes himself a cavalry officer, and makes speeches, that others write for him, in a field marshal's uniform. Sometimes he fancies himself 'Glorious Apollo', plays 'Hailstones of Brunswick' on the base fiddle, and qualifies his friends to perform 'Cuckolds all on a row'. His concerns are very much deranged. Not long ago he imported a vast quantity of Italian images at enormous prices, upon credit, and hoarded them up in a waterside cotton warehouse. Since then, things have gone all against him, and he has been in a very desponding state. It is of the utmost consequence to himself that he should be at his post, or he may lose his place; one of his predecessors some time ago having been cashiered for his misconduct. If this should meet his eye, it is earnestly requested that he will return to his duty, and he will be kindly received and no questions asked.

N.B. He has not a friend in the world except the advertiser and a few others, who never had an opportunity of speaking to him and letting him know the real state of his affairs.

PUBLIC OFFICE, LUDGATE HILL.

1st September, 1820.

WHEREAS that well known old established Public House, (formerly a *free* house) called the POLITICAL HOUSE THAT JACK BUILT, has been feloniously entered into and damaged, and the property therein carried off to a large amount, by a numerous gang of desperate

"The *Fat* in the Fire!"

Villains, who, by various vile arts and contrivances, have not only kept possession thereof, but also of the Head Waiter, who was intrusted by Mr BULL, the owner, with the management of the concern, and was a very promising young man when Mr Bull first knew him, and might have done very well if he had followed the advice of his old friends, and not suffered these desperadoes to get him into their clutches; since when he seems to have forgotten himself, and by neglecting his duty sadly, and behaving ill to the customers who support the House, has almost ruined the Business, and has also dreadfully injured the Sign, which Mr Bull had had fresh painted after he dismissed a former waiter for his bad manners. Whoever will assist Mr Bull in bringing the offenders to Justice, will be doing a great service to the young man, and he will still be retained in his situation, unless he has actually destroyed or made away with the Sign, which Mr Bull very much admires, it being a *heir-loom*. If offered to be pawned or sold it is requested the parties may be stopped, and notice given as above. As the young man has not been seen for some time, there is no doubt the ruffians have either done him a serious mischief, or secreted him somewhere to prevent Mr Bull, who is really his friend, from speaking to him.

THE END.

THE HANGMAN AND THE JUDGE

THE wide use of the death penalty in England, from the time of the Tudors well into the nineteenth century, is one of the proofs that—beneath a veneer of civilisation—our ancestors were savages at heart. It is on record that the people of India regarded with horror the murderous punishments introduced under British rule in the eighteenth century; for among the benefits of British Justice which John Company imposed upon the Heathen in his Darkness was a code which recognised (according to Sir William Blackstone) 160 Capital offences, including thefts of property valued at over five shillings. Small wonder that Thompson and Garrett in their *Rise and Fulfilment of British Rule in India*, could say of a British military campaign that 'whole populations fled in terror, not from the soldiery but from the High Court that was believed to be accompanying them'.

The attitude of Indians is only mentioned, however, to show that English practice was not universally accepted in principle, though unfortunately the Public Executioner (like trade and the missionary) followed the Flag. But—like Charity—he began at home and it is his career in England with which we are here concerned. His customers, up to 1772, including persons accused of felony, who refused to 'plead'. Unless a man would say 'Guilty' or 'Not Guilty' there could be no trial and no conviction, therefore his goods could not be confiscated. But the law had a way of persuading such persons to be reasonable by *peine forte et dure*, and the obstinate were pressed to death by heavy weights, a slow and uncomfortable way of leaving this world.

Among capital offences still recognised in 1780, one could be hanged for illegally felling a tree, robbing a rabbit-warren, associating with gypsies or posing as a Greenwich Pensioner. 'Drawing and quartering' were still in use, and Sir Samuel Romilly was accused of 'breaking down the bulwarks of the Constitution' when he tried to have these practices abolished. The arguments used against Romilly followed the same general lines as those still in use whenever the death penalty is discussed—the desirability of the gallows as a deterrent, and the assumption that people who object to hanging show a lack of sympathy for the victims of crime. Lest we should feel too superior when we consider our ancestors, it may be well to remember the arguments used by contemporary sages in defence of ritual murder in our own time. When the screen version of *Now Barabbas* first appeared (a film which treats a condemned murderer sympathetically) it was actually argued by the *Daily Telegraph* critic, Mr Campbell Dixon, that 'Human beings can feel only so much'; *ergo* he concluded that any sympathy for the murderer must necessarily be withdrawn from his victim. It was precisely for this reason that our ancestors, unwilling to appear unsympathetic with the victims of juvenile delinquency, strung up little boys and girls *pour encourager les autres*.

Several nineteenth century examples are mentioned by Roy Calvert in his book, *Capital Punishment in the Twentieth Century*, e.g. 'a cartload of girls who were executed at Tyburn, and the boys whom Greville saw sentenced to death to their own excessive amazement' (of whom the diarist remarked: 'Never did I see boys cry so'). Others included John Bell, aged thirteen, who was hanged at Maidstone in 1831. And in the year that this pamphlet of Wakefield's appeared (1833) a boy of *nine* was sentenced to be hanged by the neck till he was dead for breaking a shop window and helping himself to a few trifles. This sentence, however, was not carried out, for the revolt against judicial infanticide had already begun. Various Quakers and other busy-bodies (such as Wakefield's cousin, Elizabeth Fry) who were doubtless completely callous with regard to the sufferings of shopkeepers and such like innocent persons, had been trying to spoil the market for the Executioner, fortified by Blackstone's assurance that 'so dreadful a list' (of capital crimes) 'instead of diminishing, increases the number of offenders'. Sir Samuel Romilly, though unsuccessful in his efforts to limit the use of the death penalty, in a series of Parliamentary campaigns between 1808 and 1818 certainly influenced public opinion. At the time when Wakefield wrote *The Hangman and the Judge* the butchery had been substantially reduced, beginning with an Act introduced by Sir Robert Peel, as Home Secretary, in 1823. An Act of 1832 had recently substituted transportation for capital punishment in the case of many offences such as the theft of sheep, horses and cattle; but the position was unstable, and these timid reforms were frankly regarded as a rather daring experiment at the time when Wakefield wrote.

Edward Gibbon Wakefield was opposed to capital punishment, but he was also opposed to transportation, which he regarded as a most unsuitable alternative. Not only did he object as the leading advocate of colonial expansion, on the ground that convicts were not the ideal Pilgrim Fathers for the Antipodes; but he also held that transportation had ceased to be a punishment and savoured more of a reward, because of the great opportunities for becoming wealthy in Australia. If, he argued, criminals were to be rewarded, there might well be a great increase in crime which would be used to justify a return to the wider use of the death penalty, or at least to obstruct attempts to limit it further. What Wakefield feared most was therefore a false antithesis— the assumption that the only alternative to murdering a petty thief in the name of justice was to reward him on the pretext of punishment.

As usual, in such periods of reform, practice was a long way in advance of theory. Juries were frequently known to refuse a verdict of guilty, in the teeth of the evidence, because of the terrible penalty attaching to a conviction. Alternately they would so assess the value of stolen objects, regardless of the facts, as to keep some poor wretch out of the halter's range.

It is an odd reflection that over a thousand bankers signed a petition, presented by Brougham in 1830, urging a more lenient penalty for forgery on the grounds that the existing punishment (death) made juries unwilling to convict and therefore added to general insecurity. In this instance, the wordly wisdom of the banking firms proved more humane than the Levitical zeal of the bishops, six of whom (and an archbishop) had voted in the House of Lords against Romilly's proposal to limit the use of the death penalty, in 1810. Judging by recent efforts to abolish this savage punishment altogether, some bishops may still be counted among its last supporters.[1]

The increasing humanity of juries did not encourage the smooth and certain operation of the law, and doubtless the realisation of this helped to bring about the reforms of 1823 and after. The Government itself showed increasing reluctance in using its powers to the full. Such figures as we have indicate that even in the time of Henry VIII less than 2,000 people a year were hanged—a small proportion, surely, of the total number of convictions on capital charges. By the beginning of the nineteenth century the proportion of those sentenced to death who actually suffered that penalty was rapidly declining—less than one in seven from 1809 to 1816, it was just over one in twelve from 1818 to 1825. By 1829 it was less than one in eighteen, and by 1830 about one in forty.

Edward Gibbon Wakefield was born of Quaker parents. He had experience of prison, having been sentenced to three years' imprisonment (1827–1830) for carrying off a sixteen-year-old heiress from a

[1] The Archbishop of Dublin, mentioned by Wakefield as having written in defence of hanging, was Richard Whately.

boarding school and marrying her at Gretna Green. (This was rather unusual behaviour in a product of the Society of Friends, the more so as it was Edward's second run-away marriage, his first wife having been another heiress with whom he had also eloped.) As a result of his personal experience of jail life Wakefield wrote some valuable records and indictments, among the most notable being his account of a service in the prison chapel at Newgate, before the execution of four men (one a youth of eighteen) who were to be hanged—three for theft and one for forgery. It is one of the most terrible and moving accounts ever written of the horrors attending capital punishment. In the extract which follows the writer assumes the character of the Executioner and addresses a contemporary Judge as his colleague, Mr Justice Alderson having referred at Salisbury, while on circuit, to the 'experiment' of substituting a lesser penalty for death in the case of certain crimes. The letter to Alderson was signed 'Jack Ketch', and was an able sequel to Wakefield's previous work, *The Punishment of Death in the Metropolis*, which had been published in 1831 and was largely responsible for that tentative change in the law which was the 'experiment' in question.

Recent pronouncements by Judges on the partial abolition of flogging as a legal punishment show how little change there has been in the senile delinquents of the Bench since this pamphlet was published in 1833.

THE HANGMAN AND THE JUDGE

By Edward Gibbon Wakefield

TO MY HONORED MASTER, JUDGE ALDERSON

My Lord,

ONE killing-day, in the time of George the Third, of pious memory, I dispatched two forgers, a sheep-stealer, a coiner and nine utterers of bad notes; in all thirteen; eight men, two women and three lads. While the sheriffs and ordinary were at breakfast in our slaughter-house, the carcases outside grew cold: I took them down, and then, with Mrs. Ketch and a few friends, went to dine at the Magpie and Stump in Newgate Street. We had bacon and greens, pork chops and roast goose with brown stout and rum punch hot. My wife, being full and merry, would play at cross questions and crooked answers. Seeing, by a glance of her eye, that she had asked the ordinary's clerk,—What's the use of my Jack? I guessed the answer—To hang people. Thought I to myself, I'll pay you for that, ma'am: so when it came to my turn to question her, said I,—'My love, what's the use of a judge?' Then said she,—'I was asked, What's the use of a judge? and the answer was, To hang people'. 'A forfeit!' cried I; 'that's not a crooked answer'. Nor was it, my lord; for Mr Justice Blackstone holds, that you and I belong to the same profession. And so we do. You tell me to hang them, by the neck, till they be dead; and, till they be dead, I, by the neck, do hang them. Your black cap and my cord are tools of the same trade: you are my learned master; I am your handy journeyman. The ordinary of Newgate is your partner or mine, which you please. You provide the animals for slaughter; and Dr Cotton breaks their hearts, so that they may stand quiet, without kicking or bellowing, while I butcher them. On the whole, I consider his share of the work by far the most troublesome;

but, at any rate, you, he and I, are engaged in one business. Wherefore, I am going, with his reverence's help, to write to your lordship on a matter of the greatest importance to us, all three.

Our business is to hang people. As the judges are in the same concern with me, I need say no more of myself. But what would a judge be, without his black cap? Who would respect his horse-hair wig, when it should not remind one of the terrible vengeance of the law? Of what use crimson robes, but as they give the idea of blood? Put down hanging, and down goes the majesty of the law and the dignity of judges. At present, there is something awful about a judge. When the common people see a judge, they draw in their breath and whisper, shuddering. The arm of the law is so frightful, because it holds a rope. Why do prisoners, witnesses and jurors, speak to the judge as though he were half a god? why tremble so, why stammer and blush, why turn pale, as if I had got hold of them, when his lordship does but raise his voice or frown? why? Because a judge has power over the lives of men; because, as your lordship observes, it is his business to *destroy that which can never be replaced*. Put an end to hanging; and away goes the vengeance of the law, the dignity, the importance, the greatness, the awfulness of judges. This is one reason why the judges have a deep interest in saving me from ruin.

Another reason is, that if I should be ruined, some of the judges would be ruined likewise. You live by your pay, as I do by mine: you, upon so much a year; I, upon so much a neck; but we are both paid for hanging. Judges are paid because they are wanted; judges are wanted because there are criminals. Putting this and that together, what is the sum? it is, that judges have an interest in keeping up the stock of criminals. Suppose that our people should obey the law, as is the case, I hear, in America, of what use would be so many judges? Few criminals, few judges: for the sake of the judges, then, let crime flourish! Dr Cotton says, the conclusion is undeniable. Now, add to this, that hanging encourages crime. I speak from my own knowledge; but as your lordship may want to learn precisely how the thing comes about, I shall try to explain it all.

The common people, who furnish the greater part of criminals, have a more lively belief in hell-fire than any of the higher ranks: for, while the gentry and nobility just allow that some will suffer everlasting punishment in a world to come, the others enter into all the particulars of damnation; the scorching heat, the raging thirst, the horrid joy of the evil one, and the piercing shrieks of the damned, by day and night, for uncountable millions of years. Is this punishment severe enough?

Wellington would say,—Yes; this is the right sort of punishment, to strike terror and check crime. But when does a belief in this terrifying punishment hinder some one from calling his brother a fool? seldom indeed. The clergy are the first to say, that believers live like unbelievers. Amongst the common people believers live like unbelievers, because they believe so much. The punishment in which they believe is too frightful to be thought of: wherefore they turn, loathing, from the picture of hell, and dwell, fondly, on that of heaven.

I see this take place with nearly all who pass through my hands. For weeks or months before I touch them, Dr Cotton has preached to them about the torments of hell: he has led them to believe firmly in the torments. But has he led them to expect those torments? On the contrary, by leading them to believe in the torments, he has led them to feel sure that a punishment so very horrid will not fall upon them: he has frightened them so much, that they are no longer frightened. They are launched into eternity, as your lordship might say, confident that the gates of heaven will open to receive them. This is a clear case: take another.

What with funerals all in black, loud grief for the dead and marks of disgust at the sight of a corpse, people are brought up to dread death. After the pains of hell, what so fearful as death? The agony of death! Yet who lives as if he expected to die? Fearing death so much, we could not live if we expected to die: we should die of the unceasing terror. It is because we dread that which must happen, that we turn from the thought of it, to hope for something pleasant which may not happen. Thousands have refused to make a will, saying,—if I do, I shall die: because the making of a will would have put them in mind of death, which they could not bear to think of: their fear of that for which they ought to have got ready, prevented them from getting ready for it. More or less, all the world tremble at the thought of dying, and, therefore, behave as if they were born to live for ever. Dr Cotton says that nature commonly opposes one irregularity by another, to keep all straight.

I once saw a plain proof of it. A murderer, waiting in Newgate for trial, swallowed a tenpenny nail to cheat me of my due. He grew fat, however, under Dr Cotton's care; and I got my fee. When he was cut up, they found the nail within a soft skin or bag, which, said the surgeons, nature had formed to protect the tender coats of his stomach.

It is just so with the hanging laws. When you make a law to punish with death, you fly in the face of nature; and she beats you hollow. You mean to frighten the people, and you frighten them overmuch. You want them to think of the punishment, which is so dreadful that they will not think of it. Nay, when, by chance, one of them does think of it, the effect is to make him hope, or rather expect, contrary to reason, that he will escape, even though all others like him should be hanged. From my experience, I do believe, that if all capital convicts were hanged, not one would fully expect to be hanged short of the condemned sermon, if so soon. Nature would, somehow or other, save them all from the torment of expecting death on the gallows.

But at no time were all hanged, whom the judges had made over to me: about nine out of ten of them have slipped thro' my fingers, in the best of times. Moreover, for ten capital convicts, there cannot be less than twenty capital offenders, who are not convicted, owing to the softness of prosecutors, witnesses and juries. Thus, whoever is tempted to commit a capital offence may say to himself,—The chances are two to one that I shall not be convicted, and twenty-nine to one that I shall not be hanged. You offer him an excellent prospect of escape; and from what? from that which is so dreadful, that he would not expect it, even if he had no prospect of escape. With heavy odds against the law being executed, the law is so frightful as to make the criminal turn his thoughts from the one chance against him, and fix them steadily on the twenty-nine chances in his favour. The nature of the punishment causes the risk of punishment to be very slight; and it is the nature of the punishment which keeps out of view that very slight risk. Many who, before they had been criminal, used to shiver at the thought of us, my lord, have never thought of us at all since they became liable to die by our hands. What is the object of a law which says, that if any one do so and so he shall be punished? the object is that all who think of doing the act, shall also think of the punishment; so that the motive for not doing the act may be stronger than the temptation for doing it. But if the punishment be such, that people cannot bear to think of it, and still less to think of feeling it, why, then, the result is, that the law promotes crime; the law, instead of making a crime and a punishment, makes nothing but a crime! This surely, is the best way in the world to have plenty of criminals. Dr. Cotton, who can chop logic with any man, says I have proved the case.

But this is not the only way in which hanging causes crime. Did your lordship ever attend at killing time in the Old Bailey? If not, pray favour me with your company; not on the gallows, but staying in the street, amidst the crowd that always assembles when I am at work for the judges. It will add to the zest, if you come when I have a young woman to stiffen, supplied by yourself; some shame-faced puss, who is to die for her fear of the world's contumely. The fluttering of her petticoats, as she swings in the wind, will produce a sound most pleasant to your judicial ears, my learned master. But fail not to watch the people; the men, women and children, good, bad and indifferent, who have gathered to behold the sacred majesty of the law. You will see such flashing of eyes and grinding of teeth: you will hear sighs and groans, and words of rage and hatred, with fierce curses on yourself and me: and then laughter, such as it is, of an unnatural kind, that will make you start; and jests on the dead, to turn you sick. You will feel—no—why should you feel any more than your faithful journeyman?—but you will go to breakfast with a good appetite, and a firm conviction that every hanging bout changes many sneaking pilferers into savage robbers fit for murder.

Last year, I was called out of town, to hang a little boy for killing with malice aforethought. If guilty, he must have been in the habit of going to executions. Ten thousand people came to dabble in the young murderer's blood. That was the youngest fellow-creature I ever handled in the way of our business; and a beautiful child he was too, as you may have seen by the papers, with a straight nose, large blue eyes and golden hair. I have no heart, no feelings: who has, in our calling? but those who came to see me strangle that tender youngster have hearts and feelings, as we had once. Have—no—had; for what they saw was fit to make them as hard as your servant or his master. They saw the stripling lifted fainting on to the gallows, his smooth cheeks of the colour of wood-ashes, his limbs trembling, and his bosom heaving sigh after sigh, as if body and soul were parting without my help. It was not a downright murder; for there was scarce any life to take out of him. When I began to pull the cap (not yours but mine) over his baby face, he pressed his small hands together (his arms, you know, were corded fast to his body) and gave me a beseeching look; just as a calf will lick the butcher's hand. But cattle do not speak: this creature muttered,— 'Pray, sir, don't hurt me'. 'My dear,' answered I, 'you should have spoken to my master: I'm only the journeyman and must do as I'm bid'. This made him cry, which seemed a relief to him; and I do think I should have cried, myself, if I had not heard shouts from the crowd: poor lamb! shame! murder! Quick, said the sheriff; ready, said I; the reverend chaplain gave me the wink: the drop fell: one kick, and he swayed to and fro, dead as the feelings of an English judge.

The crowd dispersed; some weeping, with passionate exclamations; some swearing, as if hell had broke loose, and some laughing, while they cracked blackguard jokes on the judge and me, and the parson and the dangling corpse. They had come for the sight: they would have come to see an angel murdered. They had come to get drunk with strong excitement: they went back, reeling and filthy with the hot debauch. They had come to riot in the passions of fear and pity: they went back, some in a fever of rage, some burning with hate, some hardened in heart, like me or you; all sunk down in their own respect, ready to make light of pain and blood, corrupted by the indecent show, and more fit than ever to create work for us, the judge and the hangman. Oh, wise law-makers, who thought to soften the hearts of the people, to make them gentle and good, to give them a feeling of respect for themselves and others, by showing them sights like this!

In order to have plenty of criminals, the grand point is to brutalize the people. For brutalizing the people, there is nothing like public executions. Add this to what I have settled before; that laws for hanging encourage crime by holding out a prospect of escape and leading offenders to think only of that prospect; and what follows? It follows, that the hangman and the judge, who live by the number of criminals, have a common interest in preserving the punishment of death. Dr. Cotton, who also lives by our business, says the proof is perfect.

This brings me to the matter in hand. Sir Robert Peel and I have always said that reform would ruin the country; and our words are fast coming true. The first reformer was an Italian fellow named Beccaria. If he had been hanged, as he deserved, we might not have been troubled with your Benthams, Romillies, Montagues, Buxtons, Ewarts, and the like. Your lordship, may-be, never heard of Bentham: he died on his back last year, which is a sad pity: for I yet hope, that a time may come when such as he shall get their deserts from hands like ours. As for Romilly, one of the profession, a traitor! I would have suffered myself for the pleasure of stopping his breath. He is gone; but, along with his memory, the others live for mischief. To truss them, and string them in a row, would give me the greatest satisfaction. No, not the greatest; for the most exquisite pleasure in life is to hang a quaker. The pleasure consists in observing the agony of the broadbrim's brethren, when, as he mounts the scaffold, they give him the last kiss of love; so they call it. Those quakers are reformers, radicals, destructives, all of them. Oh, that they had but one neck within my hempen collar! But where's the use of wishing: let us come to the point.

Whilst these reformers contented themselves with talking and writing, it was better to let them alone; for I have remarked that discussion about hanging always hurts our cause. But now, by our cap and cord! the case is altered. Under this king's good father, when a common morning's work for me was to turn off a baker's dozen, it mattered little what any one said or wrote about the punishment of death: I cannot complain of Sir Robert Peel, under Gentleman George: but this Sailor king, as they say, this William the Reformer or Reform Bill, has made my place a sinecure. As a loyal subject I am willing to lay the blame on his minister Lord Melbourne, whom I wish I had by the neck to make room for Sir Robert. In Peel's time, truly, we never hanged above a tythe of the condemned; which was all right, as I have shown before, to encourage crime by holding out the prospect of escape; but since Peel retired to private life, the joke has been carried a great deal too far. Here, in London, session after session passes without a killing day. The judge uses his black cap, tells me to hang dozens by the neck till they be dead, and I am ever ready to use my rope: what right has the secretary of state to come between us; insulting my master, whose dignified commands are set at nought; spoiling me, who have not work enough to keep my hand in; and ruining our business, my lord, which depends upon keeping the public accustomed to deeds of blood. There's the rub. The very thought of any one dying by our hands now distresses many who, three years ago, used to read with indifference, that we had 'launched some unfortunate beings into eternity'. Only the other day, I was near getting a job by mistake; and what a fuss about nothing! As if it had not been a common practice with the privy council to send me jobs by mistake! I have disposed of many, whom I should never have touched if the privy council had been a public court; but let that pass. Why all this to do about Job Cox and your partner, my dear old master, the recorder, who was an ornament to the bench, with his cadaverous complexion? I will tell your lordship why: because since we lost Peel, so few have been hanged that people are growing soft upon the subject of hanging. Morbid sensibility! as Sir Robert would say.

Thus it is, that reform creeps on. Peel's successor begins by sparing nearly all whom the judges have made over to me: scarce any body is hanged: after a while, it seems shocking to hang any body; and then up jumps the minister, saying,—The time is come for mitigating the severity of our criminal code.

That is the way with all your noble reformers. Whatever the subject may be, reform of parliament, church reform or law reform, they let the public mind be poisoned by the newspapers; and then, as soon as a part of the constitution is brought into contempt, they say,—The time is come for a change. Having so little to do, I read the debates; by which it seems to my poor judgement, that none of our great men are much in love with reform for its own sake, but that the only question between them is, whether or not the time be come. When we take the condemned out of their cells to pinion them, we say, The time is come; meaning, that there is no use in arguing about what must be done, whether you like it or not, sulky! When a minister says, The time is come, I see directly that it is all over with some venerable institution; that he feels the necessity of yielding to a power which is too strong for him. The power which compels a minister to say, The time is come, is called by the newspapers the force of public opinion. Let us not blame Lord Melbourne for yielding to this force: if Peel had been in, when Ewart of Liverpool proposed to abolish hanging for forgery, he would have said, The time is come. The grand point, my lord, is to prevent the time from coming.

If things go on in this way for three years more, the time will be come for putting an end to our business. What is to be done to preserve our vested rights? In this case, I fear, it will be quite useless to cry,— Spoliation! even with the help of the bishops; God bless them for not taking part against us! Our object is, to prevent the repeal of any more hanging laws; to beat the quakers, hang them! But how, and by whom, is this great object to be accomplished? As for me, a poor journeyman, I can only sit at home, reflecting on what my masters, the judges, might do for themselves and me. Here follow some of my notions on the subject.

That with which we have to contend is public opinion. Whatever turns public opinion against hanging is bad for us: whatever turns public opinion in favour of hanging is good for us. As all depends upon which set of things shall have the greater force, it behoves the judges to diminish the force of one set, and to increase the force of the other, by all the means in their power. But, unfortunately, the judges have little or no power over those things which turn public opinion against hanging; the beastly education, as dear Mr. Cobbett says, that is going on all over the country, the hankering after new-fangled laws, the growing inquisitiveness of the people, the obstinacy of the quakers and the increase of newspapers and books. Still, the other things, those which turn public opinion in favour of hanging, are very much under the control of the judges. In fact, there is but one thing on our side, though it depends on many other things. That one thing is the increase of crime since the late laws against hanging. This is my only comfort: upon this alone rest all my hopes of preserving your cap and my cord, your pay and my fees, your dignity and my very name; in a word, the profit and pleasure of our majestic trade.

For us, my master, the late increase in crime is all in all. Mark its effects! the alarm of the bankers, the many plans for making forgery more difficult, the sorrow expressed by Under-secretary Lamb for having consented to do away with hanging for forgery, the archbishop of Dublin's argument in favour of hanging, the scheme of the government for killing people by slow torture at the other side of the world, and the disappointment of the quakers. These, our greatest enemies, hoped that forgeries would diminish when a dislike to meddling in our butcherly business should no longer hinder prosecutions for forgery: and, now, they turn up the whites of their eyes, howling,—Verily, the end differeth from our hopes. Yea, friend Allen, friend Hanbury and friend Capper, the experiment has been tried and has completely failed. The experiment! thank you for that word, master Alderson; with thanks to your brother Parke, who also used the word with evident glee.[1] The experiment! let us stick to that! But wherefore go on to say, that 'sufficient time has not been allowed to ascertain whether crime have increased since the alteration?' Sufficient time! why, the thing is notorious, town talk, in every body's mouth, matter of triumph to those who hate innovation and of grief to all our enemies. Sufficient time! why, the bankers have had time to lose their money, the ministers to repent of their softness, the archbishop to write a pamphlet, and the Humanity people to learn a song of lamentation. What could induce you to tell such a thundering fib? I see it: ah! you sly fellow, you want to set the public upon watching the experiment. Good, excellent, the very thing I was going to propose to you: great wits jump, saith the proverb.

My dear master! the experiment must fail: it was sure to fail before it was tried: the government was told that it would fail; and if Melbourne had been a man of business, instead of a lazy lord, he would have known that it must fail. No one expected its success; save only the Humanity men, whose feelings ran away with them to such a degree that they expected what they wished, against all reason, just as our chickens always expect to escape being trussed until the operation begins. That it was impossible the experiment should succeed, may be proved in two minutes.

Suppose that you were ordered to leave off your wig, by way of

[1] 'Home Circuit. Croydon, August 3, 1833. John Knight Draper was found guilty of forgery and uttering a check on the Godalming bank. Mr Justice Parke sentenced the prisoner to transportation for life. In doing so, he observed that *this experiment* of abolishing the punishment of death, in nearly all instances of the crime of forgery, had been made for the purpose of endeavouring to check it, by the certainty of severe secondary punishment. Unless this mitigation were found to have the desired effect, *the government would be under the painful necessity of reviving the now abolished punishment.*' Daily Papers. August 5, 1833.

experiment, to see whether any body would respect you without it: in that case, if you should not substitute for the horse-hair something fit to gain respect, such as gentleness, decency and truth; if you should still say to prisoners,—'*Man, go away:* that *alone* for which life is valuable is to work out, through misery, degradation and sorrow, the salvation of your soul', then, Master Alderson, the experiment would fail: that is, leaving off your wig, and putting nothing respectable in its place, you would be despised. This is a like case: the punishment of death was repealed, and in its place there was put, what? Nothing, a mere mockery, a sham of punishment; the great advantage to some of being sent, cost free, to a fine country, where man is so dear that a hardened criminal is worth as much as a new steam-engine in England. Hanging laws fix attention on the chances of escape, and, therefore, promote crime; but this transportation law does more: it holds out, not a chance, but a certainty, not of escape, but of reward. How transportation is a reward I will show presently. Meanwhile, let us be grateful to brother Best, the learned Wynford, for that 'wise and prudent measure', by which the experiment has been turned into a plan, sure to answer, for encouraging crime. The experiment! Ah, you deep dogs! stick to that, my masters, and we shall yet be a match for the quakers.

When Ewart of Liverpool proposed to do away with hanging for forgery, and Under-secretary Lamb said, The time is come, I was sadly cast down; like one of the doomed, *before* Dr Cotton had led him to expect salvation by talking to him about damnation. I took it for granted that the government would manage, by hook or by crook, to put some real punishment in the place of death; some punishment, thought I, which, without being so cruel as to fix attention on the chances of escape, or so shocking as to set prosecutors, witness and juries, against the law, will, nevertheless, be severe enough to create a motive for not forging, stronger than the temptation to forge. This was my stupid expectation; ass that I was not to calculate on the motives of lords and members of parliament for keeping up the costly farce of transportation. But when the profound Wynford had led his brother lords to decree that all forgers should emigrate, I recovered my usual spirits, chuckled and snapped my fingers, saying—Fol de rol; the man-killers are safe for this time. I was right; for how stands the case? What I foresaw has happened. Certain criminals being no longer punished with death, being no longer punished at all, being rewarded with a free passage to the colonies, some crimes, for which we used to hang now and then, are rapidly increasing. The great increase of those crimes is turning the public mind in favour of our cap and cord. Thousands, who used to whine about 'the severity of the criminal code', say with brother Parke—'The government will be under the painful necessity of reviving the now abolished punishment'. Not so fast brother Parke: we shall never go back to hanging for forgery; but we shall keep all that remains of the butcherman business; if, provided, the judges take care to preserve the system of transportation. Many things which encourage crime (and about which I may perhaps write to your lordship some other day) are more or less under the control of the judges; but this one thing, this sham of punishment, is peculiarly under the control of the judges, who might upset it at a blow by seriously protesting against it, and who may greatly help to preserve it by swearing, as you did at Salisbury, that emigration is worse than death.[1]

Here, brother Alderson, I have a crow to pick with you. Lies about transportation will serve our turn, provided they be addressed to the law-making class; but if the judges would turn brother Wynford's 'wise and prudent measure' to the best account, they must tell the truth, about transportation, to the common people or law-bearing class. What you said to Thomas Williams at Salisbury, you ought to have said to the grand jury; giving Thomas Williams a true description of his own excellent prospects. Another time, befool the grand jury to their heart's content; but do not deceive the prisoner. Tell him the plain truth; make an effort for once: it will go against the grain, I know, considering how long you have dealt with the fictions of law; but, remember, our all is at stake. In order that, when you next go to the circuit, you may speak the truth about transportation, the whole truth and nothing but the truth, I have, with Dr Cotton's help and a world of trouble, written the following Speech, which I hope that you will address to the first convict on whom you may pass sentence of transportation for life.

'*Man! go away* to one of the finest countries in the world, where the sun shines bright, the sky is blue, the earth fruitful, the hills and vallies pleasant, and convicts by the hundred are lords of the soil. You will go free of expense, in a first-rate ship, attended by a surgeon, with plenty of food and company, and more cared for, as to health and comfort, than most who emigrate of their own accord. Perhaps you are sorry to quit the country of your birth; but this sorrow is felt by all who emigrate: it was felt last year by more than 100,000 people, not convicts,

---

[1] Mr Stanley, the colonial minister, used the very words in the house of commons on the 16th of August, saying: 'He should take an early opportunity of laying before the house some important information relative to the classification of convicts in Van Dieman's Land, and on the different degrees of punishment; some, indeed, amounting to a degree of severity, of which many persons in this country could not be aware; in some cases approaching almost to *worse than death*.'

THE GAME LAWS;

Or, THE SACRIFICE OF THE PEASANT TO THE HARE.

who left home to share in the prosperity of such countries as New South Wales. No one brings himself to emigrate without some painful feelings; but tens of thousands, every year, bring themselves to emigrate, led on by the pleasures of hope. If you were a gentleman, well off, keeping your carriage, like many convicts in New South Wales, of course you would not wish to emigrate: and here you may see the reason why our gentry, who keep carriages and make laws, fancy that transportation must be a punishment. Why, those convicts in New South Wales, who keep their carriages, would consider transportation back to England a punishment: in short, no one, who is quite at his ease, likes to move far in any direction. But as yet, you are not at your ease, though you will be soon. At present, you belong to that uncomfortable set who take pains to emigrate, hoping to better their fortune by removing from a country where man is dirt cheap, to one where he is more precious than gold; from a country where the profits of trade and wages of labour are very low, to one where they are very high. You are going to a country, where farmers and shopkeepers make forty per cent. of their money, and common workmen earn seven shillings a day. So far, then, your prospects are most cheering.

'But, you will be a slave, says the law: let me explain that legal fiction. It is true that, on reaching New South Wales, you will be made over to a tradesman or farmer, who will set you to work, unless you have money to pay him for letting you be idle: but, in the worst case, if you work with moderate industry, about half as hard as ploughmen or weavers in England, your master will treat you with great kindness; will clothe, feed and lodge, you far better than the common people here are clothed, fed and lodged; and will encourage you, besides, by presents of spirits, tobacco and hard cash. His motive for doing all this will be a sense of your very great value; for it is only by means of your labour, that he will be able to make forty per cent. of his money. Cheer up, my man. The moment you land, you will have the strongest proof of your own importance: you will see twenty settlers scrambling for you, running to the governor, fawning upon the secretary, coaxing the treasurer and quarrelling with each other, on your account. Such is the nature of these new countries, where man is worth his weight in silver if not in gold. You ought then to rejoice in the prospect of being sent, without cost or trouble, to any new country, even as a convict.'

[The letter is signed: *Jack Ketch*.]

[*Extract*]

A LETTER TO ISAAC TOMKINS, GENT.

ONE of the most popular among the radicals of the early eighteen-thirties was Henry Brougham. As the adviser and defender of Queen Caroline he had stirred the whole country, as we have seen, when the 'Bill of Pains and Penalties' was before the House of Lords. In 1830, when a Whig Government took office, he accepted the position of Lord Chancellor and played a leading part in pushing through the Reform Act of 1832. The Whigs could be as oppressive as the Tories; and after they took office they lost no time in proving it. Cobbett (whom they prosecuted, unsuccessfully, in 1831) even maintained, on plausible grounds, that the Whigs were worse in their tyranny and injustice. The Reform Act was almost their only contribution to progress, and by present-day standards even the Reform Act registered only very timid and inadequate reforms in the electoral system; but it was mainly due to Brougham that it was not a great deal worse, and his personal efforts forced the House of Lords to realise the imperative necessity for withdrawing their opposition.

It should not be forgotten that one reason for the Reform Act was the hope of the Whig Aristocracy (the 'New Nobility' of the Sixteenth and Seventeenth centuries) that electoral reform would benefit their own party. In a previous note we have referred to the buying up of 'Rotten Boroughs' by the *nouveaux riches* from India—where Englishmen were then making enormous fortunes in a very short time, and seldom with any questions asked. One such, Paul Benfield, had been attacked by Burke, who spoke of him as a 'wholesale upholsterer' for the House of Commons. Benfield, he said, 'amidst his charitable toils for the relief of India did not forget the poor rotten constitution of his native country'. He had made, said Burke, 'reckoning himself, no fewer than eight members of the last Parliament. What copious streams of pure blood must he not have transfused into the present . . .'

The abolition of the 'Rotten Boroughs' meant a sharp curtailment of the influence exercised in the Lower House by these 'Nabobs', and by war profiteers and other persons whom the 'New Nobility' of the Reformation and of the Great Revolution could already afford to regard as upstarts. Brougham himself, who (almost alone of the Whig Cabinet) seems genuinely to have desired reform as a matter of principle, could reflect the snobbery upon which he relied to rally support in the House of Lords, where a large number of the Whigs were themselves dubious with regard to the proposed measure.

'That a Peer,' he told them, 'or a speculating attorney, or a jobbing Jew, or a gambler from the Stock Exchange, by vesting in his own person the old walls of Sarum, or a few pigsties at Bletchingley, or a summer-house at Gatton . . . is in itself a monstrous abuse. . . . An end must at length be put to the abuse which suffers the most precious rights of Government to be made the subject of common barter, to be conveyed by traffic . . . or to be made over for a gaming debt.' Gradually the Whig Aristocracy was becoming convinced that such a reform would enable it to recover its lost position; and it was not an unreasonable hope so long as a sufficiently high property qualification was attached to the franchise, so as to maintain a nice balance between the anomaly of pocket-boroughs (no longer tolerable when a considerable majority were owned by the Tories) and a universal franchise, which might have destroyed both the established parties unless they drastically revised their policies.

But just as William III had provided the Whigs with that majority in the House of Lords which they had once enjoyed, so in more recent years the same policy had been pursued by George III, under Pitt's guidance, to strengthen the ranks of the New Tories, subservient tools of the monarchy in a last attempt at absolutism. The third George had discovered the stage props of the Stuarts and (Jacobite hopes being dead) formed a useful alliance with the Tories which had provided for them a majority in the Lords and for the king a reliable Upper House, very largely made in his own image. The problem of the Reformers in 1832 was therefore the fact that the Tories not only had a solid permanent block of seats in the Commons. They had also a majority among the Peers, where pliable *parvenus* had bought themselves honour, and His Majesty's Ministers had sold something which cost nothing at all in return for solid cash and the political allegiance of the 'King's Friends'—a very good bargain for George III and his Ministers, but a bad headache for the Whigs. In 1832 the Whigs could still muster sufficient strength, if unity could be preserved (no easy task in itself) to force the Reform Bill through the House of Commons; but it was not clear at first whether the Bill could be carried in the Lords without yet another vintage of aristocracy—a Whig phalanx to be created by the new king (William IV), always supposing that he could be persuaded to do so, expressly for the purpose of trampling down the Tory opposition.

The story of the deadlock which followed, of Wellington's failure to form an alternative government, of the pressure exercised by a united nation upon the king and the House of Lords, is sufficiently well known. If the Whigs could not govern their own way, they were determined to resign, leaving the Tories to try the experiment of governing without a majority in the Lower House. That this meant the end of all effective government, and a choice between chaos and revolution, was clear to everyone. The Whigs had no mind to precipitate a revolution; but they knew their opponents well enough to judge that the mere threat was sufficient: if somebody had to withdraw in order to save the situation they were determined that it should be the Duke of Wellington, who was left only one line of retreat. The King yielded and agreed to the creation of new peers if necessary; but once more the threat sufficed. The victor of Waterloo was too experienced a commander to lead the Tories to certain destruction, and their Lordships withdrew in good order.

It is easy to see that at this time (as so often in English history, when the Peers have tried their strength against the people) any attack on the aristocracy must have been sure of a ready public. Brougham was not a very stable or a very consistent character, but he knew how to use his opportunities and—such as they were—his real opinions probably come out best in his anonymous work. Fond of popularity, a Lord among Lords, a lawyer among lawyers, a Whig among Whigs, a radical among radicals, Brougham was probably too conscious of his own merits to take a back seat gracefully in any company. Yet he was not without underlying sincerity, and anonymity could give it fair play, as this pamphlet shows. The poses of a politician, it is true, becomes habits of mind that are not easily laid aside; but in the *Letter to Isaac Tomkins* the real man seems to emerge more clearly than in many of Brougham's speeches and writings which are so often carefully levelled (with a barrister's precision) at the personal target they were designed to impress. And, oddly enough—call him a snob, a turn-coat, a wily lawyer, or what you will—Brougham was really both a great man and a tolerably good one, which is probably the reason why Carlyle never lost an opportunity to sneer at him. Indeed to have been sneered at by Carlyle would be almost *per se* a proof of greatness in any man, as we shall demonstrate in a later note.

The *Letter to Isaac Tomkins* was a supposed 'reply' to another of Brougham's pamphlets (also pseudonymous) in which the supposed

'Isaac Tomkins' had discussed the aristocracy, stressing the corruption of the Church and the Army, which provided sinecures for the younger sons of the aristocracy. In a typical passage Brougham had expressed here his well-known views on education, beginning with the public schools—'the best education in England, and one utterly below contempt'—from which the young patrician passed in due course to Oxford, which 'eradicates whatever feelings of humanity, whatever reasonable opinions, the expanding faculties of the mind may have engrafted upon the barren stocks of Henry the Sixth and William of Wickham'. Hence, said Brougham, arose 'the peculiar jealousy with which the House of Lords, as if instinctively, regards . . . those haunts of bigotry and intolerance'. Brougham's views on Oxford may be compared with the very similar opinions expressed, a generation earlier, by Gibbon. In the eighteen-thirties such strictures were still by no means unreasonable.

'Peter Jenkins', in the pamphlet that follows, replies in similar vein. The pamphlet was first published in 1835. Though later he pandered often to the prejudices of the Peers and even imitated them in many forms of snobbery (to the point of making himself ridiculous upon occasion) Brougham was too shrewd a judge of human nature to have been much deceived. We may safely assume that he never really lost his contempt for the House of Lords, even when he had made a comfortable nest in it for himself.

The personal targets—Sir Roger Gresley, Hall Dare, Bingham Baring (later Lord Ashburton) and Captain (later Vice-Admiral Sir George) Pechell—have long since been forgotten and their records are not worth recalling.

A LETTER TO ISAAC TOMKINS, GENT.

By Peter Jenkins (i.e. Lord Brougham)

Dear Sir,

I HAVE had the great satisfaction of reading your able and just remarks upon that Aristocracy which form the chief bane of all Policy, as well as all Society in this country, and which tends not much more to destroy good government over us than to sap good morals among us. You deserve all our thanks for the striking exposition you have made of this prevailing evil. But why do you stop short? Why do you dwell so much on the slighter part of the subject? What can be more insignificant to the nation at large, than the way in which Lords and Ladies spend their time at their Grandee Palaces? Let their society be ever so refined, or ever so gross—let their talk be as solid as that of rational creatures, or as silly and unsubstantial as you describe it, I care not—we and our fellow-citizens of the middle classes value not a rush the admission to that intercourse, and could well bear our perpetual exclusion from it, if that were all we had to suffer from the present Aristocratical government of the country. I want you, therefore to consider and to discourse upon our *real grievances*—those burthens by which the Aristocracy grind the faces of their inferiors.

Look only at the House of Commons—to take an example from what indeed lies at the root of the evil tree, whose bitter fruits we are all of us now eating. The Aristocracy represent us in Parliament; and, at the late election, as at all such times, they were clothed in fine smooth words—full of expressions to overflowing—glittering in pledges and promises; while they smiled from ear to ear in kindness and curtesy towards us. They would take off the malt-tax; and who, as Sir Roger Greisley said to the Derby gulls of farmers, who dared accuse *them* of ever breaking a promise? They would oppose ministers, and restore

117

reformers to power—as the Copelands, the Richards's, and I know not how many more so solemnly vowed. They were no party men to bring in a Whig Aristocracy, any more than to keep in a Tory one. But to reforming men and reforming measures they would look—and they would devote themselves to give cheap food to the country; and a reforming—a real reforming ministry to the King.

Next look at what these honest and faithful stewards have been doing ever since. They had a majority on the first vote—a strong vote indeed it was felt to be—the Speakership. What next? They did not venture to make an amendment on the Address, which was worth one farthing; they took an alteration just strong enough to disgrace the ministers—not strong or even plain enough to help on the cause of reform one single step. Do I blame Lord John Russell for proposing so weak a thing? Far from it. He knew well the stuff his majority was made of, and that if he had made it one syllable stronger or more intelligible, he would have been in a minority of fifty, instead of the majority of seven, which, by paring, and clipping, and weakening, he with difficulty obtained. Do not let us disguise the truth from ourselves. *Our Representatives have deceived us: do not let us deceive ourselves. A considerable majority of the House of Commons is against all Reform.* That majority, in its heart, hates the people. Its fears are pointed to the progress of improvement; its care is for the privileged orders; its darling object is to keep all things as much as possible in their present state, and just to give us as much relief as they cannot either resist or evade giving. They do not, in substance or effect, differ from the House of Lords, which is their natural ally, and their only lawful superior, to whose interests they are quite willing to sacrifice their constituents at any moment they can do it in safety. The Lords will not oppose a reform, when they are afraid of being swept away if they do. The bulk of the Commons—a majority of 100 at the least—will let reform pass, which they dare not resist without being sure of losing their seats. Do I, or does any body think the Lords friendly to any kind of reform, merely because they let some reforms pass? Not at all: they do it because they cannot help it. Does any one dream that above 200, or at most, 250, of the Commons really love reform, merely because the other reformers, the merely *nominal liberals*, do not dare throw out reform-bills and motions? Not a bit of it: they hate reform bitterly—hate it for its own sake—hate it for their sakes—hate it for the sake of the House of Lords, whom they really love, and where most of them hope to sit. But they fear us as well as detest us, and they must vote whether they will or no on many questions. Only see the effects of this.

It is like the argument of *measures not men*. Those members only give us just as much support and protection as they cannot possibly withhold; and in all other cases they refuse to stir for us. Hence neither Lord John Russell could frame an amendment worth a straw, excepting for merely party purposes; nor could Mr Hume support the people's most important right, to stop supplies till grievances were redressed. Hence all motions of any value are put off, because there is a struggle to turn out one set of Aristocrats, and to put another in their place. Hence, if the hearts of a very large majority of the House, and even a considerable number of the opposition were opened, and we could endure so hideous a sight—we should find not one trace of the country's good—not one vestige of the people's welfare—not the faintest impression of the public opinion—but all would be heats, hatreds, furies, fears, (not a reflection of the public wishes) about selfish objects, never rising nearer to the tone and temper of patriotism than so far as party feeling now and then borrows its hues for an ornament, and wears its garb for a disguise. Those men who I know are the majority of the House—who, I am almost certain, are some of the opposition—vote from a fifth to a fourth because they dread the loss of their seats, some because there are places which they possess or expect. They will try to patch up an expiring and impossible ministry, or to hatch a middle scheme to gratify jobbers, and frustrate all the hopes of the country, or make a new cabinet altogether; in which it is a hundred to one that we, the people, shall hardly find any men who are thoroughly disposed to do us justice, and whose heart is in the work of helping the people. I do not blame those men—the chiefs of the liberal and popular portion of the Whig party; on the contrary, I feel the debt of gratitude we owe them. But what can they do with such a system? They dare not break with the Aristocracy, to which almost all of them—more than nine in every ten—actually belong; they dare not fly in the face of the Court, which, as things are now arranged, may turn out a minister without notice, and without the least reason assigned; and, after plunging the country in confusion, retreat and suffer no kind of penalty, or even inconvenience, from its intrigue. They cannot work miracles in such a House of Commons, or make bricks without straw. They could not act for our true interests, even if they really felt as they ought, and actually wished what we desire; because they are only supported by a mixed body in the House of Commons, and opposed by a very determined and interested mass of steady, unflinching, unscrupulous enemies to all reform. *Our* friends are the minority; and the rest of the opposition, who in case of a change will be the ministerial body, is composed of men in whom the country never can again place any trust; because they have got into Parliament under false pretences; wheedling us one day with promises of strong votes, and breaking these promises the next; gaining their seats by pledges of reform, and forfeiting those pledges the moment they were sworn in.

It is easy to declaim against such men as your Greisleys and Hall Dares—your Bingham Barings and your Pechels. Whose fault was it that the son of a Tory minister was chosen on promise of voting with the liberals?—Whose but the liberals of Winchester, who preferred the man that gave out he should oppose his own father, to the man that had faithfully served them before? Whose fault was it that Captain Pechel turned out Mr. Faithful?—Whose but the Brighton liberals, who opposed an honest Tory, and preferred to an honest reformer a man notoriously receiving pay as a servant in the King's household? Nobody can pity either Winchester or Brighton. They have met exactly what their silly conduct, to call it no worse, deserves. Winchester is wholly inexcusable, for it had been treated in the same way before by the same individual.

But the persons whom we really have a right to complain of, and whom all honest men must blame, and all men of spirit despise, are the forty or fifty pretended liberals, who have not gone over openly to the enemy. These rotten members are the true cause of all the mischief that is befalling us. They will possibly make it impracticable to form a good liberal ministry: they will almost certainly cause any Government that is formed to be ill constructed,—patched of feeble men,—unpopular statesmen, and puny reformers, if reformers at all; and they will assuredly make it quite impossible for even such a ministry to last; so that we shall be driven very soon back to the Tories; and that vile and intolerable dominion will be perpetuated over us to the lasting disgrace of the country.

What remedy is there? The people must be on their guard: they must require their representatives to act like honest men, if they are not so. The people must keep a jealous eye on all that those men do in Parliament. A fit motion, by Mr Hume or Mr O'Connell, to separate the wheat from the chaff, and show the country which of those that cry out 'reform' are really reformers, is much wanted. By its results let the eye of the people be steadily and constantly directed to watch the conduct of the time-servers and waverers.

Then, and above all, let the people carefully attend to the new ministry which shall be formed, if indeed any can now be gotten together. Let all eyes be upon their conduct, and let no fear of driving them out again be suffered to suspend our admonitions, and our opposition to them; nor any apprehension of their joining in whole or in part the Tory liberals, as some call the less rancorous of the court party. Let them join, in God's name—so much the better for the country. The people must rally round those faithful men who are their real friends—who will never take office to hamper their exertions—who have even no relish, and some of them no capacity, for office, but who will be always ready to stand in the breach, and fight the battles of reform. Your true friend,

PETER JENKINS.

BALLOT

AMONG the abuses of the electoral system, in addition to those already mentioned (at which the first blow was struck by the Reform Act of 1832), the intimidation of voters was very common in the days before the secret ballot.

The supposed secrecy of the ballot-box is not, of course, a complete safeguard against intimidation. When Hitler held elections in Germany, it was commonly stated that the principal object was to locate the centres of resistance so that appropriate measures might be taken and spies strategically placed. More recently, in Northern Ireland, electors known to be unfavourable to a Unionist candidate have been menaced in such a way that only the bravest would dare to approach the ballot-box. Yet the ballot-box has been generally admitted to be the best safeguard against intimidation that has so far been devised, and the demand for some such method of voting increased in the years that followed the first Reform Act.

Intimidation arose principally from two sources. There was the economic intimidation exercised by the landlord over his tenants and the wealthy customer over the small shopkeeper, etc. (As the working class still had no representation, intimidation of their employees by employers of labour did not at that time arise.) There was also the direct intimidation that could be exercised by an angry crowd or a hired gang when the voting took place in public. When a sufficient number of people was sufficiently roused—as was the case in 1830—it is possible that the capacity of the voteless multitude to intimidate the enfranchised minority may have more than offset the economic threats and sanctions of the squirearchy. Ironically enough, we may owe the success of the Reformers in 1830 partly to the fact that voting, though restricted to so few, was *not* done in secret.

But after the Reform Act the demand for secrecy grew rapidly, and for obvious reasons. Those newly enfranchised were mainly of the lower middle-class, and they had more reason than most of the older electors to fear intimidation from the top. They had also—however much they may have owed to the popular fury that had pushed through the Act—no desire to be menaced from below. The ballot was therefore much discussed, and the extract which follows from Sydney Smith's pamphlet on the subject (first published in 1839) states the case against the ballot very ably—a *tour de force*, because there was in reality no case against the ballot except that of vested interests which were threatened.

The writer's point of view is frankly that of the Old Régime, to which he was naturally attached as a well-to-do clergyman who moved on the best possible terms with 'The Quality'. Sydney Smith is not really concerned with what effect the ballot might have on the balance of Whig versus Tory. He thinks that the gains and losses there will cancel each other, and in any case the world as he has known and enjoyed it will go on very comfortably whichever party is in power. One may also, probably, discount the anxiety expressed by the writer about the awful prospect of people promising a vote to one candidate and secretly giving it to another. Sydney Smith knew perfectly well that there are many things which civilised people prefer to do in private, and that a man is no more compelled to lie by using a ballot box than he is by having a lock on the door of the bathroom, the bedroom, or the privy. But such pseudo-moral arguments come readily to hand when big interests are at stake, and what really worried Sydney Smith comes out at the end of this pamphlet: the fear that the old Whig and Tory See-Saw might be upset by a breath of real democracy.

One of the ablest replies to the general line of argument of which this pamphlet is typical will be found in Perronet Thompson's *Catechism on the Ballot* (1859). It was not until the year 1872 that the Ballot Act was passed (following the example of Australia) and public voting abolished.

Sydney Smith's pamphlet has the merit of being, at least, remarkably well written, and the reader who most disagrees with its substance may still find himself smiling at the writer's wit or admiring the turn of a phrase. We have used the third edition of this pamphlet for present purposes, as it contains some interesting additions not to be found in the original publication. The daring and absurdity of Sydney Smith's false analogies and his frequent use of *non sequitur* might suggest that the whole pamphlet was a brilliant satire; but its intention was entirely serious.

'Mr Grote,' the protagonist of the ballot box, was George Grote, the historian. He was a 'philosophic radical' who was never really at home in the corrupt and opportunist world of politics.

BALLOT

By Sydney Smith

IT is possible, and perhaps not very difficult, to invent a machine, by the aid of which electors may vote for a candidate, or for two or three candidates, out of a greater number, without its being discovered for whom they vote; it is less easy than the rabid, and foaming Radical supposes; but I have no doubt it may be accomplished. In Mr Grote's dagger ballot box, which has been carried round the country by eminent patriots, you stab the card of your favourite candidate with a dagger. I have seen another, called the mouse-trap ballot box, in which you poke your finger into the trap of the member you prefer, and are caught and detained till the trap-clerk below (who knows by means of a wire when you are caught) marks your vote, pulls the liberator, and releases you. Which may be the most eligible of these two methods I do not pretend to determine.

Landed proprietors imagine they have a right to the votes of their tenants; and instances, in every election, are numerous where tenants have been dismissed for voting contrary to the wishes of their land-lords. In the same manner strong combinations are made against tradesmen who have chosen to think, and act for themselves in political matters, rather than yield their opinions to the solicitations of their customers. There is a great deal of tyranny and injustice in all this. I should no more think of asking what the political opinions of a shop-keeper were, than of asking whether he was tall or short, or large or small: for a difference of $2\frac{1}{2}$ per cent. I would desert the most aristocratic butcher that ever existed, and deal with one who

> Shook the arsenal, and fulmin'd over Greece.

On the contrary, I would not adhere to the man who put me in uneasy habiliments, however great his veneration for trial by jury, or however ardent his attachment to the liberty of the subject. A tenant I never had; but I firmly believe that if he had gone through certain pecuniary formalities twice a year, I should have thought it a gross act of tyranny to have interfered either with his political, or his religious opinions.

I distinctly admit that every man has a right to do what he pleases with his own. I cannot, by law, prevent any one from discharging his tenants and changing his tradesmen for political reasons; but I may judge whether that man exercises his right to the public detriment, or for the public advantage. A man has a right to refuse dealing with any tradesman who is not five feet eleven inches high; but if he acts upon this rule, he is either a madman or a fool. He has a right to lay waste his own estate, and to make it utterly barren; but I have also a right to point him out as one who exercises his right in a manner very injurious to society. He may set up a religious or a political test for his tradesmen; but admitting his right, and deprecating all interference of law, I must tell him he is making the aristocracy odious to the great mass, and that he is sowing the seeds of revolution. His purse may be full, and his fields may be wide; but the moralist will still hold the rod of public opinion over his head, and tell the money bloated blockhead that he is shaking those laws of property which it has taken ages to extort from the wretchedness and rapacity of mankind; and that what he calls his own will not long be his own, if he tramples too heavily upon human patience.

All these practices are bad; but the facts and the consequences are exaggerated.

In the first place, the plough is not a political machine: the loom and the steam-engine are furiously political, but the plough is not. Nineteen tenants out of twenty care nothing about their votes, and pull off their opinions as easily to their landlords as they do their hats. As far as the great majority of tenants are concerned, these histories of persecution are mere declamatory nonsense; they have no more predilection for whom they vote than organ pipes have for what tunes they are to play. A tenant dismissed for a fair and just cause, often attributes his dismissal to political motives, and endeavours to make himself a martyr with the public: a man who ploughs badly, or who pays badly, says he is dismissed for his vote. No candidate is willing to allow that he has lost his election by his demerits; and he seizes hold of these stories, and circulates them with the greatest avidity: they are stated in the House of Commons; John Russell and Spring Rice fall a crying; there is lamentation of Liberals in the land; and many groans for the territorial tyrants.

A standing reason against the frequency of dismissal of tenants is, that it is always injurious to the pecuniary interests of a landlord to dismiss a tenant; the property always suffers in some degree by a going off tenant; and it is therefore always the interest of a landlord not to change when the tenant does his duty as an agriculturist.

To part with tenants for political reasons always makes a landlord unpopular. The Constitutional, price 4d.; the Cato, at 3½d.; and the Lucius Junius Brutus, at 2d., all set upon the unhappy scutiger; and the squire, unused to be pointed at, and thinking that all Europe and part of Asia are thinking of him and his farmers, is driven to the brink of suicide, and despair. That such things are done is not denied, that they are scandalous when they are done is equally true; but these are reasons why such acts are less frequent than they are commonly represented to be. In the same manner, there are instances of shopkeepers being materially injured in their business from the votes they have given; but the facts themselves, as well as the consequences, are grossly exaggerated. If shopkeepers lose Tory they gain Whig customers; and it is not always the vote which does the mischief, but the low vulgar impertinence, and the unbridled scurrility of a man who thinks that by dividing to mankind their rations of butter and of cheese, he has qualified himself for legislation, and that he can hold the rod of empire because he has wielded the yard of mensuration. I detest all inquisition into political opinions, but I have very rarely seen a combination against any tradesman who modestly, quietly, and conscientiously took his own line in politics. But Brutus and butterman, cheesemonger and Cato, do not harmonise well together; good taste is offended, the coxcomb loses his friends, and general disgust is mistaken for combined oppression. Shopkeepers, too, are very apt to cry out before they are hurt; a man who sees after an election one of his customers buying a pair of gloves on the opposite side of the way, roars out that his honesty will make him a bankrupt, and the county papers are filled with letters from Brutus, Publicola, Hampden, and Pym.

This interference with the freedom of voting, bad as it is, produces no political deliberation; it does not make the Tories stronger than the Whigs, nor the Whigs than the Tories, for both are equally guilty of this species of tyranny; and any particular system of measures fails or prevails, much as if no such practice existed. The practice had better not be at all, but if a certain quantity of the evil does exist, it is better that it should be equally divided among both parties, than that it should be exercised by one, for the depression of the other. There are politicians always at a white heat, who suppose that there are landed tyrants only on one side of the question; but human life has been distressingly abridged by the flood, there is no time to spare, it is impossible to waste it upon such senseless bigotry.

If a man is sheltered from intimidation, is it at all clear that he would vote from any better motive than intimidation? If you make so tremendous an experiment, are you sure of attaining your object? The landlord has perhaps said a cross word to the tenant; the candidate for whom the tenant votes in opposition to his landlord has taken his second son for a footman, or his father knew the candidate's grandfather: how many thousand votes, sheltered (as the ballotists suppose) from intimidation, would be given from such silly motives as these? how many would be given from the mere discontent of inferiority? or from that strange simious schoolboy passion of giving pain to others, even when the author cannot be found out?—motives as pernicious as any which could proceed from intimidation. So that all voters screened by ballot would not be screened for any public good.

The Radicals (I do not use this word in any offensive sense, for I know many honest and excellent men of this way of thinking), but the Radicals praise and admit the lawful influence of wealth, and power. They are quite satisfied if a rich man of popular manners gains the votes, and affections of his dependants; but why is not this as bad as intimidation? The real object is to vote for the good politician, not for the kind-hearted, or agreeable man: the mischief is just the same to the country whether I am smiled into a corrupt choice, or frowned into a corrupt choice,—what is it to me whether my landlord is the best of landlords, or the most agreeable of men? I must vote for Joseph Hume, if I think Joseph more honest than the Marquis. The more mitigated Radical may pass over this, but the real carnivorous variety of the animal should declaim as loudly against the fascinations as against the threats of the great. The man who possesses the land should never speak to the man who tills it. The intercourse between landlord and tenant should be as strictly guarded as that of the sexes in Turkey. A funded duenna should be placed over every landed grandee.—And then intimidation! Is intimidation confined to the aristocracy? Can any thing be more scandalous and atrocious than the intimidation of mobs? Did not the mob of Bristol occasion more ruin, wretchedness, death, and alarm than all the ejection of tenants, and combinations against shopkeepers, from the beginning of the century? and did not the Scotch philosophers tear off the clothes of the Tories in Mintoshire? or at least such clothes as the customs of the country admit of being worn?—and did not they, without any reflection at all upon the customs of the country, wash the Tory voters in the river?

Some sanguine advocates of the ballot contend that it would put an end to all canvassing: why should it do so? Under the ballot, I canvass (it is true) a person who may secretly deceive me. I cannot be sure he will not do so—but I am sure it is much less likely he will vote against me, when I have paid him all the deference and attention which a representative bestows on his constituents, than if I had totally neglected him: to any other objections he may have against me, at least I will not add that of personal incivility.

Scarcely is any great virtue practised without some sacrifice; and the admiration which virtue excites, seems to proceed from the contemplation of such sufferings, and of the exertions by which they are endured: a tradesman suffers some loss of trade by voting for his country; is he not to vote? he might suffer some loss of blood in fighting for his country; is he not to fight? Every one would be a good Samaritan, if he was quite sure his compassion would cost him nothing. We should all be heroes, if it was not for blood and fractures; all saints, if it were not for the restrictions, and privations of sanctity; all patriots, if it were not for the losses and misrepresentations to which patriotism exposes us. The ballotists are a set of Englishmen glowing with the love of England and the love of virtue, but determined to hazard the most dangerous experiments in politics, rather than run the risk of losing a penny in defence of their exalted feelings.

An abominable tyranny exercised by the ballot is, that it compels those persons to conceal their votes, who hate all concealment, and who glory in the cause they support. If you are afraid to go in at the front door, and to say in a clear voice what you have to say, go in at the back door, and say it in a whisper—but this is not enough for you; you make me, who am bold and honest, sneak in at the back door as well as yourself: because you are afraid of selling a dozen or two of gloves less than usual; you compel me, who have no gloves to sell, or who would dare and despise the loss, if I had; to hide th e best feelings of my heart, and to lower myself down to your mean morals. It is as if a few cowards, who could only fight behind walls and houses, were to prevent the whole regiment from showing a bold front in the field: what right has the coward to degrade me who am no coward, and put me in the same shameful predicament with himself? If ballot is established, a zealous voter cannot do justice to his cause, there will be so many false Hampdens, and spurious Catos, that all men's actions, and motives will be mistrusted. It is in the power of any man to tell me that my colours are false, that I declaim with simulated warmth, and canvass with fallacious zeal; that I am a Tory, though I call *Russell* for ever, or a Whig in spite of my obstreperous panegyrics of *Peel*. It is really a curious condition that all men must imitate the defects of a few, in order that it may not be known who have the natural imperfection, and who put it on from conformity. In this way in former days, to hide the grey hairs of the old, every body was forced to wear powder and pomatum.

It must not be forgotten that, in the ballot, concealment must be absolutely *compulsory*. It would never do to let one man vote openly, and another secretly. You may go to the edge of the box, and say 'I vote for A', but who knows that your ball is not put in for B? There must be a clear plain opportunity for telling an undiscoverable lie, or the whole invention is at an end. How beautiful is the progress of man!—printing has abolished ignorance—gas put an end to darkness—steam has conquered time and distance—it remained for Grote and his box to remove the incumbrance of truth from human transactions. May we not look now for more little machines to abolish the other cardinal virtues?

But if all men are suspected; if things are so contrived that it is impossible to know what men really think, a serious impediment is created to the formation of good public opinion in the multitude. There is a town (No. 1) in which live two very clever and respectable men, Johnson and Pelham, small tradesmen, men always willing to run some risk for the public good, and to be less rich, and more honest than their neighbours. It is of considerable consequence to the formation of opinion in this town, as an example, to know how Johnson and Pelham vote. It guides the affections, and directs the understandings, of the whole population, and materially affects public opinion in this town; and in another borough, No. 2, it would be of the highest importance to public opinion if it were certain how Mr Smith, the ironmonger, and Mr Rogers, the London carrier, voted; because they are both thoroughly honest men, and of excellent understanding for their condition of life. Now, the tendency of ballot would be to destroy all the Pelhams, Johnsons, Rogers', and Smiths, to sow a universal mistrust, and to exterminate the natural guides, and leaders of the people: political influence, founded upon honour and ancient honesty in politics, could not grow up under such a system. No man's declaration could get believed. It would be easy to whisper away the character of the best men; and to assert that, in spite of all his declarations, which are nothing but a blind, the romantic Rogers has voted on the other side, and is in secret league with our enemies.

'Who brought that mischievous profligate villain into Parliament? Let us see the names of his real supporters. Who stood out against the strong and uplifted arm of power? Who discovered this excellent and hitherto unknown person? Who opposed the man whom we all know to be one of the first men in the country?' Are these fair and useful questions to be veiled hereafter in impenetrable mystery? Is this sort of publicity of no good as a restraint; is it of no good as an incitement to and a reward for exertions? Is not public opinion formed by such feelings? and is it not a dark and demoralising system to draw this veil over human actions, to say to the mass, be base, and you will not be despised; be virtuous, and you will not be honoured? Is this the way in which Mr Grote would foster the spirit of a bold, and indomitable people? Was the liberty of that people established by fraud? Did America lie herself into independence? Was it treachery which enabled Holland to shake off the yoke of Spain? Is there any instance since the beginning of the world, where human liberty has been established by little systems of trumpery and trick? These are the weapons of monarchs against the people, not of the people against monarchs. With their own right hand, and with their mighty arm, have the people gotten to themselves the victory, and upon them may they ever depend; and then comes Mr Grote, a scholar and a gentleman, and knowing all the histories of public courage, preaches cowardice and treachery to England; tells us that the bold cannot be free, and bids us seek for liberty by clothing ourselves in the mask of falsehood, and trampling on the cross of truth.[1]

*　　　*　　　*　　　*

It is urged that the lower order of voters, proud of such a distinction, will not be anxious to extend it to others; but the lower order of voters will often find that they possess this distinction in vain—that wealth and education are too strong for them; and they will call in the multitude as auxiliaries, firmly believing that they can curb their inferiors and conquer their superiors. Ballot is a mere illusion, but universal suffrage is not an illusion. The common people will get nothing by the one, but they will gain every thing, and ruin every thing, by the last.

Some members of Parliament who mean to vote for ballot, in the fear of losing their seats, and who are desirous of reconciling to their conscience such an act of disloyalty to mankind, are fond of saying that ballot is harmless; that it will neither do the good nor the evil that

[1] Mr Grote is a very worthy, honest, and able man; and, if the world were a chess-board, would be an important politician.

is expected from it; and that the people may fairly be indulged in such an innocent piece of legislation. Never was such folly and madness as this: ballot will be the cause of interminable hatred and jealousy among the different orders of mankind; it will familiarise the English people to a long tenor of deceit; it will not answer its purpose in protecting the independent voter, and the people, exasperated and disappointed by the failure, will indemnify themselves by insisting upon unlimited suffrage. And then it is talked of as an experiment, as if men were talking of acids and alkalies, and the galvanic pile; as if Lord John could get on the hustings and say, 'Gentlemen, you see this ballot does not answer; do me the favour to give it up, and to allow yourselves to be replaced in the same situation as the ballot found you'. Such, no doubt, is the history of nations and the march of human affairs; and, in this way, the error of a sudden and foolish largess of power to the people, might, no doubt, be easily retrieved. The most unpleasant of all bodily feelings is a cold sweat: nothing brings it on so surely as perilous nonsense in politics. I lose all warmth from the bodily frame when I hear the ballot talked of as an *experiment*.

I cannot at all understand what is meant by this indolent opinion. Votes are coerced now; if votes are free, will the elected be the same? if not, will the difference of the elected be unimportant? Will not the ballot stimulate the upper orders to fresh exertions, and is their increased jealousy and interference of no importance? If ballot, after all, is found to hold out a real protection to the voter, is universal lying of no importance? I can understand what is meant by calling ballot a great good, or a great evil; but, in the mighty contention for power which is raging in this country, to call it indifferent appears to me extremely foolish in all those in whom it is not extremely dishonest.

If the ballot did succeed in enabling the lower order of voters to conquer their betters, so much the worse. In a town consisting of 700 voters, the 300 most opulent and powerful (and therefore probably the best instructed) would make a much better choice than the remaining 400; and the ballot would, in that case, do more harm than good. In nineteen cases out of twenty, the most numerous party would be in the wrong. If this is the case, why give the franchise to all; why not confine it to the first division? *because even with all the abuses which occur, and in spite of them, the great mass of the people are much more satisfied with having a vote occasionally controlled, than with having none.* Many agree with their superiors, and therefore feel no control. Many are persuaded by their superiors, and not controlled. Some are indifferent which way they exercise the power, though they would not like to be utterly deprived of it. Some guzzle away their vote, some sell it, some brave their superiors, a few are threatened and controlled. The election, in different ways, is affected by the superior influence of the upper orders; and the great mass (occasionally and justly complaining) are, beyond all doubt, better pleased than if they had no votes at all. The lower orders always have it in their power to rebel against their superiors; and occasionally they will do so, and have done so, and occasionally and justly carried elections[1] against gold, and birth, and education. But it is madness to make laws of society which attempt to shake off the great laws of nature. As long as men love bread, and mutton, and broad cloth, wealth, in a long series of years, must have enormous effects upon human affairs, and the strong box will beat the ballot box. Mr Grote has both, but he miscalculates their respective powers. Mr Grote knows the relative values of gold and silver; but by what moral rate of exchange is he able to tell us the relative values of liberty and truth?

It is hardly necessary to say anything about universal suffrage, as there is no act of folly or madness which it may not in the beginning produce. There would be the greatest risk that the monarchy, as at present constituted, the funded debt, the established church, titles, and hereditary peerage, would give way before it. Many really honest men may wish for these changes; I know, or at least believe, that wheat and barley would grow if there was no Archbishop of Canterbury, and domestic fowls would breed if our Viscount Melbourne was again called Mr Lamb; but they have stronger nerves than I have who would venture to bring these changes about. So few nations have been free, it is so difficult to guard freedom from kings, and mobs, and patriotic gentlemen; and we are in such a very tolerable state of happiness in England, that I think such changes would be very rash; and I have an utter mistrust in the sagacity and penetration of political reasoners who pretend to foresee all the consequences to which they would give birth. When I speak of the tolerable state of happiness in which we live in England, I do not speak merely of nobles, squires, and canons of St Paul's, but of drivers of coaches, clerks in offices, carpenters, blacksmiths, butchers, and bakers, and most men who do not marry upon nothing, and become burthened with large families before they have arrived at years of maturity. The earth is not sufficiently fertile for this:

Difficilem victum fundit durissima tellus.

After all, the great art in politics and war is to choose a good position for making a stand. The Duke of Wellington examined and fortified

---

[1] The 400 or 500 voting against the 200 are right about as often as juries are right in differing from judges; and that is very seldom.

NOT SO *VERY* UNREASONABLE!!! EH?

.....ORN.—"MY MISTRESS SAYS SHE HOPES YOU WON'T CALL A MEETING OF HER CREDITORS; BUT IF YOU WILL LEAVE YOUR BILL IN THE USUAL
WAY, IT SHALL BE PROPERLY ATTENDED TO."

the lines of Torres Vedras a year before he had any occasion to make use of them, and he had previously marked out Waterloo as the probable scene of some future exploit. The people seem to be hurrying on through all the well known steps to anarchy; they must be stopped at some pass or another: the first is the best and the most easily defended. The people have a right to ballot or to any thing else which will make them happy; and they have a right to nothing which will make them unhappy. They are the best judges of their immediate gratifications, and the worst judges of what would best conduce to their interests for a series of years. Most earnestly and conscientiously wishing their good, I say,

No Ballot.

[*Extracts*]

ON SLAVERY, AND ITS REMEDY

THIS short pamphlet needs longer introduction. Its interest lies in the confident assertion of the author that slavery does not pay, and in the figures which he gives.

Joseph Pease was a well-known Quaker and M.P. for Durham from 1832 until 1841, being the first member of the Society of Friends to sit in Parliament. (He created a precedent by his insistence on making an affirmation in place of the Oath of Allegiance, which was permitted after consideration by a select committee.) In spite of the hard-boiled argument which he employed on this occasion, the question of slavery was one that really moved Pease, as it did many humane people at that time; and there is no reason to assume that a campaign so energetically conducted over many years by people who had no economic interests themselves in the matter was anything but a genuine expression of their belief in human freedom. In many—including Pease himself—this belief had a religious origin, which did not preclude a hard-headed early nineteenth century industrialist from urging arguments which (he felt) should have some appeal to the business acumen of the slave-owning planters. Nor did it preclude many of the abolitionists—such as Wilberforce himself, and even John Bright—from taking up a very unsatisfactory attitude in regard to child labour at home and factory legislation generally. The contrast was noted by many, and made the subject (in the case of Wilberforce) of some bitter comments by Cobbett.

When Joseph Pease wrote this pamphlet, in 1841, slavery had been theoretically abolished in the British colonies by the Act of 1833. How unsatisfactory the position still was for the former slaves in the West Indies we shall note in discussing a later pamphlet. But the work of Joseph Pease is of special interest because it illustrates the wider interests of many Englishmen in the nineteenth century. A sense of world citizenship was already coming into being, and it is significant that Joseph Pease, who was active in the cause of world peace, should have concerned himself not only with what was happening in Britain, or even in the British Colonies, but with a social evil which was at that time more widespread in the United States than in any other country.

This short pamphlet affords an interesting comparison with the extracts from Anthony Benezet's *Caution and Warning*, published in our first volume. In the latter the appeal is purely humanitarian, and is addressed by a colonist to his fellow colonists. Here we have an Englishman addressing the world and appealing to economic interest. And all that remains to explain is how the same man who was honestly shocked by the idea of slavery was not also shocked by the exploitation of Indian 'free' labour, as plainly shown in his own words. To understand that, however, is to understand the whole complex problem of Victorian social morality.

The whole story of the abolition of slavery is remarkable, not only because it was a triumph achieved by a small group of idealists against powerful vested interests, but because abolition was eventually accomplished after every imaginable blunder had been committed by weak and hesitating statesmen, who hovered between moral right and political expediency, in such a way as to satisfy neither—a familiar pose of politicians in all ages. An Act of 1807, by which it had been attempted to abolish the slave trade, without abolishing slavery itself, had actually led to a great increase in the number of Negroes shipped from Africa, as the slave traders then had to allow for the number they were obliged to throw overboard if they met a British warship. The number thrown overboard was estimated at two-thirds of the annual 'cargo' of these bootleggers in human flesh. This contraband trade continued so long as slavery provided a good market at the other end; but the number of Negroes who survived such trips was not large enough to satisfy the planters, the slave population declined, and conditions on the plantations actually deteriorated after the theoretical cessation of the slave trade.

The Act of 1833, which was intended to end slavery itself in the British Colonies, had given excellent financial compensation to the slave-owners, and directed that the slaves should be bound as 'apprentices' to their former owners for seven years, under pain of corporal punishment—children under six excepted. When Pease wrote, the seven years' period was over—it had, in fact, been reduced to five years, in practice, owing to opposition in the House of Commons to Governmental 'gradualism'. Not for the last time in our history it had been clear that the Government was going slowly, not on account of any insuperable obstacles, but merely as a matter of habit. One might even call it a matter of principle were it not that in time of war our governments have been known to move so quickly that in half an hour they have undone whole centuries of progress.

ON SLAVERY, AND ITS REMEDY

By Joseph Pease

THE shortest, surest way of destroying the Slave Trade and Slavery all over the world, is what we all most ardently desire. If there be a *shorter* way, I would not stop surely to convince the dark heart of the Planter that he ought to set his Slaves free from a sense of justice.

I would surely not stop to convince the despotic Planter that he must yield up the delightful, arbitrary rule of his Slaves to reap the advantage of free labour.

Has not the fifty years in the great Anti-Slavery struggle demonstrated how little was to be obtained in our West India Colonies by converting the Planters?—let us inquire how many Planters set their Slaves free from a sense of justice?—let us inquire how many yielded their despotic power to avail themselves of the profit from free labour?

Then what has caused the conversion of the West India Planters?—England giving them twenty millions sterling for their Slaves, which were not worth ten millions!

When five hundred thousand human beings are annually torn from their native country and carried into miserable, hopeless Slavery; whilst five millions of the great human family are dragging out a miserable existence in cruel bondage, does not every year of delay involve us in an awful responsibility? The weight of these considerations has rested for years with great force upon my mind, and led me to turn my attention, as it were, everywhere, seeking for a remedy.

The important question at this moment is, whether the remedy is not offered to us by British India?

THE FOLLOWING FACTS SHOW

A Comparative Statement of the Expense of Labour in the Brazils and Cuba, and in the Presidency of Bengal, in the East Indies.

In Brazils and Cuba, 1,000 Slave labourers will, on the very *lowest* average, cost the proprietor of an estate, £20 per annum each, or £20,000.

In Bengal, 1,000 free labourers will, at the very *highest* average cost (according to Sir Geo. Stevens's statement), the renter or proprietor of an estate £3 12s. per annum each, or £3,600.

Balance in favour of the East Indies, upon every 1,000 labourers, is £16,400.

Again; evidence given on the 16th of March, 1840, before the Select Committee of the House of Commons, Lord Seymour in the chair:—

Andrew Sym, the great East India Planter, states, that in the manufacture of this India sugar, ordinary labourers receive 1¾d per day—can by any possibility the Slave labour of Cuba and the Brazils meet in the market the East India sugar, cotton, or any other of the Indian produce raised by 1¾d a day labour, which is about £2 12s 6d per annum, when the lowest estimate of the Cuba and Brazils Slave labour is £20 per annum.

Further, a great Planter, one of my friends, in Madras, hires the little farmers to cultivate his land, for which he has to pay only 2s per day, for 8 men, 16 oxen and 8 ploughs; and what would *these* cost by *Slave labour* in the Brazils and Cuba?

Mr. Sym says the whole expense of labour before the cane is ripe is 9s per acre, and we charge 6s an acre rent for sugar land, making 15s an acre, which yields 320 lb. or near 3 cwt., which is 5s per cwt. or £5 per ton, and all the *costs* till delivered in bond, may vary from £7 to £10 per ton.

Three large East India Planters tell me, now that the duty on rum is equalised, that they can afford to deliver sugar, free from all expense, in bond, at £15 a ton, of the same quality and value as the sugar for which we have been paying £46 a ton. Other Planters assure me they can lay this sugar in bond for £12 a ton.[1]

I will conclude these remarks with the opinion given by the enlightened and benevolent James Cropper, several years ago, viz., 'that if *slavery* and the *slave trade* had been left to a competition with free labour,

---

[1] £15 East Indies—£45 or £46 we pay;—home consumption, say 200,000 tons per annum, which we could purchase for £30 a ton *less*. Does not this make England pay six millions sterling more for her Sugar than the East Indies would furnish us at.

and we had neither made laws to abolish them nor given our money for their support, both the one and the other would ere this have ceased to exist in the slave countries.

'Nearly fifty years of time, and fifty millions of money, are surely enough to have spent on erroneous views. Oh! that the friends of the cause could be aware that the continuance of oppression will rest wholly on themselves, so long as they refuse to look at the question in all its bearings, which many of them have hitherto done.'

When I reflect on the years of misery in which millions of our fellow-creatures have been toiling out their deplorable existence— when I reflect on the millions of the great human family, torn from their native country and destroyed by the slave trade—since this pious man gave us the warning[1]—all that is within me seems at times as it were to shrink from our awful responsibility.

JOSEPH PEASE.

No. 2, Christopher Street, Finsbury Square.
6th Mo. 28, 1841.

[1] 'This pious man' (i.e. James Cropper, a wealthy Quaker engaged in East India trade) was the object of one of Cobbett's most bitter attacks, in the *Register* of July and August, 1821. Cobbett quoted Dr Francis Buchanan, an acknowledged authority, to prove that slavery existed on the Indian plantations, and that the condition of the slaves there was worse than that of slaves in the West Indies. [ED.]

CHEAP CLOTHES AND NASTY

KINGSLEY'S *Cheap Clothes and Nasty* explains itself so well that it may be said to need no more introduction than its author requires. What is perhaps more necessary is an apologia for the re-publication here of a work so well known and so often published in the past.

The answer is that we were anxious to provide at least one descriptive pamphlet which would give a true picture of working-class life in the mid-nineteenth century. It was from that life, and as a protest against it, that the various working-class movements arose which shaped so much of the political literature in the hundred years since Kingsley's pamphlet appeared in 1850. We chose this pamphlet because it is easily the best of its kind—an account which is written with knowledge, yet never becomes a tedious rigmarole of statistics, like so much of the Fabian literature, a generation later. Even Kingsley's figures come to life; and the vigour with which he writes makes it easy to forgive him his faults and prejudices, for we are listening to a man who really feels passionately the wrongs of others.

We were also anxious to include at least one example of the literature produced by the 'Christian Socialists', who did so much at this time to arouse the conscience of the country with regard to many glaring social evils. This pamphlet, alone of all that these 'muscular Christians' produced, seemed suitable for our present purpose. They were a curious, muddle-headed group. (Kingsley in this pamphlet shows more than a trace of anti-Semitism; he believed quite fanatically in the 'Nordic' races, was rabid in his Protestanism and—like Ruskin—had some odd views about the moral regeneration that might be found in a really good war.) But there is no doubting the sincerity of 'Parson Lot' in this historic description and indictment of the Jungle Law which resulted from the principles enunciated by Edmund Burke and Sir Thomas Turton in previous pamphlets.

TRACTS BY CHRISTIAN SOCIALISTS

II

CHEAP CLOTHES AND NASTY

By "Parson Lot" (Charles Kingsley)

(Second Edition)

'Nata servituti mancipia semel veneunt, atque ultro à domino aluntur: Britanni servitutem suam quotidie emunt, quotidie pascunt.'—TACITUS AGRICOLA.

KING RYENCE, says the legend of Prince Arthur, wore a paletot trimmed with kings' beards. In the first French Revolution (so Carlyle assures us) there were at Meudon, tanneries of human skins. Mammon, at once tyrant and revolutionary, follows both these noble examples—in a more respectable way, doubtless, for Mammon hates cruelty; bodily pain is his devil—the worst evil of which he, in his effeminacy, can conceive. So he shrieks benevolently when a drunken soldier is flogged; but he trims his paletots, and adorns his legs, with the flesh of men and the skins of women, with degradation, pestilence, heathendom, and despair; and then chuckles self-complacently over the smallness of his tailors' bills. Hypocrite!—straining at a gnat, and swallowing a camel! What is flogging, or hanging, King Ryence's paletot, or the tanneries of Meudon, to the slavery, starvation, waste of life, year-long imprisonment in dungeons, narrower and fouler than those of the Inquisition, which goes on among thousands of free English clothes-makers at this day?

'The man is mad,' says Mammon, smiling supercilious pity. Yes, Mammon; mad as Paul before Festus; and for much the same reason, too. Much learning has made us mad. From two articles in the *Morning Chronicle* of Friday, December 14th, and Tuesday, December 18th,

1849, on the Condition of the Working Tailors, we learnt too much to leave us altogether masters of ourselves. But there is method in our madness; we can give reasons for it—satisfactory to ourselves, perhaps also to Him who made us, and you, and all tailors likewise. Will you, freshly bedizened, you and your footmen, from Nebuchadnezzar and Co.'s 'Emporium of fashion', hear a little about how your finery is made? You are always calling out for facts, and have a firm belief in salvation by statistics. Listen to a few.

The Metropolitan Commissioner of the *Morning Chronicle* called two meetings of the Working Tailors, one in Shadwell, and the other at the Hanover-square Rooms, in order to ascertain their condition from their own lips. Both meetings were crowded. At the Hanover-square Rooms there were more than one thousand men; they were altogether unanimous in their descriptions of the misery and slavery which they endured. It appears that there are two distinct tailor trades—the 'honourable' trade, now almost confined to the West End, and rapidly dying out there, and the 'dishonourable' trade of the show-shops and slop-shops—the plate-glass palaces, where gents—and, alas! those who would be indignant at that name—buy their cheap-and-nasty clothes. The two names are the tailors' own slang; slang is true and expressive enough, though, now and then. The honourable shops in the West End number only sixty; the dishonourable, four hundred and more; while at the East End the dishonourable trade has it all its own way. The honourable part of the trade is declining at the rate of one hundred and fifty journeymen per year; the dishonourable increasing at such a rate that, in twenty years, it will have absorbed the whole tailoring trade, which employs upwards of twenty-one thousand journeymen. At the honourable shops, the work is done, as it was universally thirty years ago, on the premises and at good wages. In the dishonourable trade, the work is taken home by the men, to be done at the very lowest possible prices, which decrease year by year, almost month by month. At the honourable shops, from 36s to 24s is paid for a piece of work for which the dishonourable shop pays from 22s to 9s. But not to the workmen; happy is he if he really gets two-thirds, or half of that. For at the honourable shops, the master deals directly with his workmen; while at the dishonourable ones, the greater part of the work, if not the whole, is let out to contractors, or middle-men—'*sweaters*', as their victims significantly call them—who, in their turn, let it out again, sometimes to the workmen, sometimes to fresh middle-men; so that out of the price paid for labour on each article, not only the workmen, but the sweater, and perhaps the sweater's sweater, and a third, and a fourth, and a fifth, have to draw their profit. And when the labour price has been already beaten down to the lowest possible, how much remains for the workmen after all these deductions, let the poor fellows themselves say!

One working tailor (at the Hanover-square Rooms meeting) 'mentioned a number of shops, both at the east and west ends, whose work was all taken by sweaters; and several of these shops were under royal and noble patronage. There was one notorious sweater who kept his carriage. He was a Jew, and of course he gave a preference to his own sect. Thus another Jew received it from him second hand and at a lower rate; then it went to a third—till it came to the unfortunate Christian at perhaps the eighth rate, and he performed the work at barely living prices: this same Jew required a deposit of 5 *l.* in money before he would give out a single garment to be made. He need not describe the misery which this system entailed upon the workmen. It was well known; but it was almost impossible, except for those who had been at the two, to form an idea of the difference between the present meeting and one at the East End, where all who attended worked for slop-shops and sweaters. The present was a highly respectable assembly: the other presented no other appearance but those of misery and degradation'.

Another says—'We have all worked in the honourable trade, so we know the regular prices from our own personal experience. Taking the bad work with the good work, we might earn 11s a week upon an average. Sometimes we do earn as much as 15s; but, to do this, we are obliged to take part of our work home to our wives and daughters. We are not always fully employed. We are nearly half our time idle. Hence, our earnings are, upon an average throughout the year, not more than 5s 6d a week'. 'Very often I have made only 3s 4d in the week,' said one. 'That's common enough with us all, I can assure you,' said another. 'Last week my wages was 7s 6d,' declared one. 'I earned 6s 4d,' exclaimed the second. 'My wages came to 9s 2d. The week before I got 6s 3d.' 'I made 7s 9d,' and 'I, 7s or 8s, I can't exactly remember which.' 'This is what we term the best part of our winter season. The reason why we are so long idle is because more hands than are wanted are kept on the premises, so that in case of a press of work coming in, our employers can have it done immediately. Under the day-work system no master tailor had more men on the premises than he could keep continually going; but since the change to the piece-work system, masters made a practice of engaging double the quantity of hands that they have any need for, so that an order may be executed 'at the shortest possible notice', if requisite. A man must not leave the premises when unemployed,—if he does, he loses his chance of work coming in. I have been there four days together, and had not a stitch of work to do.' 'Yes; that is common enough.' 'Ay, and then you're told if you complain, you can go, if you don't like it. I am sure twelve hands would do all they have done at home, and yet they keep forty of us. It's generally remarked, that however strong and healthy a man may be when he goes to work at that shop, in a month's time he'll be a complete shadow, and have almost all his clothes in pawn. By Sunday morning, he has no money at all left, and he has to subsist till the following Saturday upon about a pint of weak tea, and four slices of bread and butter per day!!!'

'Another of the reasons for the sweaters keeping more hands than they want is, the men generally have their meals with them. The more men they have with them the more breakfasts and teas they supply, and the more profit they make. The men usually have to pay 4d, and very often 5d, for their breakfast, and the same for their tea. The tea or breakfast is mostly a pint of tea or coffee, and three to four slices of bread and butter. *I worked for one sweater who almost starved the men: the smallest eater there would not have had enough if he had got three times as much. They had only three thin slices of bread and butter, not sufficient for a child, and the tea was both weak and bad. The whole meal could not have stood him in 2d a head, and what made it worse was, that the men who worked there couldn't afford to have dinners, so that they were starved to the bone.* The sweater's men generally lodge where they work. A sweater usually keeps about six men. These occupy two small garrets; one room is called the kitchen, and the other the workshop; and here the whole of the six men, and the sweater, his wife, and family, live and sleep. One sweater *I worked with had four children and six men, and they, together with his wife, sister-in-law, and himself, all lived in two rooms, the largest of which was about eight feet by ten. We worked in the smallest room, and slept there as well—all six of us. There were two turn-up beds in it, and we slept three in a bed. There was no chimney, and indeed, no ventilation whatever. I was near losing my life there—the foul air of so many people working all day in the place, and sleeping there at night, was quite suffocating. Almost all the men were consumptive, and I myself attended the dispensary for disease of the lungs. The room in which we all slept was not more than six feet square. We were all sick and weak, and loath to work.* Each of the six of us paid 2s 6d a week for our lodging, or 15s altogether, and I am sure such a room as we slept and worked in might be had for 1s a week; you can get a room with a fire-place for 1s 6d. The usual sum that the men working for sweaters pay for their tea, breakfasts, and lodging is 6s 6d to 7s a week, and they seldom earn more money in the week. Occasionally at the week's end, they are in debt to the sweater. This is seldom for more than 6d, for the sweater will not give them victuals if he has no work for them to do. Many who live and work at the sweater's are married men, and are obliged to keep their wives and children in lodgings by themselves. Some send them to the workhouse, others to their friends in the country. Besides the profit of the board and lodging, the sweater takes 6d out of the price paid for every garment under 10s; some take 1s, and I do know of one who takes as much as 2s. This man works for a large show-shop at the West End. The usual profit of the sweater, over and above the board and lodging, is 2s out of every pound. Those who work for sweaters soon lose their clothes, and are unable to seek for other work, because they have not a coat to their back to go and seek it in. *Last week, I worked with another man at a coat for one of her Majesty's ministers, and my partner never broke his fast while he was making his half of it.* The minister dealt at a cheap West-end show shop. All the workman had, the whole of the day-and-a-half he was making the coat, was a little tea. But sweaters' work is not so bad as government work after all. At that, we cannot make more than 4s or 5s a-week altogether—that is, counting the time we are running after it, of course. *Government contract work is the worst of all, and the starved-out and sweated-out tailor's last resource.* But still, government does not do the regular trade so much harm as the cheap show and slop-shops. These houses have ruined thousands. They have cut down the prices, so that men cannot live at the work; and the masters who did and would pay better wages, are reducing the workmen's pay every day. They say they must either compete with the large show-shops or go into the *Gazette*.'

Sweet competition! Heavenly maid!—Now-a-days hymned alike by penny-a-liners and philosophers as the ground of all society—the only real preserver of the earth! Why not of Heaven, too? Perhaps there is competition among the angels, and Gabriel and Raphael have won their rank by doing the maximum of worship on the minimum of grace? We shall know some day. In the meanwhile, 'these are thy works, thou Parent of all good!' Man eating man, eaten by man, in every variety of degree and method! Why does not some enthusiastic political economist write an epic on 'The Consecration of Cannibalism'?

But if any one finds it pleasant to his soul to believe the poor journeyman's statements exaggerated, let him listen to one of the sweaters themselves:—

'I wish,' says he, 'that others did for the men as decently as I do. I know there are many who are living entirely upon them. Some employ as many as fourteen men. I myself worked in the house of a man who did this. The chief part of us lived, and worked, and slept together in two rooms, on the second floor. They charged 2s 6d per head for the lodging alone. Twelve of the workmen, I am sure, lodged in the house, and these paid altogether 30s a-week rent to the sweater. I should think the sweater paid 8s a-week for the rooms—so that he gained at least 22s clear, out of the lodging of these men, and stood at no rent himself. For the living of the men he charged—5d for breakfasts, and the same for teas, and 8d for dinner—or at the rate of 10s 6d each per head. Taking one with the other, and considering the manner in which they lived, I am certain that the cost for keeping each of them could not have been more than 5s. This would leave 5s 6d clear profit on the board of each of the twelve men, or, altogether, 3l 6s per week; and this, added to the 1l 2s profit on the rent, would give 4l 8s for the sweater's gross profit on the board and lodging of the workmen in his place. But, besides this, he got 1s out of each coat made on his premises, and there were twenty-one coats made there, upon an average, every week; so that, altogether, the sweater's clear gains out of the men, were 5l 9s every week. Each man made about a coat and a half in the course of the seven days (*for they all worked on a Sunday—they were generally told to ' borrow a day of the Lord'*.) For this coat and a half, each hand got 1l 2s 6d, and out of it he had to pay 13s for board and lodging; so that there was 9s 6d clear left. These are the profits of the sweater, and the earnings of the men engaged under him, when working for the first-rate houses. But many of the cheap houses pay as low as 8s for the making of each dress and frock coat, and some of them as low as 6s. Hence the earnings of the men at such work would be from 9s to 12s per week, and the cost of their board and lodging without dinners, for these they seldom have, would be from 7s 6d to 8s per week. Indeed, the men working under sweaters at such prices generally consider themselves well off if they have a shilling or two in their pockets for Sunday. The profits of the sweater, however, would be from 4l to 5l out of twelve men, working on his premises. The usual number of men working under each sweater is about six individuals: and the average rate of profit, about 2l 10s, without the sweater doing any work himself. It is very often the case that a man working under a sweater is obliged to pawn his own coat to get any pocket-money that he may require. Over and over again the sweater makes out that he is in his debt from 1s to 2s at the end of the week, and when the man's coat is in pledge, he is compelled to remain imprisoned in the sweater's lodgings for months together. In some sweating places, there is an old coat kept called a 'reliever', and this is borrowed by such men as have none of their own to go out in. There are very few of the sweater's men who have a coat to their backs or a shoe to their feet to come out into the streets on Sunday. Down about Fulwood's-rents, Holborn, I am sure I would not give 6d for the clothes that are on a dozen of them; and it is surprising to me, working and living together in such numbers and in such small close rooms, in narrow close back courts as they do, that they are not all swept off by some pestilence. I myself have seen half-a-dozen men at work in a room that was a little better than a bedstead long. It was as much as one could do to move between the wall and the bedstead when it was down. There were two bedsteads in this room, and they nearly filled the place when they were down. The ceiling was so low, that I couldn't stand upright in the room. There was no ventilation in the place. There was no fireplace, and only a small window. When the window was open, you could nearly touch the houses at the back, and if the room had not been at the top of the house, the men could not have seen at all in the place. The staircase was so narrow, steep, and dark, that it was difficult to grope your way to the top of the house—it was like going up a steeple. This is the usual kind of place in which the sweater's men are lodged. The reason why there are so many Irishmen working for the sweaters is, because they are seduced over to this country by the prospect of high wages and plenty of work. They are brought over by the Cork boats at 10s a-head, and when they once get here, the prices they receive are so small, that they are unable to go back. In less than a week after they get here, their clothes are all pledged, and they are obliged to continue working under the sweaters.

'The extent to which this system of "street-kidnapping" is carried on is frightful. Young tailors, fresh from the country, are decoyed by the sweaters' wives into their miserable dens, under extravagant promises of employment, to find themselves deceived, imprisoned, and starved, often unable to make their escape for months—perhaps years; and then only fleeing from one dungeon to another as abominable.'

In the meantime, the profits of the beasts of prey who live on these poor fellows—both masters and sweaters—seem as prodigious as their cruelty.

Hear another working tailor on this point:—'In 1844, I belonged to the honourable part of the trade. Our house of call supplied the present show-shop with men to work on the premises. The prices then paid were at the rate of 6d per hour. For the same driving capes that they paid 18s then, they give only 12s for now. For the dress and frock coats they gave 15s then, and now they are 14s. The paletots and shooting coats were 12s: there was no coat made on the premises under that sum. At the end of the season, they wanted to reduce the paletots to 9s. The men refused to make them at that price, when other houses were paying as much as 15s for them. The consequence of this was, the house discharged all the men, and got a Jew middleman from the neighbourhood of Petticoat-lane, to agree to do them all at 7s 6d a-piece. The Jew employed all the poor people who were at work for the slop warehouses in Houndsditch and its vicinity. This Jew makes on an average 500 paletots a week. The Jew gets 2s 6d profit out of each, and having no sewing trimmings allowed to him, he makes the workpeople find them. The saving in trimmings alone to the firm, since the workmen left the premises, must have realized a small fortune to them. Calculating men, women, and children, I have heard it said that the cheap house at the West-end employs 1000 hands. The trimmings for the work done by these, would be about 6d a-week per head, so that the saving to the house since the men worked on the premises has been no less than 1300l a-year, and all this taken out of the pockets of the poor. The Jew who contracts for making the paletots is no tailor at all. A few years ago he sold sponges in the street, and now he rides in his carriage. The Jew's profits are 500 half-crowns, or 60l odd, per week—that is upwards of 3000l a-year. Women are mostly engaged at the paletot work. When I came to work for the cheap show-shop I had 5l 10s in the saving bank; now I have not a halfpenny in it. All I had saved went little by little to keep me and my family. I have always made a point of putting some money by when I could afford it, but since I have been at this work it has been as much as I could do to *live*, much more to *save*. One of the firm for which I work has been heard publicly to declare that he employed 1000 hands constantly. Now the earnings of these at the honourable part of the trade would be upon an average, taking the skilful with the unskilful, 15s a-week each, or 39,000l a-year. But since they discharged the men from off their premises, they have cut down the wages of the workmen one-half—taking one garment with another —*though the selling prices remain the same to the public*, so that they have saved by the reduction of the workmen's wages no less than 19,500l per year. Every other quarter of a year something has been 'docked' off our earnings, until it is almost impossible for men with families to live decently by their labour; and now, for the first time, they pretend to feel for them. They even talk of erecting a school for the children of their workpeople; but where is the use of their erecting schools, when they know as well as we do that, at the wages they pay, the children must be working for their fathers at home? They had much better erect workshops, and employ the men on the premises at fair living wages, and then the men could educate their own children, without being indebted to their charity'.

On this last question of what the master-cannibals had 'much better do,' we have somewhat to say presently. In the meantime, hear another of the things which they had much better *not* do. 'Part of the fraud and deception of the slop trade consists in the mode in which the public are made believe that the men working for such establishments earn more money than they really do. The plan practised is similar to that adopted by the army clothier, who made out that the men working on his establishment made per week from 15s to 17s each; whereas, on inquiry, it was found that a considerable sum was paid out of that to those who helped to do the looping for those who took it home. When a coat is given to me to make, a ticket is handed to me with the garment, similar to this one which I have obtained from a friend of mine.

448
  Mr *Smith* 6675 Made by *M*
  Ze = 12s = *lined lustre*
      quilted double stitched
       each side seams
448. No. 6675.
       o'clock *Friday*
 Mr *Smith*

On this you see the price is marked at 12s,' continued my informant, 'and supposing that I, with two others, could make three of these garments in the week, the sum of thirty-six shillings would stand in the books of the establishment, as the amount earned by me in that space of time. This would be sure to be exhibited to the customers, immediately that there was the least outcry made about the starvation price they paid for their work, as a proof that the workpeople engaged on their establishment received the full prices; whereas, of that 36s entered against my name, *I should have had to pay 24s. to those who assisted me*: besides this, my share of the trimmings and expenses would have been 1s 6d, and probably my share of the fires would be 1s more; so that the real fact would be, that I should make 9s 6d clear, and this it would be almost impossible to do, if I did not work long over hours. I am obliged to keep my wife continually at work helping me, in order to live.

In short, the condition of these men is far worse than that of the wretched labourers of Wilts or Dorset. Their earnings are as low and often lower; their trade requires a far longer instruction, far greater skill and shrewdness; their rent and food are more expensive; and their hours of work, while they have work, more than half as long again. Conceive sixteen or eighteen hours of skilled labour in a stifling and fetid chamber, earning not much more than 6s 6d or 7s a week! And, as has been already mentioned in one case, the man who will earn even that, must work all Sunday. He is even liable to be thrown out of his work for refusing to work on Sunday. Why not? Is there anything about one idle day in seven to be found among the traditions of Mammon? When the demand comes, the supply must come; and will, in spite of foolish auld-warld notion about keeping days holy—or keeping contracts holy either, for, indeed, Mammon has no conscience —right and wrong are not words expressible by any commercial laws yet in vogue; and therefore it appears that to earn this wretched pittance is by no means to get it. 'For,' says one, and the practice is asserted to be general, almost universal, 'there is at our establishment a mode of reducing the price of our labour even lower than we have mentioned. The prices we have stated are those *nominally* paid for making the garments; but it is not an uncommon thing in our shop for a man to make a garment, and to receive nothing at all for it. I remember a man once having a waistcoat to do, the price of making which was 2s, and when he gave the job in he was told that he owed the establishment 6d. The manner in which this is brought about is by a system of fines. We are fined if we are behind time with our job, 6d the first hour, and 3d for each hour that we are late.' 'I have known as much as 7s 6d to be deducted off the price of a coat on the score of want of punctuality,' one said; 'and, indeed, very often the whole money is stopped. It would appear, as if our employers themselves strove to make us late with our work, and so have an opportunity of cutting down the price paid for our labour. They frequently put off giving out the trimmings to us till the time at which the coat is due has expired. If to the trimmer we return an answer that is considered "saucy", we are fined 6d or 1s, according to the trimmer's temper.' 'I was called a thief,' another of the three declared, 'and because I told the man I would not submit to such language, I was fined 6d. These are the principal of the in-door fines. The out-door fines are still more iniquitous. There are full a dozen more fines for minor offences; indeed, we are fined upon every petty pretext. We never know what we have to take on a Saturday, for the meanest advantages are taken to reduce our wages. If we object to pay these fines, we are told that we may leave; but they know full well that we are afraid to throw ourselves out of work.'

Folks are getting somewhat tired of the old rodomontade that a slave is free the moment he sets foot on British soil! Stuff!—are these tailors free? Put any conceivable sense you will on the word, and then say—are they free? We have, thank God, emancipated the black slaves; it would seem a not inconsistent sequel to that act to set about emancipating these white ones. Oh! we forgot: there is an infinite difference between the two cases—the black slaves worked for our colonies; the white slaves work for *us*. But, indeed, if, as some preach, self-interest is the mainspring of all human action, it is difficult to see who will step forward to emancipate the said white slaves; for all classes seem to consider it equally their interest to keep them as they are; all classes, though by their own confession they are ashamed, are yet not afraid to profit by the system which keeps them down.

Not only the master tailors and their underlings, but the retail tradesmen, too, make their profit out of these abominations. By a method which smacks at first sight somewhat of benevolence, but proves itself in practice to be one of those 'previous balms which break,' not 'the head', (for that would savour of violence, and might possibly give some bodily pain, a thing intolerable to the nerves of Mammon) but the heart—an organ which, being spiritual, can of course be recognised by no laws of police or commerce. The object of the State, we are told, is 'the consecration of body and goods'; there is nothing in that about broken hearts; nothing which should make it a duty to forbid such a system as a working tailor here describes—

'Fifteen or twenty years ago, such a thing as a journeyman tailor having to give security before he could get work was unknown; but now I and such as myself could not get a stitch to do first handed, if we did not either procure the security of some householder, or deposit 5*l* in the hands of the employer. The reason of this is, the journeymen are so badly paid, that the employers know they can barely live on what they get, and consequently they are often driven to pawn the garments given out to them, in order to save themselves and their families from starving. If the journeyman can manage to scrape together 5*l*, he has to leave it in the hands of his employer all the time that he is working for the house. I know one person who gives out the work for a fashionable West End slop-shop will not take household security, and requires 5*l* from each hand. I am informed by one of the parties who worked for this man that he has as many as 150 hands in his employ, and that each of these has placed 5*l* in his hands, so that altogether the poor people have handed over 750*l* to increase the capital upon which he trades, and for which he pays no interest whatsoever.'

This recals a similar case, (mentioned by a poor stay-stitcher in another letter, published in the *Morning Chronicle*), of a large wholesale staymaker in the City, who had amassed a large fortune by beginning to trade upon the 5*s* which he demanded to be left in his hands by his workpeople before he gave them employment.

'Two or three years back one of the slop-sellers at the East End became bankrupt, and the poor people lost all the money that had been deposited as security for work in his hands. The journeymen who get the security of householders are enabled to do so by a system which is now in general practice at the East End. Several bakers, publicans, chandler-shop keepers, and coal-shed keepers, make a trade of becoming security for those seeking slop-work. They consent to be responsible for the workpeople upon the condition of the men dealing at their shops. The workpeople who require such security are generally very good customers, from the fact of their either having large families, all engaged in the same work, or else several females or ma!es working under them, and living at their house. The parties who become securities thus not only greatly increase their trade, but furnish a second-rate article at a first-rate price. It is useless to complain of the bad quality or high price of the articles supplied by the securities, for the shop-keepers know, as well as the workpeople, that it is impossible for the hands to leave them without losing their work. I know one baker whose security was refused at the slop-shop because he was already responsible for so many, and he begged the publican to be his deputy, so that by this means the workpeople were obliged to deal at both baker's and publican's too. I never heard of a butcher making a trade of becoming security, *because the slop-work people cannot afford to consume much meat*.

'The same system is also pursued by lodging-house keepers. They will become responsible if the workmen requiring security will undertake to lodge at their house.'

But of course the men most interested in keeping up the system are those who buy the clothes of these cheap shops. And who are they? Not merely the blackguard Gent—the butt of Albert Smith and Punch, who flaunts at the Casinos and Cremorne Gardens in vulgar finery wrung out of the souls and bodies of the poor; not merely the poor lawyer's clerk or reduced half-pay officer who has to struggle to look as respectable as his class commands him to look on a pittance often no larger than that of the day-labourer—no, strange to say—and yet not strange, considering our modern eleventh commandment 'Buy cheap and sell dear',—the richest as well as the poorest imitate the example of King Ryence and the tanners of Meudon. At a great show establishment—to take one instance out of many—the very one where, as we heard just now, 'however strong and healthy a man may be when he goes to work at that shop, in a month's time he will be a complete shadow, and have almost all his clothes in pawn'—

'We have also made garments for Sir —— ——, Sir —— ——, Alderman ——, Dr —— and Dr ——. We make for several of the aristocracy. We cannot say whom, because the tickets frequently come to us as Lord —— and the Marquis of ——. This could not be a Jew's trick, because the buttons on the liveries had coronets upon them. And again, we know the house is patronized largely by the aristocracy, clergy, and gentry, by the number of court-suits and liveries, surplices, regimentals, and ladies' riding-habits that we continually have to make up. *There are more clergymen among the customers than any other class, and often we have to work at home upon the Sunday at their clothes, in order to get a living.* The customers are mostly ashamed of dealing at this house, for the men who take the clothes to the customers' houses in the cart have directions to pull up at the corner of the street. We had a good proof of the dislike of gentle-folks to have it known that they dealt at that shop for their clothes, for when the trowsers buttons were stamped with the name of the firm, we used to have the garments returned, daily, to have other buttons put on them, and now the buttons are unstamped!'

We shall make no comment on this extract. It needs none. If these men know how their clothes are made, they are past contempt. Afraid of man, and not afraid of God! As if His eye could not see the cart laden with the plunder of the poor because it stopped round the corner! If, on the other hand, they do *not* know these things,—and doubtless the majority do not,—it is their sin that they do not know it. Woe to a society whose only apology to God and man is, 'Am I my brother's keeper?' Men ought to know the condition of those by whose labour they live. Had the question been the investment of a few pounds in a speculation, these gentlemen would have been careful enough about good security. Ought they to take no security when they invest their money in clothes, that they are not putting on their backs accursed garments, offered in sacrifice to devils, reeking with the sighs of the starving, tainted—yes, tainted, indeed, for it comes out now that diseases numberless are carried home in these same garments from the miserable abodes where they are made. Evidence to this effect was given in 1844; but Mammon was too busy to attend to it. These wretched creatures, when they have pawned their own clothes and bedding, will use as substitutes the very garments they are making. So Lord ——'s coat has been seen covering a group of children blotched with small pox. The Rev D—— finds himself suddenly unpresentable from a cutaneous disease, which it is not polite to mention on the south of the Tweed, little dreaming that the shivering dirty being who made his coat has been sitting with his arms in the sleeves for warmth while he stitched at the tails. The charming Miss C—— is swept off by typhus or scarlatina, and her parents talk about 'God's heavy judgment and visitation'—had they tracked the girl's new riding habit back to the stifling undrained hovel where it served as a blanket to the fever-stricken slop-worker, they would have seen *why* God had visited them, seen that His judgments are true judgments, and give His plain opinion of the system which 'speaketh good of the covetous whom God abhorreth'—a system, to use the words of the *Morning Chronicle's* correspondent, 'unheard of and unparalleled in the history of any country—a scheme so deeply laid for the introduction and supply of under-paid labour to the market, that it is impossible for the working-man not to sink and be degraded by it into the lowest depths of wretchedness and infamy'—'a system which is steadily and gradually increasing, and sucking more and more victims out of the honourable trade, who are really intelligent artizans, living in comparative comfort and civilization, into the dishonourable or sweating trade in which the slop-workers are generally almost brutified by their incessant toil, wretched pay, miserable food, and filthy homes.'

But to us, almost the worst feature in the whole matter is, that the government are not merely parties to, but actually the originators of this system. The contract system, as a working tailor stated in the name of the rest, 'had been mainly instrumental in destroying the living wages of the working-man. Now, the government were the sole originators of the system of contracts and of sweating. Forty years ago, there was nothing known of contracts, except government contracts; and at that period the contractors were confined to making slops for the navy, the army, and the West India slaves. It was never dreamt of then, that such a system was to come into operation in the better classes of trade, till ultimately it was destructive of masters as well as men. The government having been the cause of the contract system, and, consequently of the sweating system, he called upon them to abandon it. The sweating system had established the show shops and the ticket system, both of which were countenanced by the government, till it had become a fashion to support them.'

'Even the court assisted to keep the system in fashion, and the royal arms and royal warrants were now exhibited common enough by slop-sellers.'

'Government said, its duty was to do justice. But was it consistent with justice to pay only 2s 6d for making navy jackets, which would be paid 10s for by every 'honourable' tradesman? Was it consistent with justice for the government to pay for Royal Marine clothing (private's coat and epaulettes) 1s 9d? Was it consistent with justice for the government to pay for making a pair of trowsers (four or five hours' work) only 2½d? And yet, when a contractor, noted for paying just wages to those he employed, brought this under the consideration of the Admiralty, they declared they had nothing to do with it. Here is their answer:—

'Admiralty, March 19, 1847.

'Sir—Having laid before my Lords Commissioners of the Admiralty, your letter of the 8th instant, calling their attention to the extremely low prices paid for making up articles of clothing, provided for her Majesty's naval service, I am commanded by their lordships to acquaint you, that they have no control whatever over the wages paid for making up contract clothing. Their duty is to take care that the articles supplied are of good quality, and well made: the cost of the material and the workmanship are matters which rest with the contractor; and if the public were to pay him a higher price than that demanded, it would not ensure any advantage to the men employed by him, as their wages depend upon the amount of competition for employment amongst themselves.

'I am, Sir, your most obedient servant,

'H. G. WARD.'

'W. Shaw, Esq.'

Oh most impotent conclusion, however officially cautious, and 'philosophically' correct! Even if the wages did depend entirely on the amount of competition, on whom does the amount of competition depend? Merely on the gross numbers of the workmen? Somewhat too, one would think, on the system according to which the labour and the wages are distributed. But right or wrong, is it not a pleasant answer for the poor working tailors, and one likely to increase their faith, hope, and charity towards the present commercial system, and those who deny the possibility of any other?

'The government,' says another tailor at the same meeting, 'had really been the means of reducing prices in the tailoring trade to so low a scale that no human being, whatever his industry, could live and be happy in his lot. The government were really responsible for the first introduction of female labour. He would clearly prove what he had stated. He would refer first to the army clothing. Our soldiers were comfortably clothed, as they had a right to be; but surely the men who made the clothing which was so comfortable, ought to be paid for their labour so as to be able to keep themselves comfortable and their famil'es virtuous. But it was in evidence, that the persons working upon army clothing could not, upon an average, earn more than 1s a-day. Another government department, the post-office, afforded a considerable amount of employment to tailors; but those who worked upon the post-office clothing earned, at the most, only 1s 6d a-day. The police clothing was another considerable branch of tailoring; this, like the others, ought to be paid for at living prices; but the men at work at it could only earn 1s 6d a-day, supposing them to work hard all the time, fourteen or fifteen hours. The custom house clothing gave about the same prices. Now, all these sorts of work were performed by time-workers, who, as a natural consequence of the wages they received, were the most miserable of human beings. Husband, wife, and family all worked at it; they just tried to breathe upon it; to live, it never could be called. *Yet the same government which paid such wretched wages, called upon these wretched people to be industrious, to be virtuous, and happy.* How was it possible, whatever their industry, to be virtuous and happy? The fact was, the men who, at a slack season, had been compelled to fall back upon these kinds of work, became so beggared and broken down by it, notwithstanding the assistance of their wives and families, that they were never able to rise out of it.'

And now comes the question—What is to be done with these poor tailors, to the number of between fifteen and twenty thousand? Their condition, as it stands, is simply one of ever-increasing darkness and despair. The system which is ruining them is daily spreading, deepening. While we write, fresh victims are being driven by penury into the slop-working trade, fresh depreciations of labour are taking place. Like Ulysses' companions in the cave of Polyphemus, the only question among them is, to scramble so far back as to have *a chance of being eaten last.* Before them is ever-nearing slavery, disease, and starvation. What can be done?

First—this can be done. That no man who calls himself a Christian—no man who calls himself a man—shall ever disgrace himself by dealing at any show-shop or slop-shop. It is easy enough to know them. The ticketed garments, the impudent puffs, the trumpery decorations, proclaim them—every one knows them at first sight. He who pretends not to do so, is simply either a fool or a liar. Let no man enter them—they are the temples of Moloch—their thresholds are rank with human blood. God's curse is on them, and on those who, by supporting them, are partakers of their sins. Above all, let no clergyman deal at them. Poverty—and many clergymen are poor—doubly poor, because society often requires them to keep up the dress of gentlemen on the income of an artizan; because, too, the demands on their charity are quadruple those of any other class—yet poverty is no excuse. The thing is damnable—not Christianity only, but common humanity cries out against it. Woe to those who dare to outrage in private the principles which they preach in public! God is not mocked; and his curse will find out the priest at the altar, as well as the nobleman in his castle.

But it is so hard to deprive the public of the luxury of cheap clothes! Then let the public look out for some other means of procuring that priceless blessing. If that, on experiment, be found impossible—if the comfort of the few be for ever to be bought by the misery of the many—if civilization is to benefit every one except the producing class—then this world is truly the devil's world, and the sooner so ill-constructed and infernal a machine is destroyed by that personage the better.

But let, secondly, a dozen, or fifty, or a hundred journeymen say to one another: 'It is competition that is ruining us, and competition is division, disunion, every man for himself, every man against his brother. The remedy must be in association, co-operation, self-sacrifice for the sake of one another. We can work together at the honourable tailor's workshop—we can work and live together in the sweater's den for the profit of our employers; why should we not work and live together in our own workshops, or our own homes, for our own profit? The journeymen of the honourable trade are just as much interested as the slop-workers in putting down sweaters and slop-sellers, since their numbers are constantly decreasing, so that their turn must come some day. Let them, if no one else does, lend money to allow us to set up a workshop of our own, a shop of our own. If the money be not lent, still let us stint and strain ourselves to the very bone, if it were only to raise one sweater's security-money, which one of us should pay into the slop-sellers' hands, in his own name, but on behalf of all; that will at least save one sweater's profit out of our labour, and bestow it upon ourselves; and we will not spend that profit, but hoard it, till we have squeezed out all the sweaters one by one. Then we will open our common shop, and sell at as low a price as the cheapest of the show-shops. We *can* do this—by the abolition of sweater's profits— by the using, as far as possible, of one set of fires, lights, rooms, kitchens, and washhouses—above all, by being true and faithful to one another, as all partners should be. And, then, all that the master slop-sellers had better do, will be simply to vanish and become extinct.'

And again, let one man, or half-a-dozen men arise, who believe that the world is not the devil's world at all, but God's; that the multitude of the people is not, as Malthusians aver, the ruin, but as Solomon believed, 'the strength of the rulers'; that men are not meant to be beasts of prey, eating one another up by competition, as in some confined pike-pond, where the great pike having dispatched the little ones, begin to devour each other, till one overgrown monster is left alone to die of starvation—Let a few men who have money, and believe that, arise to play the man.

Let them help and foster the growth of association by all means. Let them advise the honourable tailors, while it is time, to save themselves from being degraded into slop-sellers by admitting their journeymen to a share in profits. Let them encourage the journeymen to compete with Nebuchadnezzar and Co. at their own game. Let them tell those journeymen that the experiment is even now being tried, and, in many instances successfully, by no less than one hundred and four associations of journeymen in Paris. Let them remind them of that Great Name which the Parisian 'ouvrier' so often forgets—of Him whose everlasting Fatherhood is the sole ground of all human brotherhood, whose wise and living will is the sole source of all perfect order and government. Let them, as soon as an association is formed, provide for them a proper ventilated workshop, and let it out to the associate tailors at a low, fair rent. I believe that they will not lose by it—because it is right. God will take care of their money. The world, it comes out now, is so well ordered by Him, that model lodging-houses, public baths, wash-houses, insurance offices, all pay a reasonable profit to those who invest money in them—perhaps associate workshops may do the same. At all events, the owners of these show-shops realize a far higher profit than need be, while the buildings required for a tailoring establishment are surely not more costly than those absurd plate-glass fronts, and brass scroll-work chandeliers, and puffs, and paid poets. A large house might thus be taken, in some central situation, the upper floors of which might be fitted up as model lodging-houses for the tailor's trade alone. The drawing-room floor might be the work-room; on the ground-floor the shop; and if possible a room of call or registration office for unemployed journeymen, and a reading-room. Why should not this succeed, if the owners of the house and the workers who rent it are only true to one another? Every tyro in political economy knows that association involves a saving both of labour and of capital. Why should it not succeed, when every one connected with the establishment, landlords and workmen, will have an interest in increasing its prosperity, and none whatever in lowering the wages of any party employed?

But above all, so soon as these men are found working together for common profit, in the spirit of mutual self-sacrifice, let every gentleman and every Christian, who has ever dealt with, or could ever have dealt with, Nebuchadnezzar and Co., or their fellows, make it a point of honour and conscience to deal with the associated workmen, and get others to do the like. *It is by securing custom, far more than by gifts or loans of money, that we can help the operatives.* We should but hang a useless burthen of debt round their necks by advancing capital, without affording them the means of disposing of their produce.

Be assured, that the finding of a tailors' model lodging-house, work-rooms, and shop, and the letting out of the two latter to an association, would be a righteous act to do. If the plan does not pay, what then? only a part of the money can be lost; and to have given that to a hospital or an almshouse would have been called praiseworthy and Christian charity; how much more to have spent it, not in the cure, but in the prevention of evil—in making almshouses less needful, and lessening the number of candidates for the hospital!

Regulations as to police, order, and temperance, the workmen must, and, if they are worthy of the name of free men, they can organize for themselves. Let them remember that an association of labour is very different from an association of capital. The capitalist only embarks his money on the venture; the workman embarks his time—that is, much at least of, his life. Still more different is the operatives' association from the single capitalist, seeking only to realize a rapid fortune, and then withdraw. The association knows no withdrawal from business; it must grow in length and in breadth, outlasting rival slop-sellers, swallowing up all associations similar to itself, and which might end by competing with it. 'Monopoly!' cries a free-trader, with hair on end. No so, good friend; there will be no real free trade without association. Who tells you that tailors' associations are to be the only ones?

Some such thing, as I have hinted, might surely be done. Where there is a will, there is a way. No doubt there are difficulties—Howard and Elizabeth Fry, too, had their difficulties. Brindley and Brunel[1] did not succeed at their first trial. It is the sluggard only who is always crying, 'There is a lion in the streets'. Be daring—trust in God, and he will fight for you; man of money, whom these words have touched, godliness has the promise of this life, as well as of that to come. The thing must be done, and speedily; for if it be not done by fair means, it will surely do itself by foul. The continual struggle of competition, not only in the tailors' trade, but in every one which is not, like the navigator's or engineer's, at a premium from its novel and extraordinary demand, will weaken and undermine more and more the masters, who are already many of them speculating on borrowed capital, while it will depress the workmen to a point at which life will become utterly intolerable; increasing education will serve only to make them the more conscious of their own misery; the boiler will be strained to bursting pitch, till some jar, some slight crisis, suddenly directs the imprisoned forces to one point, and then—

What then?

Look at France and see.

PARSON LOT

[1] Celebrated engineers. (ED.)

OCCASIONAL DISCOURSE ON THE NIGGER QUESTION

CARLYLE'S *Occasional Discourse* actually appeared in *Fraser's Magazine* in 1849, before the previous pamphlet was published, but did not make its appearance among the 'Latter Day Pamphlets' until 1853.

All that Carlyle really had to say—though he took some 13,000 words to say it, from which we have extracted only a portion—was that the Negroes in the West Indies found it possible to live on very little, and that in order to force them to produce wealth for English planters and delicacies for Mr Carlyle's table they should be reduced once more to something that differed only in name from slavery.

As a specimen of venomous hatred against people the writer had never met, whose only crime was their unwillingness to work themselves to death in order to provide wealth and luxury for others, this diatribe is probably unsurpassed. We include it for this reason alone. In due course Carlyle's 'Hero' appeared on the scene in the form of E. J. Eyre, Governor of Jamaica, who provoked a rebellion by his harshness, and crushed it with such inhumanity that even the British Government was shocked and Eyre was dismissed from his post. In a subsequent pamphlet (*Shooting Niagara*) Carlyle, who—in company with Ruskin, Tennyson and others—espoused the cause of Governor Eyre, denounced those who took the opposite view as 'a small loud group or knot of rabid nigger-philanthropists barking furiously in the gutter'. This referred to John Bright, T. H. Huxley, and other contemporaries of the 'Sage', who is still, for some reason, honoured in the Borough of Chelsea.

A glance at the late Hugh Kingsmill's *Invective and Abuse* (Edition of 1944) will show the reader that Carlyle lavished similar epithets upon Wordsworth, Coleridge, Lamb, Keats, George Sand, Shelley, Leigh Hunt, Harriet Martineau and O'Connell. This may help to explain our statement, in a previous note, that to have been sneered at by Carlyle was almost in itself a proof of any man's greatness.

It will be noticed that, whereas Burke and others justified economic oppression in Britain by Adam Smith's 'Law of Supply and Demand',

Carlyle justified the 'beneficent whip' for Negroes when the 'Law of Supply and Demand' ceased to favour the interests of the ruling race and class. The 'happiness' of the ex-slaves was, of course, an official fiction; and it may be necessary to point out that the £20,000,000 to which Carlyle refers was not paid to the Negroes, but was compensation (greatly over-rated, according to Joseph Pease) paid to the former owners of human cattle.

'Exeter Hall' symbolised the Christian Abolitionist Movement of the period, and much more than that. For 'Broad-brimmed' compare page 105. This reference is, of course, to the style in hats which distinguished Quakers at that time.

Shorn of its verbiage and of a certain silly facetiousness, this pamphlet expresses the essence of the Nazi racial policy and of the racial policy still pursued in South Africa.

OCCASIONAL DISCOURSE ON THE NIGGER QUESTION

By Thomas Carlyle

My Philanthropic Friends,

IT is my painful duty to address some words to you, this evening on the Rights of Negroes. Taking, as we hope we do, an extensive survey of social affairs, which we find all in a state of the frightfullest embroilment, and as it were, of inextricable final bankruptcy, just at present; and being desirous to adjust ourselves in that huge upbreak, and unutterable welter of tumbling ruins, and to see well that our grand proposed Association of Associations, the UNIVERSAL ABOLITION-OF-PAIN ASSOCIATION, which is meant to be the consummate golden flower and summary of modern Philanthropisms all in one, do *not* issue as a universal 'Sluggard-and-Scoundrel Protection Society,'—we have judged that, before constituting ourselves, it would be very proper to commune earnestly with one another, and discourse together on the leading elements of our great Problem, which surely is one of the greatest. With this view the Council has decided, both that the Negro Question, as lying at the bottom, was to be the first handled, and if possible the first settled; and then also, what was of much more questionable wisdom, that—that, in short, I was to be Speaker on the occasion. An honourable duty; yet, as I said, a painful one!—Well, you shall hear what I have to say on the matter; and probably you will not in the least like it.

West-Indian affairs, as we all know, and as some of us know to our cost, are in a rather troublous condition this good while. In regard to West Indian affairs, however, Lord John Russell is able to comfort us with one fact, indisputable where so many are dubious, That the

Negroes are all very happy and doing well. A fact very comfortable indeed. West Indian Whites, is it admitted, are far enough from happy; West Indian Colonies not unlike sinking wholly into ruin: at home, too, the British Whites are rather badly off; several millions of them hanging on the verge of continual famine; and in single towns, many thousands of them very sore put to it, at this time, not to live 'well', or as a man should, in any sense temporal or spiritual, but to live at all:—these, again, are uncomfortable facts; and they are extremely extensive and important ones. But, thank Heaven, our interesting Black population, —equalling almost in number of heads one of the Ridings of Yorkshire, and in *worth* (in quantity of intellect, faculty, docility, energy, and available human valour and value) perhaps one of the streets of Seven Dials,—are all doing remarkably well. 'Sweet blighted lilies,'—as the American epitaph on the Nigger child has it,—sweet blighted lilies, they are holding up their heads again! How pleasant, in the universal bankruptcy abroad, and dim dreary stagnancy at home, as if for England too there remained nothing but to suppress Chartist riots, banish united Irishmen, vote the supplies, and *wait* with arms crossed till black Anarchy and Social Death devoured us also, as it has done the others; how pleasant to have always this fact to fall back upon: Our beautiful Black darlings are at least happy; with little labour except to the teeth, *which* surely, in those excellent horse-jaws of theirs, will not fail!

Exeter Hall, my philanthropic friends, has had its way in this matter. The Twenty Millions, a mere trifle despatched with a single dash of the pen, are paid; and far over the sea, we have a few black persons rendered extremely 'free' indeed. Sitting yonder with their beautiful muzzles up to the ears in pumpkins, imbibing sweet pulps and juices; the grinder and incisor teeth ready for ever new work, and the pumpkins cheap as grass in those rich climates: while the sugar-crops rot round them uncut, because labour cannot be hired, so cheap are the pumpkins;— and at home we are but required to rasp from the breakfast loaves of our own English labourers some slight 'differential sugar-duties', and lend a poor half-million or a few poor millions now and then, to keep that beautiful state of matters going on. A state of matters lovely to contemplate, in these emancipated epochs of the human mind; which has earned us not only the praises of Exeter Hall, and loud long-eared hallelujahs of laudatory psalmody from the Friends of Freedom everywhere, but lasting favour (it is hoped) from the Heavenly Powers themselves;—and which may, at least, justly appeal to the Heavenly Powers, and ask them, If ever in terrestrial procedure they saw the match of it? Certainly in the past history of the human species it has no parallel: nor, one hopes, will it have in the future. [*Some emotion in the audience: which the Chairman suppressed.*]

Sunk in deep froth-oceans of 'Benevolence', 'Fraternity,' 'Emancipation-principle,' 'Christian Philanthropy,' and other most amiable-looking, but most baseless, and in the end baleful and all-bewildering jargon,—sad product of a sceptical Eighteenth Century, and of poor human hearts left *destitute* of any earnest guidance, and disbelieving that there ever was any, Christian or Heathen, and reduced to believe in rosepink Sentimentalism alone, and to cultivate the same under its Christian, Antichristian, Broad-brimmed, Brutus-headed, and other forms,—has not the human species gone strange roads, during that period? And poor Exeter Hall, cultivating the Broad-brimmed form of Christian Sentimentalism, and long talking and bleating and braying in that strain, has it not worked out results? Our West Indian Legislatings, with their spoutings, anti-spoutings, and interminable jangle and babble; our Twenty millions down on the nail for Blacks of our own; Thirty gradual millions more, and many brave Brtish lives to boot, in watching Blacks of other people's; and now at last our ruined sugar-estates, differential sugar-duties, 'immigration loan,' and beautiful Blacks sitting there up to the ears in pumpkins, and doleful Whites sitting here without potatoes to eat; never till now, I think, did the sun look down on such a jumble of human nonsenses;—of which, with the two hot nights of the Missing-Despatch Debate,[1] God grant that the measure might now at last be full! But no, it is not yet full; we have a long way to travel back, and terrible flounderings to make, and in fact an immense load of nonsense to dislodge from our poor heads, and manifold cobwebs to rend from our poor eyes, before we get into the road again, and can begin to act as serious men that have work to do in this Universe, and no longer as windy sentimentalists that merely have speeches to deliver and despatches to write. O Heaven, in West-Indian matters, and in all manner of matters, it is so with us: the more is the sorrow!—

The West Indies, it appears, are short of labour; as indeed is very conceivable in those circumstances. Where a Black man, by working about half an hour a-day (such is the calculation), can supply himself, by aid of sun and soil, with as much pumpkin as will suffice, he is likely to be a little stiff to raise into hard work! Supply and demand, which,

---

[1] Does any reader now remember it? A cloudy reminiscence of some such thing, and of noise in the Newspapers upon it, remain with us,—fast hastening to abolition for every man. (*Note of* 1849.)—This Missing Despatch Debate, what on earth was it? (*Note of* 1853.)

science says, should be brought to bear on him, have an uphill task of it with such a man. Strong sun supplies itself gratis, rich soil in those unpeopled or half-peopled regions almost gratis; these are *his* 'supply'; and half an hour a-day, directed upon these, will produce pumpkin which is his 'demand'. The fortunate Black man, very swiftly does he settle *his* account with supply and demand:—not so swiftly the less fortunate White man of those tropical localities. A bad case, his, just now. He himself cannot work; and his black neighbour, rich in pumpkin, is in no haste to help him. Sunk to the ears in pumpkin, imbibing saccharine juices, and much at his ease in the Creation, he can listen to the less fortunate white man's 'demand', and take his own time in supplying it. Higher wages, massa; higher, for your cane-crop cannot wait; still higher,—till no conceivable opulence of cane-crop will cover such wages. In Demerara, as I read in the blue book of last year, the cane-crop, far and wide, stands rotting; the fortunate black gentlemen, strong in their pumpkins, having all struck till the 'demand' rise a little. Sweet blighted lilies, now getting up their heads again!

Science, however, has a remedy still. Since the demand is so pressing, and the supply so inadequate (equal in fact to *nothing* in some places, as appears), increase the supply; bring more Blacks into the labour-market, then will the rate fall, says science. Not the least surprising part of our West Indian policy is this recipe of 'immigration'; of keeping down the labour-market in those islands by importing new Africans to labour and live there. If the Africans that are already there could be made to lay down their pumpkins, and labour for their living, there are already Africans enough. If the new Africans, after labouring a little, take to pumpkins like the others, what remedy is there? To bring in new and ever new Africans, say you, till pumpkins themselves grow dear; till the country is crowded with Africans; and black men there, like white men here, are forced by hunger to labour for their living? That will be a consummation. To have 'emancipated' the West Indies into a *Black Ireland*: 'free' indeed, but an Ireland, and Black! The world may yet see prodigies; and reality be stranger than a nightmare dream.

Our own white or sallow Ireland, sluttishly starving from age to age on its act-of-parliament 'freedom', was hitherto the flower of mis-management among the nations: but what will this be to a Negro Ireland, with pumpkins themselves fallen scarce like potatoes! Imagination cannot fathom such an object; the belly of Chaos never held the like. The human mind, in its wide wanderings, has not dreamt yet of such a 'freedom' as that will be. Towards that, if Exeter Hall and science of supply and demand are to continue our guides in the matter, we are daily travelling, and even struggling, with loans of half-a-million and such-like, to accelerate ourselves.

Truly, my philanthropic friends, Exeter Hall Philanthropy is wonderful. And the Social Science,—not a 'gay science', but a rueful,—which finds the secret of this Universe in 'supply and demand', and reduces the duty of human governors to that of letting men alone, is also wonderful. Not a 'gay science', I should say, like some we have heard of; no, a dreary, desolate, and indeed quite abject and distressing one; what we might call, by way of eminence, the *dismal science*. These two, Exeter Hall Philanthropy and the Dismal Science, led by any sacred cause of Black Emancipation, or the like, to fall in love and make a wedding of it,—will give birth to progenies and prodigies; dark extensive moon-calves, unnameable abortions, wide-coiled monstrosities, such as the world has not seen hitherto! [*Increased emotion, again suppressed by the Chairman.*]

In fact, it will behove us of this English nation to overhaul our West Indian procedure from top to bottom, and ascertain a little better what it is that Fact and Nature demand of us, and what only Exeter Hall wedded to the Dismal Science demands. To the former set of demands we will endeavour, at our peril,—and worse peril than our purse's, at our soul's peril,—to give all obedience. To the latter we will very frequently demur, and try if we cannot stop short where they contradict the former,—and especially *before* arriving at the black throat of ruin, whither they appear to be leading us. Alas, in many other provinces besides the West Indian, that unhappy wedlock of Philanthropic Liberalism and the Dismal Science has engendered such all-enveloping delusions, of the moon-calf sort, and wrought huge woe for us, and for the poor civilized world, in these days! And sore will be the battle with said moon-calves; and terrible the struggle to return out of our delusions, floating rapidly on which, not the West Indies alone, but Europe generally, is nearing the Niagara Falls. [*Here various persons, in an agitated manner, with an air of indignation, left the room: especially one very tall gentleman in white trousers, whose boots creaked much. The President, in a resolved voice, with a look of official rigour, whatever his own private feelings might be, enjoined 'Silence, Silence!' The meeting again sat motionless.*]

My philanthropic friends, can you discern no fixed headlands in this wide-weltering deluge, of benevolent twaddle and revolutionary grape-shot, that has burst forth on us; no sure bearings at all? Fact and Nature, it seems to me, say a few words to us, if happily we have still an ear for Fact and Nature. Let us listen a little and try.

And first, with regard to the West Indies, it may be laid down as a principle, which no eloquence in Exeter Hall, or Westminster Hall, or elsewhere, can invalidate or hide, except for a short time only, That no Black man who will not work according to what ability the gods have given him for working, has the smallest right to eat pumpkin, or to any fraction of land that will grow pumpkin, however plentiful such land may be; but has an indisputable and perpetual *right* to be compelled, by the real proprietors of said land, to do competent work for his living. This is the everlasting duty of all men, black or white, who are born into this world. To do competent work, to labour honestly according to the ability given them; for that and for no other purpose was each one of us sent into this world; and woe is to every man who, by friend or by foe, is prevented from fulfilling this the end of his being. That is the 'unhappy' lot; lot equally unhappy cannot otherwise be provided for man. Whatsoever prohibits or prevents a man from this his sacred appointment to labour while he lives on earth,—that I say, is the man's deadliest enemy; and all men are called upon to do what is in their power or opportunity towards delivering him from that. If it be his own indolence that prevents and prohibits him, then his own indolence is the enemy he must be delivered from: and the first 'right' he has,— poor indolent blockhead, black or white,—is, That every *un*prohibited man, whatsoever wiser, more industrious person may be passing that way, shall endeavour to 'emancipate' him from his indolence, and by some wise means, as I said, compel him, since inducing will not serve, to do the work he is fit for. Induce him, if you can: yes, sure enough, by all means try what inducement will do; and indeed every coachman and carman knows that secret, without our preaching, and applies it to his very horses as the true method:—but if your Nigger will not be induced? In that case, it is full certain, he must be compelled; should and must; and the tacit prayer he makes (unconsciously he, poor block-head), to you, and to me, and to all the world who are wiser than himself, is 'Compel me!' For indeed he *must*, or else do and suffer worse,—he as well as we. It were better the work did come out of him! It was the meaning of the gods with him and with us, that his gift should turn to use in this Creation, and not lie poisoning the thoroughfares, as a rotten mass of idleness, agreeable to neither heaven nor earth. For idleness does, in all cases, inevitably *rot*, and become putrescent;—and I say deliberately, the very Devil is in *it*.

None of you, my friends, have been in Demerara lately, I apprehend? May none of you go till matters mend there a little. Under the sky there are uglier sights than perhaps were seen hitherto! Dead corpses, the rotting body of a brother man, whom fate or unjust men have killed, this is not a pleasant spectacle; but what say you to the dead soul of a man,—in a body which still pretends to be vigorously alive, and can drink rum? An idle White gentleman is not pleasant to me; though I confess the real work for him is not easy to find, in these our epochs; and perhaps he is seeking, poor soul, and may find at last. But what say you to an idle Black gentleman, with his rum-bottle in his hand (for a little additional pumpkin you can have red herrings and rum, in Demerara),—rum-bottle in his hand, no breeches on his body, pumpkin at discretion, and the fruitfullest region of the earth going back to jungle round him? Such things the sun looks down upon in our fine times; and I, for one, would rather have no hand in them.

Yes, this is the eternal law of Nature for a man, my beneficent Exeter-Hall friends; this, that he shall be permitted, encouraged, and if need be, compelled to do what work the Maker of him has intended by the making of him for this world! Not that he should eat pumpkin with never such felicity in the West India Is'ands is, or can be, the blessed-ness of our Black friend; but that he should do useful work there, according as the gifts have been bestowed on him for that. And his own happiness, and that of others round him, will alone be possible by his and their getting into such a relation that this can be permitted him, and in case of need, that this can be compelled him. I beg you to understand this; for you seem to have a little forgotten it, and there lie a thousand inferences in it, not quite useless for Exeter Hall, at present. The idle Black man in the West Indies had, not long since, the right, and will again under better form, if it please Heaven, have the right (actually the first 'right of man' for an indolent person) to be *compelled* to work as he was fit, and to *do* the Maker's will who had constructed him with such and such capabilities, and prefigurements of capability. And I incessantly pray Heaven, all men, the whitest alike and the blackest, the richest and the poorest, in other regions of the world, had attained precisely the same right, the divine right of being compelled (if 'permitted' will not answer) to do what work they are appointed for, and not to go idle another minute, in a life which is so short, and where idleness so soon runs to putrescence! Alas, we had then a perfect world; and the Millennium, and true 'Organization of Labour', and reign of complete blessedness, for all workers and men, had then arrived,—which in these our own poor districts of the Planet, as we all lament to know, it is very far from having yet done. [*More withdrawals: but the rest sitting with increased attention.*]

Do I, then, hate the Negro? No; except when the soul is killed out of him, I decidedly like poor Quashee; and find him a pretty kind of man.

With a pennyworth of oil, you can make a handsome glossy thing of Quashee, when the soul is not killed in him! A swift, supple fellow; a merry-hearted, grinning, dancing, singing, affectionate kind of creature, with a great deal of melody and amenability in his composition. This certainly is a notable fact: The black African, alone of wild men, can live among men civilized. While all manner of Caribs and others pine into annihilation in presence of the pale faces, he contrives to continue; does not die of sullen irreconcilable rage, of rum, or brutish laziness and darkness, and fated incompatibility with his new place; but lives and multiplies, and evidently means to abide among us, if we can find the right regulation for him. We shall have to find it; we are now engaged in the search; and have at least discovered that of two methods, the old Demerara method, and the new Demerara method, neither will answer.

And now observe, my friends, it was not Black Quashee, or those he represents, that made those West India Islands what they are, or can, by any hypothesis, be considered to have the right of growing pumpkins there. For countless ages, since they first mounted oozy, on the back of earthquakes, from their dark bed in the ocean deeps, and reeking saluted the tropical Sun, and ever onwards till the European white man first saw them some three short centuries ago, those Islands had produced mere jungle, savagery, poison-reptiles, and swamp-malaria: till the white European first saw them, they were as if not yet created,— their noble elements of cinnamon, sugar, coffee, pepper black and grey, lying all asleep, waiting the white enchanter who should say to them, Awake! Till the end of human history and the sounding of the Trump of Doom, they might have lain so, had Quashee and the like of him been the only artists in the game. Swamps, fever-jungles, man-eating Caribs, rattlesnakes, and reeking waste and putrefaction, this had been the produce of them under the incompetent Caribal (what we call Cannibal) possessors, till that time; and Quashee knows, himself, whether ever he could have introduced an improvement. Him, had he by a miraculous chance been wafted thither, the Caribals would have eaten, rolling him as a fat morsel under their tongue! for him, till the sounding of the Trump of Doom, the rattlesnakes and savageries would have held on their way. It was not he, then; it was another than he! Never by art of his could one pumpkin have grown there to solace any human throat; nothing but savagery and reeking putrefaction could have grown there. These plentiful pumpkins, I say therefore, are not his: no, they are another's; they are his only under conditions. Conditions which Exeter Hall, for the present, has forgotten; but which

Nature and the Eternal Powers have by no manner of means forgotten, but do at all moments keep in mind; and, at the right moment, will, with the due impressiveness, perhaps in a rather terrible manner, bring again to our mind also!

If Quashee will not honestly aid in bringing out those sugars, cinnamons, and nobler products of the West Indian Islands, for the benefit of all mankind, then I say neither will the Powers permit Quashee to continue growing pumpkins there for his own lazy benefit; but will sheer him out, by and by, like a lazy gourd overshadowing rich ground; him and all that partake with him,—perhaps in a very terrible manner. For, under favour of Exeter Hall, the 'terrible manner' is not yet quite extinct with the Destinies in this Universe; nor will it quite cease, I apprehend, for soft sawder or philanthropic stump-oratory now or henceforth. No; the gods wish besides pumpkins, that spices and valuable products be grown in their West Indies; thus much they have declared in so making the West Indies:—infinitely more they wish, that manful industrious men occupy their West Indies, not indolent two-legged cattle, however 'happy' over their abundant pumpkins! Both these things, we may be assured, the immortal gods have decided upon, passed their eternal Act of Parliament for: and both of them, though all terrestrial Parliaments and entities oppose it to the death, shall be done. Quashee, if he will not help in bringing out the spices, will get himself made a slave again (which state will be a little less ugly than his present one), and with beneficent whip, since other methods avail not, will be compelled to work. Or, alas, let him look across to Haiti, and trace a far sterner prophecy! Let him, by his ugliness, idleness, rebellion, banish all White men from the West Indies, and make it all one Haiti,—with little or no sugar growing, black Peter exterminating black Paul, and where a garden of the Hesperides might be, nothing but a tropical dog-kennel and pestiferous jungle,—does he think that will for ever continue pleasant to gods and men? I see men, the rose-pink cant all peeled away from them, land one day on those black coasts; men *sent* by the Laws of this Universe, and inexorable Course of Things; men hungry for gold, remorseless, fierce as old Buccaneers were;—and a doom for Quashee which I had rather not contemplate! The gods are long-suffering; but the law from the beginning was, He that will not work shall perish from the earth; and the patience of the gods has limits!

Before the West Indies could grow a pumpkin for any Negro, how much European heroism had to spend itself in obscure battle; to sink, in mortal agony, before the jungles, the putrescences and waste savageries could become arable, and the Devils be in some measure chained there! The West Indies grow pine-apples, and sweet fruits, and spices; we hope they will one day grow beautiful Heroic human Lives too, which is surely the ultimate object they were made for: beautiful souls and brave; sages, poets, what not; making the Earth nobler round them, as their kindred from old have been doing; true 'splinters of the old Harz Rock'; heroic white men, worthy to be called old Saxons, browned with a mahogany tint in those new climates and conditions. But under the soil of Jamaica, before it could even produce spices or any pumpkin, the bones of many thousand British men had to be laid. Brave Colonel Fortescue, brave Colonel Sedgwick, brave Colonel Brayne,—the dust of many thousand strong old English hearts lies there; worn down in frightful travail, chaining the Devils, which were manifold. Heroic Blake contributed a bit of his life to that Jamaica. A bit of the great Protector's own life lies there; beneath those pumpkins lies a bit of the life that was Oliver Cromwell's. How the great Protector would have rejoiced to think, that all this was to issue in growing pumpkins to keep Quashee in a comfortably idle condition! No; that is not the ultimate issue; not that.

The West Indian Whites, so soon as this bewilderment of philanthropic and other jargon abates from them, and their poor eyes get to discern a little what the Facts are and what the Laws are, will strike into another course, I apprehend! I apprehend they will, as a preliminary, resolutely *refuse* to permit the Black man any privilege whatever of pumpkins till he agree for work in return. Not a square inch of soil in those fruitful Isles, purchased by British blood, shall any Black man hold to grow pumpkins for him, except on terms that are fair towards Britain. Fair; see that they be not unfair, not towards ourselves, and still more, not towards him. For injustice is *for ever* accursed: and precisely our unfairness towards the enslaved Black man has,—by inevitable revulsion and fated turn of the wheel,—brought about these present confusions. Fair towards Britain it will be, that Quashee give work for privilege to grow pumpkins. Not a pumpkin, Quashee, not a square yard of soil, till you agree to do the State so many days of service. Annually that soil will grow you pumpkins; but annually also, without fail, shall you, for the owner thereof, do your appointed days of labour. The State has plenty of waste soil; but the State will religiously give you none of it on other terms. The State wants sugar from these Islands, and means to have it; wants virtuous industry in these Islands, and must have it. The State demands of you such service as will bring these results, this latter result which includes all. Not a Black Ireland, by immigration, and boundless black supply for the demand; not that,—may the gods forbid!—but a regulated West Indies, with black working population in adequate numbers; all 'happy', if they find it possible; and *not* entirely unbeautiful to gods and men, which latter result they *must* find possible! All 'happy' enough; that is to say, all working according to the faculty they have got, making a little more divine this Earth which the gods have given them. Is there any other 'happiness',—if it be not that of pigs fattening daily to the slaughter? So will the State speak by and by.

Any poor idle Black man, any idle White man, rich or poor, is a mere eye-sorrow to the State; a perpetual blister on the skin of the State. The State is taking measures, some of them rather extensive in Europe at this very time, and already as in Paris, Berlin, and elsewhere, rather tremendous measures, to *get* its rich white men set to work; for alas, they also have long sat Negro-like up to the ears in pumpkin, regardless of 'work', and of a world all going to waste for their idleness! Extensive measures, I say and already (as, in all European lands, this scandalous Year of street-barricades and fugitive sham-kings exhibits) *tremendous* measures; for the thing is instant to be done.

The thing must be done everywhere; *must* is the word. Only it is so terribly difficult to do; and will take generations yet, this of getting our rich European white men 'set to work'! But yours in the West Indies, my obscure Black friends, your work, and the getting of you set to it, is a simple affair; and by diligence, the West Indian legislatures, and Royal governors, setting their faces fairly to the problem, will get it done. You are not 'slaves' now; nor do I wish, if it can be avoided, to see you slaves again: but decidedly you will have to be servants to those that are born *wiser* than you, that are born lords of you, servants to the Whites, if they *are* (as what mortal can doubt they are?) born wiser than you. That, you may depend on it, my obscure Black friends, is and was always the Law of the World, for you and for all men: To *be* servants, the more foolish of us to the more wise; and only sorrow, futility, and disappointment will betide both, till both in some approximate degree get to conform to the same. Heaven's laws are not repealable by Earth, however Earth may try,—and it has been trying hard, in some directions, of late! I say, no well-being and in the end no being at all, will be possible for you or us, if the law of Heaven is not complied with. And if 'slave' means essentially 'servant hired for life',—for life, or by a contract of long continuance and not easily dissoluble,—I ask once more, Whether, in all human things, the 'contract of long continuance' is not precisely the contract to be desired, were the right terms once found for it? Servant hired for life, were the right terms once found, which I do not pretend they are, seems to me much preferable to servant hired for the month, or by contract dissoluble in a day. What that amounts to, we have known, and our thirty thousand Distressed Astronomers have known; and we don't want that! [*Some assent in the small remnant of an audience. 'Silence!' from the Chair.*]

To state articulately, and put into practical Lawbooks, what on all sides is *fair* from the West-Indian White to the West-Indian Black; what relations the Eternal Maker *has* established between these two creatures of His; what He has written down with intricate but ineffaceable record, legible to candid human insight, in the respective qualities, strengths, necessities and capabilities of each of the two: this, as I told the Hon. Hickory my Carolina correspondent, will be a long problem; only to be solved by continuous human endeavour, and earnest effort gradually perfecting itself as experience successively yields new light to it. This will be to '*find* the right terms'; terms of a contract that will endure, and be sanctioned by Heaven, and obtain prosperity on Earth, between the two. A long problem, terribly neglected hitherto;—whence these West-Indian sorrows, and Exeter-Hall monstrosities, just now! But a problem which must be entered upon, and by degrees be completed. A problem which, I think, the English People also, if they mean to retain human Colonies, and not Black Irelands in addition to the White, cannot begin too soon. What are the true relations between Negro and White, their mutual duties under the sight of the Maker of them both; what human laws will assist both to comply more and more with these? The solution, only to be gained by earnest endeavour, and sincere reading of experience, such as have never yet been bestowed on it, is not yet here; the solution is perhaps still distant. But some approximation to it, various real approximations, could be made, and must be made:—this of declaring that Negro and White are *un*related, loose from one another, on a footing of perfect equality, and subject to no law but that of supply and demand according to the Dismal Science; this, which contradicts the palpablest facts, is clearly no solution, but a cutting of the knot asunder; and every hour we persist in this is leading us towards *dis*solution instead of solution!

What then is practically to be done, by us poor English, with our Demerara and other blacks? Well, in such a mess as we have made there, it is not easy saying what is first to be done! But all this of perfect equality, of cutting quite loose from one another; all this, with 'immigration loan', 'happiness of black peasantry,' and the other melancholy stuff that has followed from it, will first of all require to be *un*done, and the ground cleared of it, by way preliminary to 'doing'! After that there may several things be possible.

Already one hears of Black *Adscripti glebæ:* which seems a promising arrangement, one of the first to suggest itself in such a complicacy. It appears the Dutch Blacks, in Java, are already a kind of *Adscripts*, after the manner of the old European serfs; bound, by royal authority, to give so many days of work a year. Is not this something like a real approximation; the first step towards all manner of such? Wherever, in British territory, there exists a Black man, and needful work to the just extent is not to be got out of him, such a law in defect of better, should be brought to bear upon said Black man! How many laws of like purport, conceivable some of them, might be brought to bear upon the Black man and the White, with all despatch by way of solution instead of dissolution to their complicated case just now! On the whole it ought to be rendered possible, ought it not, for White men to live beside Black men, and in some just manner to command Black men, and produce West Indian fruitfulness by means of them? West Indian fruitfulness will need to be produced. If the English cannot find the method for that, they may rest assured there will another come (Brother Jonathan or still another) who can. He it is whom the gods will bid continue in the West Indies; bidding us ignominiously, 'Depart ye quack-ridden, incompetent'!—

[Extracts]

THE BATTLE OF DORKING

IN the year 1870 the tranquillity of Victorian England was suddenly disturbed by events on the Continent.

Not since the Hundred Days of Napoleon's last bid for power had European affairs seemed tó come so near to our shores. The 'peaceful reign' of Victoria had, it is true, been celebrated by almost continuous warfare in India or some outpost of the empire, but the distant carnage meant very little to people in England, and even the Crimean War was only a far-off rattle of sabres to be suitably celebrated by Tennyson or Tupper. The Franco-Prussian War of 1870 to 1871 brought sharply to the attention of the richest nation in the world—as we were at that time—the unpleasant fact that empires are carved with the sword and that—

> The same arts that did gain
> A power, must it maintain.

The French statesman Thiers had said of the Second Empire: 'There are no blunders left for us to make'. He was wrong; and the final blunder which led Napoleon III into war with Prussia was one from which France never completely recovered. The swift and complete defeat of the French made some people in England wonder whether British neutrality had been well-advised and what might be Bismarck's next step. Generally speaking, however, the belief that 'it can't happen here' seems to have held good; and it was at this comfortable self-assurance of his countrymen that Lt.-Col. Chesney levelled his pamphlet. Given his premises, which were in fact accepted by most Englishmen, he was remarkably near the truth. If the people of this country were to maintain indefinitely their high standard of living, based upon an elaborate system of looting the far corners of the earth, they must be prepared for more than an occasional distant border raid or the suppression of an insurrection of subject peoples. They had to be able to face the greatest power in Europe, which might at any moment challenge them; they could not, in short, enjoy the benefits of being the world's most successful brigands and expect to do so indefinitely without meeting another claimant.

The clash which Chesney foresaw did not occur until 1914; but his

GREAT AUTUMN MANŒUVRE.

HODGE. "*Lor-a-massy, me-aster! Be oi to be a 'power in t' ste-ate'? What be oi to get by tha-at?*"

MR. G. "*That, my good friend, is a mere detail. The question is, what am I to get by it!!*"

reading of the inevitable climax of power politics was a perfectly correct one. This did not prevent the pamphlet from being denounced as 'alarmist' by Gladstone, who, as head of the existing Government, felt it his duty to reassure his countrymen in their belief that imperialism and international politics were a sort of poker game in which no other country would ever call their bluff, a gamble in which they would always win and could never lose. Such, in fact, was the Victorian illusion for which we are actually paying today, when we inherit the vastly increased population encouraged by Victorian economy, whilst the means of draining the world's wealth to support it (means which seemed at one time to be increasing perpetually) have now shrunk away, leaving Britain more and more dependent upon its own inadequate resources.

We may not agree with Chesney's solution for this problem, but he stands out as a realist in a society which based its hopes upon an illusion. He writes as though he were looking back at the story of a sudden and unexpected defeat of Britain by Germany. First published anonymously as a story in *Blackwood's Magazine*, May 1871, and issued the same year as a pamphlet, Chesney's 'alarmist' fantasy attracted much attention. The middle of the pamphlet, which we have not used (although it provided the title), is a long and detailed 'eye-witness' account of the great battle of Dorking, when the German invaders defeated the unprepared and undisciplined British. The pamphlet was re-issued in 1914, at the outbreak of the war, for obvious reasons. If one forgets its propaganda purpose it can be considered as a remarkable narrative which suggests comparison with the account by H. G. Wells of an invasion from Mars.

THE BATTLE OF DORKING

By Sir George Tomkyns Chesney

You ask me to tell you, my grandchildren, something about my own share in the great events that happened fifty years ago. 'Tis sad work turning back to that bitter page in our history, but you may perhaps take profit in your new homes from the lesson it teaches. For us in England it came too late. And yet we had plenty of warnings, if we had only made use of them. The danger did not come on us unawares. It burst on us suddenly, 'tis true; but its coming was foreshadowed plainly enough to open our eyes, if we had not been wilfully blind. We English have only ourselves to blame for the humiliation which has been brought on the land. Venerable old age! Dishonourable old age, I say, when it follows a manhood dishonoured as ours has been. I declare, even now, though fifty years have passed, I can hardly look a young man in the face when I think I am one of those in whose youth happened this degradation of Old England —one of those who betrayed the trust handed down to us unstained by our forefathers.

What a proud and happy country was this fifty years ago! Free-trade had been working for more than a quarter of a century, and there seemed to be no end to the riches it was bringing us. London was growing bigger and bigger; you could not build houses fast enough for the rich people who wanted to live in them, the merchants who made the money and came from all parts of the world to settle there, and the lawyers and doctors and engineers and others, and trades-people who got their share out of the profits. The streets reached down to Croydon and Wimbledon, which my father could remember quite country places; and people used to say that Kingston and Reigate would soon be joined to London. We thought we could go on building and multiplying

for ever. 'Tis true that even then there was no lack of poverty;
the people who had no money went on increasing as fast as the rich,
and pauperism was already beginning to be a difficulty; but if the rates
were high, there was plenty of money to pay them with; and as for
what were called the middle classes, there really seemed no limit to
their increase and prosperity. People in those days thought it quite a
matter of course to bring a dozen of children into the world—or, as it
used to be said, Providence sent them that number of babies; and if they
couldn't always marry off all the daughters, they used to manage to
provide for the sons, for there were new openings to be found in all the
professions, or in the Government offices, which went on steadily
getting larger. Besides, in those days young men could be sent out to
India, or into the army or navy; and even then emigration was not
uncommon, although not the regular custom it is now. Schoolmasters,
like all other professional classes, drove a capital trade. They did not
teach very much, to be sure, but new schools with their four or five
hundred boys were springing up all over the country.

Fools that we were! We thought that all this wealth and prosperity
were sent us by Providence, and could not stop coming. In our blind-
ness we did not see that we were merely a big workshop, making up
the things which came from all parts of the world; and that if other
nations stopped sending us raw goods to work up, we could not produce them ourselves. True, we had in those days an advantage in our
cheap coal and iron; and had we taken care not to waste the fuel, it
might have lasted us longer. But even then there were signs that coal
and iron would soon become cheaper in foreign parts; while as to food
and other things, England was not better off than it is now. We were so
rich simply because other nations from all parts of the world were in
the habit of sending their goods to us to be sold or manufactured; and
we thought that this would last for ever. And so, perhaps, it might have
lasted, if we had only taken proper means to keep it; but, in our folly,
we were too careless even to insure our prosperity, and after the course
of trade was turned away it would not come back again.

And yet, if ever a nation had a plain warning, we had. If we were the
greatest trading country, our neighbours were the leading military
power in Europe. They were driving a good trade, too, for this was
before their foolish communism (about which you will hear when you
are older) had ruined the rich without benefiting the poor, and they
were in many respects the first nation in Europe; but it was on their
army that they prided themselves most. And with reason. They had
beaten the Russians and the Austrians, and the Prussians too, in

bygone years, and they thought they were invincible. Well do I remember the great review held at Paris by the Emperor Napoleon during the great Exhibition, and how proud he looked showing off his splendid Guards to the assembled kings and princes. Yet, three years afterwards, the force so long deemed the first in Europe was ignominiously beaten, and the whole army taken prisoners. Such a defeat had never happened before in the world's history; and with this proof before us of the folly of disbelieving in the possibility of disaster merely because it had never fallen upon us, it might have been supposed that we should have the sense to take the lesson to heart. And the country was certainly roused for a time, and a cry was raised that the army ought to be reorganised, and our defences strengthened against the enormous power for sudden attacks which it was seen other nations were able to put forth. And a scheme of army reform was brought forward by the Government. It was a half-and-half affair at best; and, unfortunately, instead of being taken up in Parliament as a national scheme, it was made a party matter of, and so fell through. There was a Radical section of the House, too, whose votes had to be secured by conciliation, and which blindly demanded a reduction of armaments as the price of allegiance. This party always decried military establishments as part of a fixed policy for reducing the influence of the Crown and the aristocracy. They could not understand that the times had altogether changed, that the Crown had really no power, and that the Government merely existed at the pleasure of the House of Commons, and that even Parliament-rule was beginning to give way to mob-law. At any rate, the Ministry, baffled on all sides, gave up by degrees all the strong points of a scheme which they were not heartily in earnest about. It was not that there was any lack of money, if only it had been spent in the right way. The army cost enough, and more than enough, to give us a proper defence, and there were armed men of sorts in plenty and to spare, if only they had been decently organised. It was in organisation and forethought that we fell short, because our rulers did not heartily believe in the need for preparation. The fleet and the Channel, they said, were sufficient protection. So army reform was put off to some more convenient season, and the militia and volunteers were left untrained as before, because to call them out for drill would 'interfere with the industry of the country'. We could have given up some of the industry of those days, forsooth, and yet be busier than we are now. But why tell you a tale you have so often heard already? The nation, although uneasy, was misled by the false security its leaders professed to feel; the warning given by the disasters that overtook France was allowed to pass by unheeded. We would not even be at the trouble of putting our arsenals in a safe place, or of guarding the capital against a surprise, although the cost of doing so would not have been so much as missed from the national wealth. The French trusted in their army and its great reputation, we in our fleet; and in each case the result of this blind confidence was disaster, such as our forefathers in their hardest struggles could not have even imagined.

I need hardly tell you how the crash came about. First, the rising in India drew away a part of our small army; then came the difficulty with America, which had been threatening for years, and we sent off ten thousand men to defend Canada—a handful which did not go far to strengthen the real defences of that country, but formed an irresistible temptation to the Americans to try and take them prisoners, especially as the contingent included three battalions of the Guards. Thus the regular army at home was even smaller than usual, and nearly half of it was in Ireland to check the talked-of Fenian invasion fitting out in the West. Worse still—though I do not know it would really have mattered as things turned out—the fleet was scattered abroad: some ships to guard the West Indies, others to check privateering in the China seas, and a large part to try and protect our colonies on the Northern Pacific shore of America, where, with incredible folly, we continued to retain possessions which we could not possibly defend. America was not the great power forty years ago that it is now; but for us to try and hold territory on her shores which could only be reached by sailing round the Horn, was as absurd as if she had attempted to take the Isle of Man before the independence of Ireland. We see this plainly enough now, but we were all blind then.

It was while we were in this state, with our ships all over the world, and our little bit of an army cut up into detachments, that the Secret Treaty was published, and Holland and Denmark were annexed. People say now that we might have escaped the troubles which came on us if we had at any rate kept quiet till our other difficulties were settled; but the English were always an impulsive lot: the whole country was boiling over with indignation, and the Government, egged on by the press, and going with the stream, declared war. We had always got out of scrapes before, and we believed our old luck and pluck would somehow pull us through.

Then, of course, there was bustle and hurry all over the land. Not that the calling up of the army reserves caused much stir, for I think there were only about 5,000 altogether, and a good many of these were not to be found when the time came; but recruiting was going on all over the country, with a tremendous high bounty, 50,000 more men having been voted for the army. Then there was a Ballot Bill passed for adding 55,500 men to the militia; why a round number was not fixed on I don't know, but the Prime Minister said that this was the exact quota wanted to put the defences of the country on a sound footing. Then the shipbuilding that began! Ironclads, despatch-boats, gunboats, monitors,—every building-yard in the country got its job, and they were offering ten shillings a-day wages for anybody who could drive a rivet. This didn't improve the recruiting, you may suppose. I remember, too, there was a squabble in the House of Commons about whether artisans should be drawn for the ballot, as they were so much wanted, and I think they got an exemption. This sent numbers to the yards; and if we had had a couple of years to prepare instead of a couple of weeks, I daresay we should have done very well.

It was on a Monday that the declaration of war was announced, and in a few hours we got our first inkling of the sort of preparation the enemy had made for the event which they had really brought about, although the actual declaration was made by us. A pious appeal to the God of battles, whom it was said we had aroused, was telegraphed back; and from that moment all communication with the north of Europe was cut off. Our embassies and legations were packed off at an hour's notice, and it was as if we had suddenly come back to the middle ages. The dumb astonishment visible all over London the next morning, when the papers came out void of news, merely hinting at what had happened, was one of the most startling things in this war of surprises. But everything had been arranged beforehand; nor ought we to have been surprised, for we had seen the same Power, only a few months before, move down half a million of men on a few days' notice, to conquer the greatest military nation in Europe, with no more fuss than our War Office used to make over the transport of a brigade from Aldershot to Brighton,—and this, too, without the allies it had now. What happened now was not a bit more wonderful in reality; but people of this country could not bring themselves to believe that what had never occurred before to England could ever possibly happen. Like our neighbours, we became wise when it was too late.

Of course the papers were not long in getting news—even the mighty organisation set at work could not shut out a special correspondent; and in a very few days, although the telegraphs and railways were intercepted right across Europe, the main facts oozed out. An embargo had been laid on all the shipping in every port from the Baltic to Ostend; the fleets of the two great Powers had moved out, and it was supposed were assembled in the great northern harbour, and troops were hurrying on board all the steamers detained in these places, most of which were British vessels. It was clear that invasion was intended. Even then we might have been saved, if the fleet had been ready. The forts which guarded the flotilla were perhaps too strong for shipping to attempt; but an ironclad or two, handled as British sailors knew how to use them, might have destroyed or damaged a part of the transports and delayed the expedition, giving us what we wanted, time. But then the best part of the fleet had been decoyed down to the Dardanelles, and what remained of the Channel squadron was looking after Fenian filibusters off the west of Ireland; so it was ten days before the fleet was got together, and by that time it was plain the enemy's preparations were too far advanced to be stopped by a *coup-de-main*. Information, which came chiefly though Italy, came slowly, and was more or less vague and uncertain; but this much was known, that at least a couple of hundred thousand men were embarked or ready to be put on board ships, and that the flotilla was guarded by more ironclads than we could then muster. I suppose it was the uncertainty as to the point the enemy would aim at for landing, and the fear lest he should give us the go-by, that kept the fleet for several days in the Downs; but it was not until the Tuesday fortnight after the declaration of war that it weighed anchor and steamed away for the North Sea. Of course you have read about the Queen's visit to the fleet the day before, and how she sailed round the ships in her yacht, and went on board the flag-ship to take leave of the admiral; how, overcome with emotion, she told him that the safety of the country was committed to his keeping. You remember, too, the gallant old officer's reply, and how all the ships' yards were manned, and how lustily the tars cheered as her Majesty was rowed off. The account was of course telegraphed to London, and the high spirits of the fleet infected the whole town. I was outside the Charing Cross station when the Queen's special train from Dover arrived, and from the cheering and shouting which greeted her Majesty as she drove away, you might have supposed we had already won a great victory. The leading journal, which had gone in strongly for the army reduction carried out during the session, and had been nervous and desponding in tone during the past fortnight, suggesting all sorts of compromises as a way of getting out of the war, came out in a very jubilant form next morning. 'Panic-stricken inquirers,' it said, 'ask now, where are the means of meeting the invasion? We reply that the invasion will never take place. A British fleet, manned by British sailors whose courage and enthusiasm are reflected in the people of this country, is already on the way to meet the presumptuous foe. The issue of a contest between British ships and those of any other country, under anything like equal odds, can never be doubtful. England awaits with calm confidence the issue of the impending action.'

Such were the words of the leading article, and so we all felt. It was on Tuesday, the 10th of August, that the fleet sailed from the Downs. It took with it a submarine cable to lay down as it advanced, so that continuous communication was kept up, and the papers were publishing special editions every few minutes with the latest news. This was the first time such a thing had been done, and the feat was accepted as a good omen. Whether it is true that the Admiralty made use of the cable to keep on sending contradictory orders, which took the command out of the admiral's hands, I can't say; but all that the admiral sent in return was a few messages of the briefest kind, which neither the Admiralty nor any one else could have made any use of. Such a ship had gone off reconnoitring; such another had rejoined—fleet was in latitude so and so. This went on till the Thursday morning. I had just come up to town by train as usual, and was walking to my office, when the newsboys began to cry, 'New edition—enemy's fleet in sight!' You may imagine the scene in London! Business still went on at the banks, for bills matured although the independence of the country was being fought out under our own eyes, so to say, and the speculators were active enough. But even with the people who were making and losing their fortunes, the interest in the fleet overcame everything else; men who went to pay in or draw out their money stopped to show the last bulletin to the cashier. As for the street, you could hardly get along for the crowd stopping to buy and read the papers; while at every house or office the members sat restlessly in the common room, as if to keep together for company, sending out some one of their number every few minutes to get the latest edition. At least this is what happened at our office; but to sit still was as impossible as to do anything, and most of us went out and wandered about among the crowd, under a sort of feeling that the news was got quicker at in this way. Bad as were the times coming, I think the sickening suspense of that day, and the shock which followed, was almost the worst that we underwent. It was about ten o'clock that the first telegram came; an hour later the wire announced that the admiral had signalled to form line of battle, and shortly afterwards that the order was given to bear down on the enemy and engage. At twelve came the announcement, 'Fleet opened fire about three miles to leeward of us'—that is, the ship with the cable. So far all had been expectancy, then came the first token of calamity.

'An ironclad has been blown up'—'the enemy's torpedoes are doing great damage'—'the flag-ship is laid aboard the enemy'—'the flag-ship appears to be sinking'—'the vice-admiral has signalled to'—there the cable became silent, and as you know, we heard no more till two days afterwards. The solitary ironclad which escaped the disaster steamed into Portsmouth.

Then the whole story came out—how our sailors, gallant as ever, had tried to close with the enemy; how the latter evaded the conflict at close quarters, and, sheering off, left behind them the fatal engines which sent our ships, one after the other, to the bottom; how all this happened almost in a few minutes. The Government, it appears, had received warnings of this invention; but to the nation this stunning blow was utterly unexpected. That Thursday I had to go home early for regimental drill, but it was impossible to remain doing nothing, so when that was over I went up to town again, and after waiting in expectation of news which never came, and missing the midnight train, I walked home. It was a hot sultry night, and I did not arrive till near sunrise. The whole town was quite still—the lull before the storm; and as I let myself in with my latch-key, and went softly up-stairs to my room to avoid waking the sleeping household, I could not but contrast the peacefulness of the morning—no sound breaking the silence but the singing of the birds in the garden—with the passionate remorse and indignation that would break out with the day. Perhaps the inmates of the rooms were as wakeful as myself; but the house in its stillness was just as it used to be when I came home alone from balls or parties in the happy days gone by.

*   *   *   *

We had heard of generosity in war; we found none: the war was made by us, it was said, and we must take the consequences. London and our only arsenal captured, we were at the mercy of our captors, and right heavily did they tread on our necks. Need I tell you the rest?—of the ransom we had to pay, and the taxes raised to cover it, which keep us paupers to this day?—the brutal frankness that announced we must give place to a new naval Power, and be made harmless for revenge?—the victorious troops living at free quarters, the yoke they put on us made the more galling that their requisitions had a semblance of method and legality? Better have been robbed at first hand by the soldiery themselves, than through our own magistrates made the instruments for extortion. How we lived through the degradation we daily and hourly underwent, I hardly even now understand. And what was there left to us to live for? Stripped of our colonies; Canada and the West Indies gone to America; Australia forced to separate; India lost for ever, after the English there had all been destroyed, vainly trying to hold the country when cut off from aid by their countrymen; Gibraltar and Malta ceded to the new naval Power; Ireland independent and in perpetual anarchy and revolution. When I look at my country as it is now—its trade gone, its factories silent, its harbours empty, a prey to pauperism and decay—when I see all this, and think what Great Britain was in my youth, I ask myself whether I have really a heart or any sense of patriotism that I should have witnessed such degradation and still care to live! France was different. There, too, they had to eat the bread of tribulation under the yoke of the conqueror! their fall was hardly more sudden or violent than ours; but war could not take away their rich soil; they had no colonies to lose; their broad lands, which made their wealth, remained to them; and they rose again from the blow. But our people could not be got to see how artificial our prosperity was—that it all rested on foreign trade and financial credit; that the course of trade once turned away from us, even for a time, it might never return; and that our credit once shaken might never be restored. To hear men talk in those days, you would have thought that Providence had ordained that our Government should always borrow at three per cent, and that trade came to us because we lived in a foggy little island set in a boisterous sea. They could not be got to see that the wealth heaped up on every side was not created in the country, but in India and China, and other parts of the world; and that it would be quite possible for the people who made money by buying and selling the natural treasures of the earth, to go and live in other places, and take their profits with them. Nor would men believe that there could ever be an end to our coal and iron, or that they would get to be so much dearer than the coal and iron of America that it would no longer be worth while to work them, and that therefore we ought to insure against the loss of our artificial position as the great centre of trade, by making ourselves secure and strong and respected. We thought we were living in a commercial millennium, which must last for a thousand years at least. After all, the bitterest part of our reflection is, that all this misery and decay might have been so easily prevented, and that we brought it about ourselves by our own short-sighted recklessness. There, across the narrow Straits, was the writing on the wall, but we would not choose to read it. The warnings of the few were drowned in the voice of the multitude. Power was then passing away from the class which had been used to rule, and to face political dangers, and which had brought the nation with honour unsullied through former struggles, into the hands of the lower classes, uneducated, untrained to the use of political rights, and swayed by demagogues; and the few who were wise in their generation were denounced as alarmists, or as aristocrats who sought their own aggrandisement by wasting public money on bloated armaments. The rich were idle and luxurious; the poor grudged the cost of defence. Politics had become a mere bidding for Radical votes, and those who should have led the nation stooped rather to pander to the selfishness of the day, and humoured the popular cry which denounced those who would secure the defence of the nation by enforced arming of its manhood, as interfering with the liberties of the people. Truly the nation was ripe for a fall; but when I reflect how a little firmness and self-denial, or political courage and foresight, might have averted the disaster, I feel that the judgment must have really been deserved. A nation too selfish to defend its liberty, could not have been fit to retain it. To you, my grandchildren, who are now going to seek a new home in a more prosperous land, let not this bitter lesson be lost upon you in the country of your adoption. For me, I am too old to begin life again in a strange country; and hard and evil as have been my days, it is not much to await in solitude the time which cannot now be far off, when my old bones will be laid to rest in the soil I have loved so well, and whose happiness and honour I have so long survived.

USEFUL WORK VERSUS USELESS TOIL

IT is important to realise that there is as much difference between the Socialism of the nineteenth century and what is called Socialism today as there is between the Tolpuddle Martyrs and the modern Trade Union Chief (whose objective is the House of Lords; or at the very least, a knighthood). The pioneers of trade unionism would find it very difficult to understand Lord Citrine; and the Socialists of William Morris's days would be distinctly perplexed by the sight of a Labour Government which had swallowed imperialism, monarchy and capitalism—even bolstering up a predatory economic system by introducing forced labour for private profit. 'Nationalised industries' run by boards as remote as any limited company, where the workers were still in perpetual conflict with their employers, would without doubt have horrified William Morris; and he would certainly not have recognised such a system as Socialism. For while the modern 'Socialist' preserves at all costs the distinction between employer and employee, forcing people if necessary into what the nineteenth century socialists called 'wage-slavery', and making life as hard as possible for the 'self-employed person', William Morris preached quite the opposite doctrine. He wanted a world in which *all* people were 'self-employed', either individually or collectively.

But even the Socialists of the late nineteenth century—those disturbing people who threatened the false tranquility of the complacent Victorians—had among them potential bureaucrats and plenty of those Comrades who express their belief in fraternity by imputing corruption and low intrigue to other Comrades who differ from them on some minor point. Among the bureaucratic types of Morris's days was H. M. Hyndman, who dominated the Social Democratic Federation, an honest man but unimaginative and tiresome. Morris, after trying to work with Hyndman for a while, decided that it was impossible in view of their complete difference of outlook—a difference which might not have seemed important if Hyndman had not been the kind of man who makes a big issue of a small disagreement, his supporters being ready to assist still further by making any such issue the subject of a vendetta.

Accordingly, in the last days of 1884, after a final split in the S.D.F.,

Morris and his friends walked out and founded the Socialist League. With Belfort Bax, Morris began to edit a new Socialist paper and a series of pamphlets under the collective title 'The Socialist Platform'. Here at last he had a forum for what was to him far more than an economic theory. To William Morris, Socialism meant a new attitude to life, involving something much more profound than the shallow basis of class interests in a class struggle—'a life,' he wrote, 'in which every human being should find unrestricted scope for his best powers and faculties'.

During the last phase of his connection with the S.D.F., Morris had visited Edward Carpenter and 'listened with longing heart' to Carpenter's account of his way of living, growing his own wheat and marketing fruit and flowers. 'It seems to me,' wrote Morris, 'that the real way to enjoy life is to accept all its necessary ordinary details and turn them into pleasures . . . whereas modern civilisation huddles them out of the way, has them done in a venal and slovenly manner till they become real drudgery which people can't help trying to avoid.'

This was always one of Morris's themes, and clearly it was much on his mind just at this time. On the one hand he could deplore, as every socialist did, the exploitation of labour to produce rent, interest and dividends, and the 'useless toil' that created nothing—such as the stupid waste of human lives in competitive salesmanship, competitive advertisement, and the hundred other ways in which men are employed to snatch each other's bread or merely to add up the profits of other people in large ledgers. He could denounce the absurdity of an economic system which forced them to undertake such tasks, when they might be contributing usefully to society. He knew, long before the great slumps of the twentieth century, that a society was mad which made a blessing of mere 'employment' (as though the total amount of consumer goods could be increased by a rich man employing a large staff of household servants, whom the employer was supposed in some mysterious way to 'support', and as though a wealthy man did literally 'make' his own money and other people could eat it).

All these fallacies and a hundred others on which civilisation has built since man first began to value money more than the things he bought with it, or the labour that created them, Morris exposed clearly enough, as any Socialist might have done. But he did something else that was rare even among Socialists: he replaced the stupid conception of 'employment' as the thing to be aimed at by a creative conception of work as a pleasure in itself.

The Socialist Society which Morris desired (and the dream which he

THE SOCIALIST PLATFORM.—No. 2.

USEFUL WORK

v.

USELESS TOIL

WILLIAM MORRIS.

PRICE ONE PENNY.

LONDON:

SOCIALIST LEAGUE OFFICE,

13 Farringdon Road, Holborn Viaduct, E.C.

1885.

left to haunt a world that drifts ever further from it) was therefore a world in which nobody sought 'employment'. Nor did it follow the Carlyle pattern—so ably set out by the Sage in a previous pamphlet— with drudgery as a moral tonic for one to the material benefit of another. Nor, again, was he interested in the idea of work as something to be done as rapidly as possible, taking all the pleasure out of it, in order to provide endless 'leisure' for people who knew only how to kill time and not how to use it. Work was to be useful, its motive was to be service of the community, and its incentive was to lie in its social usefulness combined with the joy of the craftsmen in the exercise of his skill and in the creation of things useful or beautiful.

Hence Morris's Socialist League pamphlet, in 1885, was a challenge not only to capitalist values but also to the dreary conception of work which Socialists had inherited from the Capitalist system.

USEFUL WORK VERSUS USELESS TOIL

By William Morris

THE above title may strike some of my readers as strange. It is assumed by most people now-a-days that all work is useful, and by most *well-to-do* people that all work is desirable. Most people, well-to-do or not, believe that, even when a man[1] is doing work which appears to be useless, he is earning his livelihood by it—he is 'employed', as the phrase goes; and most of those who are well-to-do cheer on the happy worker with congratulations and praises, if he is only 'industrious' enough and deprives himself of all pleasure and holidays in the sacred cause of labour. In short it has become an article of the creed of modern morality that all labour is good in itself—a convenient belief to those who live on the labour of others. But as to those on whom they live, I recommend them not to take it on trust, but to look into the matter a little deeper.

Let us grant, first, that the race of man must either labour or perish. Nature gives us absolutely nothing gratis; we must win it by toil of some sort or degree. Let us see, then, if she does not give us some compensation for this compulsion to labour, since certainly in other matters she takes care to make the acts necessary to the continuance of life in the individual and the race not only endurable, but even pleasurable.

Yet, first, we must say in the teeth of the hypocritical praise of all labour, whatsoever it may be, of which I have made mention, that there is some labour which is so far from being a blessing that it is a curse; that it would be better for the community and for the worker if the latter were to fold his hands and refuse to work, and either die or let us pack him off to the workhouse or prison—which you will.

[1] When the word 'man' or 'men' is used in the following pages, it is intended to include both sexes, unless otherwise stated.

Here, you see, are two kinds of work—one good, the other bad; one not far removed from a blessing, a lightening of life; the other a mere curse, a burden to life.

What is the difference between them, then? This: one has hope in it, the other has not. It is manly to do the one kind of work, and manly also to refuse to do the other.

What is the nature of the hope which, when it is present in work, makes it worth doing?

It is threefold, I think—hope of rest, hope of product, hope of pleasure in the work itself; and hope of these also in some abundance and of good quality; rest enough and good enough to be worth having; product worth having by one who is neither a fool nor an ascetic; pleasure enough for all for us to be conscious of it while we are at work; not a mere habit, the loss of which we shall feel as a fidgetty man feels the loss of the bit of string he fidgets with.

I have put the hope of rest first because it is the simplest and most natural part of our hope. Whatever pleasure there is in some work, there is certainly some pain in all work, the beast-like pain of stirring up our slumbering energies to action, the beast-like dread of change when things are pretty well with us; and the compensation for this animal pain is animal rest. We must feel while we are working that the time will come when we shall not have to work. Also the rest, when it comes, must be long enough to allow us to enjoy it; it must be longer than is merely necessary for us to recover the strength we have expended in working, and it must be animal rest also in this, that it must not be disturbed by anxiety, else we shall not be able to enjoy it. If we have this amount and kind of rest we shall, so far, be no worse off than the beasts.

As to the hope of product, I have said that nature compels us to work for that. It remains for *us* to look to it that we *do* really produce something, and not nothing, or at least nothing that we want or are allowed to use. If we look to this and use our wills we shall, so far, be better than machines.

The hope of pleasure in the work itself: how strange that hope must seem to some of my readers—to most of them! Yet I think that to all living things there is a pleasure in the exercise of their energies, and that even beasts rejoice in being lithe and swift and strong. But a man at work, making something which he feels will exist because he is working at it and wills it, is exercising the energies of his mind and soul as well as of his body. Memory and imagination help him as he works. Not only his own thoughts, but the thoughts of the men of past ages guide his hands; and, as a part of the human race, he creates. If we work thus we shall be men, and our days will be happy and eventful.

Thus worthy work carries with it the hope of pleasure in rest, the hope of the pleasure in our using what it makes, and the hope of pleasure in our daily creative skill.

All other work but this is worthless; it is slaves' work—mere toiling to live, that we may live to toil.

Therefore, since we have, as it were, a pair of scales in which to weigh the work now done in the world, let us use them. Let us estimate the worthiness of the work we do, after so many thousand years of toil, so many promises of hope deferred, such boundless exultation over the progress of civilisation and the gain of liberty.

Now, the first thing as to the work done in civilisation and the easiest to notice is that it is portioned out very unequally amongst the different classes of society. First, there are people—not a few—who do no work, and make no pretence of doing any. Next, there are people, and very many of them, who work fairly hard, though with abundant easements and holidays, claimed and allowed; and lastly, there are people who work so hard that they may be said to do nothing else than work, and are accordingly called 'the working classes', as distinguished from the middle classes and the rich, or aristocracy, whom I have mentioned above.

It is clear that this inequality presses heavily upon the 'working' class, and must visibly tend to destroy their hope of rest at least, and so, in that particular, make them worse off than mere beasts of the field; but that is not the sum and end of our folly of turning useful work into useless toil, but only the beginning of it.

For first, as to the class of rich people doing no work, we all know that they consume a great deal while they produce nothing. Therefore, clearly, they have to be kept at the expense of those who do work, just as paupers have, and are a mere burden on the community. In these days there are many who have learned to see this, though they can see no further into the evils of our present system, and have formed no idea of any scheme for getting rid of this burden; though perhaps they have a vague hope that changes in the system of voting for members of the House of Commons may, as if by magic, tend in that direction. With such hopes or superstitions we need not trouble ourselves. Moreover, this class, once thought most necessary to the State, is scant of numbers, and has now no power of its own, but depends on the support of the class next below it—the middle class. In fact, it is really composed either of the most successful men of that class, or of their immediate descendants.

As to the middle class, including the trading, manufacturing and professional people of our society, they do, as a rule, seem to work quite hard enough, and so at first sight might be thought to help the community, and not burden it. But by far the greater part of them, though they work, do not produce, and even when they do produce, as in the case of those engaged (wastefully indeed) in the distribution of goods, or doctors, or (genuine) artists and literary men, they consume out of all proportion to their due share. The commercial and manufacturing part of them, the most powerful part, spend their lives and energies in fighting amongst themselves for their respective shares of the wealth which they *force* the genuine workers to provide for them; the others are almost wholly the hangers-on of these: they are the parasites of property, sometimes, as in the case of lawyers, undisguisedly so; sometimes, as the doctors and others above-mentioned, professing to be useful but too often of no use save as supporters of the system of folly, fraud and tyranny of which they form a part. And all these we must remember, have, as a rule, one aim in view: not the production of utilities, but the gaining of a position either for themselves or their children in which they will not have to work at all. It is their ambition and the end of their whole lives to gain, if not for themselves yet at least for their children, the proud position of being obvious burdens on the community. For their work itself, in spite of the sham dignity with which they surround it, they care nothing: save a few enthusiasts, men of science, art or letters, who, if they are not the salt of the earth, are at least (and O, the pity of it!) the salt of the miserable system of which they are the slaves, which hinders and thwarts them at every turn and even sometimes corrupts them.

Here then is another class, this time very numerous and all-powerful, which produces very little and consumes enormously, and is therefore supported, as paupers are, by the real producers. The class that remains to be considered produces all that is produced, and supports both itself and the other classes, though it is placed in a position of inferiority to them; real inferiority, mind you, involving a degradation both of mind and body. But it is a necessary consequence of this tyranny and folly that again many of these workers are not producers. A vast number of them once more are merely parasites of property, some of them openly so, as the soldiers by land and sea who are kept on foot for the perpetuating of national rivalries and enmities, and for the purposes of the national struggle for the share of the product of unpaid labour. But besides this obvious burden on the producers and the scarcely less obvious one of domestic servants, there is first the army of clerks, shop-assistants and so forth who are engaged in the service of the private war for wealth, which as above said, is the real occupation of the well-to-do middle class. This is a larger body of workers than might be supposed, for it includes amongst others all those engaged in what I should call competitive salesmanship, or, to use a less dignified word, the puffery of wares, which has now got to such a pitch that there are many things which cost far more to sell than they do to make.

Next there is the mass of people employed in making all those articles of folly and luxury, the demand for which is the outcome of the existence of the rich non-producing classes; things which people leading a manly and uncorrupted life would not ask for or dream of. These things, whoever may gainsay me, I will for ever refuse to call wealth; they are not wealth, but waste. Wealth is what nature gives us and what a reasonable man can make out of the gifts of nature for his reasonable use. The sunlight, the fresh air, the unspoiled face of the earth, food, raiment and housing, necessary and decent; the storing up of knowledge of all kinds, and the power of disseminating it; means of free communication between man and man; works of art, the beauty which man creates when he is most a man, most aspiring and thoughtful —all things which serve the pleasure of people, free, manly and uncorrupted. This is wealth. Nor can I think of anything worth having which does not come under one or other of these heads. But think, I beseech you, of the product of England, the workshop of the world, and will you not be bewildered, as I am, at the thought of the mass of things which no sane man could desire, but which our useless toil makes—and sells?

Now, further, there is even a sadder industry yet forced on many, very many, of our workers—the making of wares which are necessary to them and, their brethren, *because they are an inferior class*. For if many men live without producing, nay, must live lives so empty and foolish that they *force* a great part of the workers to produce wares which no one needs, not even the rich, it follows that most men must be poor; and, living as they do on wages from those whom they support, cannot get for their use the *goods* which men naturally desire, but must put up with miserable makeshifts for them, with coarse food that does not nourish, with rotten raiment which does not shelter, with wretched houses which may well make a town-dweller in civilisation look back with regret to the tent of the nomad tribe, or the cave of the pre-historic savage. Nay, the workers must even lend a hand to the great industrial invention of the age—adulteration, and by its help produce for their own use shams and mockeries of the luxury of the rich; for the wage-earners must always live as the wage-payers bid them, and their very habits of life are *forced* on them by their masters.

But it is waste of time to try to express in words due contempt of the productions of the much-praised cheapness of our epoch. It must be enough to say that this cheapness is necessary to the system of exploiting on which modern manufacture rests. In other words, our society includes a great mass of slaves, who must be fed, clothed, housed and amused as slaves, and that their daily necessity compels them to make the slave-wares whose use is the perpetuation of their slavery.

To sum up, then, concerning the manner of work in civilised states, these states are composed of three classes—a class which does not even pretend to work, a class which pretends to work but which produces nothing, and a class which works, but is compelled by the other two classes to do work which is often unproductive.

Civilisation therefore wastes its own resources, and will do so as long as the present system lasts. These are cold words with which to describe the tyranny under which we suffer; try then to consider what they mean.

There is a certain amount of natural material and of natural forces in the world and a certain amount of labour-power inherent in the persons of the men that inhabit it. Men urged by their necessities and desires have laboured for many thousands of years at the task of subjugating the forces of nature and of making the natural material useful to them. To our eyes, since we cannot see into the future, that struggle with nature seems nearly over, and the victory of the human race over her nearly complete. And, looking backwards to the time when history first began, we note that the progress of that victory has been far swifter and more startling within the last two hundred years than ever before. Surely, therefore, we moderns ought to be in all ways vastly better off than any who have gone before us. Surely we ought, one and all of us, to be wealthy, to be well furnished with the good things which our victory over nature has won for us.

But what is the real fact? Who will dare to deny that the great mass of civilised men are poor? So poor are they that it is mere childishness troubling ourselves to discuss whether perhaps they are in some ways a little better off than their forefathers. They are poor; nor can their poverty be measured by the poverty of a resourceless savage, for he knows of nothing else than his poverty; that he should be cold, hungry, houseless, dirty, ignorant, all that is to him as natural as that he should have a skin. But for us, for the most of us, civilisation has bred desires which she forbids us to satisfy, and so is not merely a niggard but a torturer also.

Thus then have the fruits of our victory over nature been stolen from us, thus has compulsion by nature to labour in hope of rest, gain, and pleasure been turned into compulsion by man to labour in hope—of living to labour!

What shall we do then, can we mend it?

Well, remember once more that it is not our remote ancestors who achieved the victory over nature, but our fathers, nay, our very selves. For us to sit hopeless and helpless then would be a strange folly indeed: be sure that we can amend it. What, then, is the first thing to be done?

We have seen that modern society is divided into two classes, one of which is *privileged* to be kept by the labour of the other—that is, it forces the other to work for it and takes from this inferior class everything that it *can* take from it, and uses the wealth so taken to keep its own members in a superior position, to make them beings of a higher order than the others: longer lived, more beautiful, more honoured, more refined than those of the other class. I do not say that it troubles itself about its members being *positively* long lived, beautiful or refined, but merely insists that they shall be so *relatively* to the inferior class. As also it cannot use the labour-power of the inferior class fairly in producing real wealth it wastes it wholesale in the production of rubbish.

It is this robbery and waste on the part of the minority which keeps the majority poor; if it could be shown that it is necessary for the preservation of society that this should be submitted to, little more could be said on the matter, save that the despair of the oppressed majority would probably at some time or other destroy Society. But it has been shown, on the contrary, even by such incomplete experiments, for instance, as Co-operation (so-called) that the existence of a privileged class is by no means necessary for the production of wealth, but rather for the 'government' of the producers of wealth, or, in other words, for the upholding of privilege.

The first step to be taken then is to abolish a class of men privileged to shirk their duties as men, thus forcing others to do the work which they refuse to do. All must work according to their ability, and so produce what they consume—that is, each man should work as well as he can for his own livelihood, and his livelihood should be assured to him; that is to say, all the advantages which society would provide for each and all of its members.

Thus, at last, would true Society be founded. It would rest on equality of condition. No man would be tormented for the benefit of another—nay, no one man would be tormented for the benefit of Society. Nor, indeed, can that order be called Society which is not upheld for the benefit of every one of its members.

But since men live now, badly as they live, when so many people do not produce at all, and when so much work is wasted, it is clear that, under conditions where all produced and no work was wasted, not only would everyone work with the certain hope of gaining a due share of wealth by his work, but also he could not miss his due share of rest. Here, then, are two out of the three kinds of hope mentioned above as an essential part of worthy work assured to the worker. When class robbery is abolished, every man will reap the fruits of his labour, every man will have due rest—leisure, that is. Some Socialists might say we need not go any further than this; it is enough that the worker should get the full produce of his work, and that his rest should be abundant. But though the compulsion of man's tyranny is thus abolished, I yet demand compensation for the compulsion of nature's necessity. As long as the work is repulsive, it will still be a burden which must be taken up daily, and even so would mar our life, though it be not of long daily duration. What we want to do is to add to our wealth without diminishing our pleasure. Nature will not be finally conquered till our work becomes a part of the pleasure of our lives.

That first step of freeing people from the compulsion to labour needlessly will at least put us on the way towards this happy end; for we shall then have time and opportunities for bringing it about. As things are now, between the waste of labour-power in mere idleness and its waste in unproductive work, it is clear that the world of civilisation is supported by a small part of its people; when *all* were working *usefully* for its support, the share of work which each would have to do would be but small, if our standard of life were about on the footing of what well-to-do and refined people now think desirable. We shall have labour-power to spare, and shall, in short, be as wealthy as we please. It will be easy to live. If we were to wake up some morning now, under our present system, and find it 'easy to live', that system would force us to set to work at once and make it hard to live; we should call that 'developing our resources', or some such fine name. The multiplication of labour has become a necessity for us, and as long as that goes on no ingenuity in the invention of machines will be of any real use to us. Each new machine will cause a certain amount of misery among the workers whose special industry it may disturb; so many of them will be reduced from skilled to unskilled workmen, and then gradually matters will slip into their due grooves, and all will work apparently smoothly again; and if it were not that all this is preparing revolution, things would be, for the greater part of men, just as they were before the new wonderful invention.

But when revolution has made it 'easy to live', when all are working harmoniously together and there is no one to rob the worker of his time, that is to say his life; in those coming days there will be no compulsion on us to go on producing things we do not want, no compulsion on us to labour for nothing, we shall be able calmly and thoughtfully to consider what we shall do with our wealth of labour-power. Now, for my part, I think the first use we ought to make of that wealth, of that freedom, should be to make all our labour, even the commonest and most necessary, pleasant to everybody; for thinking over the matter carefully, I can see that the one course which will certainly make life happy in the face of all accidents and troubles is to take a pleasurable interest in all the details of life. And lest perchance you think that an assertion too universally accepted to be worth making, let me remind you how entirely modern civilisation forbids it; with what sordid, and even terrible, details it surrounds the life of the poor, what a mechanical and empty life she forces on the rich; and how rare a holiday it is for any of us to feel ourselves a part of nature, and unhurriedly, thoughtfully, and happily to note the course of our lives amidst all the little links of events which connect them with the lives of others, and build up the great whole of humanity.

But such a holiday our whole lives might be, if we were resolute to make all our labour reasonable and pleasant. But we must be resolute, indeed; for no half measures will help us here. It has been said already that our present joyless labour, and our lives scared and anxious as the life of a hunted beast are forced upon us by the present system of producing for the profit of the privileged classes. It is necessary to state what this means. Under the present system of wages and capital the 'manufacturer' (most absurdly so-called, since a manufacturer means a person who makes with his hands) having a monopoly of the means whereby the power to labour inherent in every man's body can be used for production, is the master of those who are not so privileged; he, and he alone, is able to make use of this labour-power, which, on the other hand, is the only commodity by means of which his 'capital', that is to say the accumulated product of past labour, can be made productive.

He therefore buys the labour-power of those who are bare of capital and can only live by selling it to him; his purpose in this transaction is to increase his capital, to make it breed. It is clear that if he paid those with whom he makes his bargain the full value of their labour, that is to say all that they produced, he would fail in his purpose. But since he is the monopolist of the means of productive labour, he can *compel* them to make a bargain better for him and worse for them than that; which bargain is that after they have earned their livelihood, estimated according to a standard high enough to ensure their peaceable submission to his mastership, the rest (and by far the larger part as a matter of fact) of what they produce shall belong to him, shall be his *property* to do as he likes with, to use or abuse at his pleasure; which property is, as we all know, jealously guarded by army and navy, police and prison; in short, by that huge mass of physical force which superstition, habit, fear of death by starvation—IGNORANCE, in one word, among the propertyless masses enables the propertied classes to use for the subjection of—their slaves.

Now at other times, other evils resulting from this system may be put forward. What I want to point out now is the impossibility of our attaining to attractive labour under this system, and to repeat that it is this robbery (there is no other word for it) which wastes the available labour-power of the civilised world, forcing many men to do nothing, and many, very many more to do nothing useful; and forcing those who carry on really useful labour to most burdensome overwork. For understand once for all that the 'manufacturer' aims primarily at producing, by means of the labour he has stolen from others, not goods but profits, that is, the 'wealth' that is produced over and above the livelihood of his workmen. Whether that 'wealth' is real or sham matters nothing to him. If it sells and yields him a 'profit' it is all right. I have said that, owing to there being rich people who have more money than they can spend reasonably, and who therefore buy sham wealth, there is waste on that side; and also that, owing to there being poor people who cannot afford to buy things which are worth making, there is waste on that side. So that the 'demand' which the capitalist 'supplies' is a false demand. The market in which he sells is 'rigged' by the miserable inequalities produced by the robbery of the system of Capital and Wages.

It is this system, therefore, which we must be resolute in getting rid of, if we are to attain to happy and useful work for all. The first step towards making labour attractive is to get the means of making labour fruitful, the Capital, including the land, machinery, factories, etc., into the hands of the community, to be used for the good of all alike, so that we might all work at 'supplying' the real 'demands' of each and all—that is to say, work for livelihood, instead of working to supply the demand for the profit market—instead of working for profit,—*i.e.*, the power of compelling other men to work against their will.

When this first step has been taken and men begin to understand that nature wills all men either to work or starve, and when they are no longer such fools as to allow some the alternative of stealing, when this happy day is come, we shall then be relieved from the tax of waste, and consequently shall find that we have, as aforesaid, a mass of labour-power available, which will enable us to live as we please within reasonable limits. We shall no longer be hurried and driven by the fear of starvation, which at present presses no less on the greater part of men in civilised communities than it does on mere savages. The first and most obvious necessities will be so easily provided for in a community in which there is no waste of labour, that we shall have time to look round and consider what we really do want, that can be obtained without over-taxing our energies; for the often-expressed fear of mere idleness falling upon us when the force supplied by the present hierarchy of compulsion is withdrawn, is a fear which is but generated by the burden of excessive and repulsive labour, which we most of us have to bear at present.

I say once more that, in my belief, the first thing which we shall think so necessary as to be worth sacrificing some idle time for, will be the attractiveness of labour. No very heavy sacrifice will be required for attaining this object, but some *will* be required. For we may hope that men who have just waded through a period of strife and revolution will be the last to put up long with a life of mere utilitarianism, though Socialists are sometimes accused by ignorant persons of aiming at such a life. On the other hand, the ornamental part of modern life is already rotten to the core, and must be utterly swept away before the new order of things is realised. There is nothing of it—there is nothing which could come of it that could satisfy the aspirations of men set free from the tyranny of commercialism.

We must begin to build up the ornamental part of life—its pleasures, bodily and mental, scientific and artistic, social and individual—on the basis of work undertaken willingly and cheerfully, with the consciousness of benefiting ourselves and our neighbours by it. Such absolutely necessary work as we should have to do would in the first place take up but a small part of each day, and so far would not be burdensome; but it would be a task of daily recurrence, and therefore would spoil our day's pleasure unless it were made at least endurable while it lasted. In other words, all labour, even the commonest, must be made attractive.

How can this be done?—is the question the answer to which will take up the rest of this paper. In giving some hints on this question, I know that, while all Socialists will agree with many of the suggestions made, some of them may seem strange and venturesome. These must be considered as being given without any intention of dogmatising, and as merely expressing my own personal opinion.

From all that has been said already it follows, that labour, to be attractive, must be directed towards some obviously useful end, unless in cases where it is undertaken voluntarily by each individual as a pastime. This element of obvious usefulness is all the more to be counted on in sweetening tasks otherwise irksome, since social morality, the responsibility of man towards the life of man, will, in the new order of things, take the place of theological morality, or the responsibility of man to some abstract idea. Next, the day's work will be short. This need not be insisted on. It is clear that with work unwasted it *can* be short. It is clear also that much work which is now a torment, would be easily endurable if it were much shortened.

Variety of work is the next point, and a most important one. To compel a man to do day after day the same task, without any hope of escape or change, means nothing short of turning his life into a prison-torment. Nothing but the tyranny of profit-grinding makes this necessary. A man might easily learn and practice at least three crafts, varying sedentary occupation with outdoor—occupation calling for the exercise of strong bodily energy for work in which the mind had more to do. There are few men, for instance, who would not wish to spend part of their lives in the most necessary and pleasantest of all work—cultivating the earth. One thing which will make this variety of employment possible will be the form that education will take in a socially-ordered community. At present all education is directed towards the end of fitting people to take their places in the hierarchy of commerce—these as masters, those as workmen. The education of the masters is more ornamental than that of the workmen, but it is commercial still; and even at the ancient universities learning is but little regarded, unless it can in the long run be made to *pay*. Due education is a totally different thing from this, and concerns itself in finding out what different people are fit for, and helping them along the road which they are inclined to take. In a duly-ordered society, therefore, young people would be taught such handicrafts as they had a turn for as a part of their education, the discipline of their minds and bodies; and adults would also have opportunities of learning in the same schools, for the development of individual capacities would be of all things chiefly aimed at by education, instead, as now, the subordination of all capacities to the great end of 'money-making' for oneself—or one's master. The amount of talent, and even genius, which the present system crushes, and which would be drawn out by such a system, would make our daily work easy and interesting.

Under this head of variety I will note one product of industry which has suffered so much from commercialism that it can scarcely be said to exist, and is, indeed, so foreign from our epoch that I fear there are some who will find it difficult to understand what I have to say on the subject, which I nevertheless must say, since it is really a most important one. I mean that side of art which is, or ought to be, done by the ordinary workman while he is about his ordinary work, and which has got to be called, very properly, Popular Art. This art, I repeat, no longer exists now, having been killed by commercialism. But from the beginning of man's contest with nature till the rise of the present capitalistic system, it was alive, and generally flourished. While it lasted, everything that was made by man was adorned by man, just as everything made by nature is adorned by her. The craftsman, as he fashioned the thing he had under his hand, ornamented it so naturally and so entirely without conscious effort, that it is often difficult to distinguish where the mere utilitarian part of his work ended and the ornamental began. Now the origin of this art was the necessity that the workman felt for variety in his work, and though the beauty produced by this desire was a great gift to the world, yet the obtaining variety and pleasure in the work by the workman was a matter of more importance still, for it stamped all labour with the impress of pleasure. All this has now quite disappeared from the work of civilisation. If you wish to have ornament, you must pay specially for it, and the workman is compelled to produce ornament, as he is to produce other wares. He is compelled to pretend happiness in his work, so that the beauty produced by man's hand, which was once a solace to his labour, has now become an extra burden on him, and ornament is now but one of the follies of useless toil, and perhaps not the least irksome of its fetters.

Besides the short duration of labour, its conscious usefulness, and the variety which should go with it, there is another thing needed to make it attractive, and that is pleasant surroundings. The misery and squalor which we people of civilisation bear with so much complacency as a necessary part of the manufacturing system, is just as necessary to the community at large as a proportionate amount of filth would be in the house of a private rich man. If such a man were to allow the cinders to be raked all over his drawing-room, and a privy to be established in each corner of his dining room, if he habitually made a dust and refuse heap of his once beautiful garden, never washed his sheets or changed his table-cloth, and made his family sleep five in a bed, he would surely find himself in the claws of a commission *de lunatico*. But such acts of miserly folly are just what our present society is doing daily under the compulsion of a supposed necessity, which is nothing short of madness. I beg you to bring your commission of lunacy against civilisation without more delay.

For all our crowded towns and bewildering factories are simply the outcome of the profit system. Capitalistic manufacture, capitalistic land-owning and capitalistic exchange force men into big cities in order to manipulate them in the interests of capital; the same tyranny contracts the due space of the factory so much that (for instance) the interior of a great weaving-shed is almost as ridiculous a spectacle as it is a horrible one. There is no other necessity for all this, save the necessity for grinding profits out of men's lives, and of producing cheap goods for the use (and subjection) of the slaves who grind. All labour is not yet driven into factories; often where it is there is no necessity for it, save again the profit-tyranny. People engaged in all such labour need by no means be compelled to pig together in close city quarters. There is no reason why they should not follow their occupations in quiet country homes, in industrial colleges, in small towns, or, in short, where they find it happiest for them to live.

As to that part of labour which must be associated on a large scale, this very factory-system, under a reasonable order of things (though to my mind there might still be drawbacks to it), would at least offer opportunities for a full and eager social life surrounded by many pleasures. The factories might be centres of intellectual activity also, and work in them might well be varied very much: the tending of the necessary machinery might to each individual be but a short part of the day's work. The other work might vary from raising food from the surrounding country to the study and practice of art and science. It is a matter of course that people engaged in such work, and being the masters of their own lives, would not allow any hurry or want of foresight to force them into enduring dirt, disorder, or want of room. Science duly applied would enable them to get rid of refuse, to minimise, if not wholly to destroy, all the inconveniences which at present attend the use of elaborate machinery, such as smoke, stench and noise; nor would they endure that the buildings in which they worked or lived should be ugly blots on the fair face of the earth. Beginning by making their factories, buildings and sheds decent and convenient like their homes, they would infallibly go on to make them not merely negatively good, inoffensive merely, but even beautiful, so that the glorious art of architecture, now for some time slain by commercial greed, would be born again and flourish.

So, you see, I claim that work in a duly-ordered community should be made attractive by the consciousness of usefulness, by its being carried on with intelligent interest, by variety, and by its being exercised amidst pleasurable surroundings. But I have also claimed, as we all do, that the day's work should not be wearisomely long. It may be said, 'How can you make this last claim square with the others? If the work is to be so refined, will not the goods made be very expensive?'

I do admit, as I have said before, that some sacrifice will be necessary in order to make labour attractive. I mean that, if we *could* be contented in a free community to work in the same hurried, dirty, disorderly, heartless way as we do now, we might shorten our day's labour very much more than I suppose we shall do, taking all kinds of labour into account. But if we did, it would mean that our new-won freedom of condition would leave us as anxious, listless and wretched as we are now, which I hold is simply impossible. We should be contented to make the sacrifices necessary for raising our condition to the standard called out for as desirable by the whole community. Nor only so. We should, individually, be emulous to sacrifice quite freely still more of our time and our ease towards the raising of the standard of life. Persons, either by themselves or associated for such purposes, would freely, and for the love of the work and for its results—stimulated by the hope of the pleasure of creation—produce those ornaments of life for the service of all, which they are now bribed to produce (or pretend to produce) for the service of a few rich men. The experiment of a civilised community living wholly without art or literature has not yet been tried. The past degradation and corruption of civilisation may force this denial of pleasure upon the society which will arise from its ashes. If that must be, we will accept the passing phase of utilitarianism as a foundation for the art which is to be. If the cripple and the starveling disappear from our streets, if the earth nourish us all alike, if the sun shine for all of us alike, if to one and all of us the glorious drama of the earth—day and night, summer and winter—can be presented as a thing to understand and love, we can afford to wait awhile till we are purified from the shame of the past corruption, and till art arises again amongst people freed from the terror of the slave and the shame of the robber.

Meantime, in any case, the refinement, thoughtfulness and deliberation of labour must indeed be paid for, but not by compulsion to labour long hours. Our epoch has invented machines which would have appeared wild dreams to the men of past ages, and of those machines we have as yet *made no use*.

They are called 'labour-saving' machines—that phrase commonly used implies what we expect of them; but we do not get what we expect. What they really do is to reduce the skilled labourer to the ranks of the unskilled, to increase the number of the 'reserve army of labour',—that is to increase the precariousness of life among the workers and to intensify the labour of those who serve the machines (as slaves their masters). All this they do by the way, while they pile up the profits of the employers of labour or force them to expend those profits in bitter commercial war with each other. In a true society these miracles of ingenuity would be for the first time used for minimising the amount of time spent in unattractive labour, which by their means might be so reduced as to be but a very light burden on each individual. All the more as these machines would most certainly be very much improved when it was no longer a question as to whether their improvement would 'pay' the individual, but rather whether it would benefit the community.

So much for the ordinary use of machinery, which would probably, after a time, be somewhat restricted when men found out that there was no need for anxiety as to mere subsistence, and learned to take an interest and pleasure in handiwork which, done deliberately and thoughtfully, could be made more attractive than machine work.

Again, as people freed from the daily terror of starvation find out what they really wanted, being no longer compelled by anything but their own needs, they would refuse to produce the mere inanities which are now called luxuries, or the poison and trash now called cheap wares. No one would make plush breeches when there were no flunkies to wear them, nor would anybody waste his time over making oleo-margerine when no one was *compelled* to abstain from real butter. Adulteration laws are only needed in a society of thieves—and in such a society they are a dead letter.

Socialists are often asked how work of the rougher and more repulsive kind could be carried out in the new condition of things. To attempt to answer such questions fully or authoritatively would be attempting the impossibility of constructing a scheme of a new society out of the materials of the old, before we knew which of those materials would disappear and which endure through the evolution which is leading us to the great change. Yet it is not difficult to conceive of some arrangement whereby those who did the roughest work, should work for the shortest spells. And again, what is said above of the variety of work applies specially here. Once more I say, that for a man to be the whole of his life hopelessly engaged in performing one repulsive and never-ending task, is an arrangement fit enough for the hell imagined by theologians, but scarcely fit for any other form of society. Lastly, if this rougher work were of any special kind we may suppose that special volunteers would be called on to perform it, who would surely be forthcoming, unless men in a state of freedom should lose the sparks of manliness which they possessed as slaves.

And yet if there be any work which cannot be made other than repulsive, either by the shortness of its duration or the intermittency of its recurrence, or by the sense of special and peculiar usefulness (and therefore honour) in the mind of the man who performs it freely. If there be any work which cannot be but a torment to the worker, what then? Well, then, let us see if the heavens will fall on us if we leave it undone, for it were better if they should. The produce of such work cannot be worth the price of it.

Now we have seen that the semi-theological dogma that all labour under any circumstances, is a blessing to the labourer, is hypocritical and false; that on the other hand labour is good when due hope of rest and pleasure accompanies it. We have weighed the work of civilisation in the balance and found it wanting, since hope is mostly lacking to it, and therefore we see that civilisation has bred a dire curse for men. But we have seen also that the work of the world might be carried on in hope and with pleasure if it were not wasted by folly and tyranny, by the perpetual strife of opposing classes.

It is Peace, therefore, which we need in order that we may live and work in hope and with pleasure. Peace so much desired, if we may trust men's words, but which has been so continually and steadily rejected by them in deeds. But for us, let us set our hearts on it and win it at whatever cost.

What the cost may be, who can tell? Will it be possible to win peace peaceably? Alas, how can it be? We are so hemmed in by wrong and folly, that in one way or other we must always be fighting against them: our own lives may see no end to the struggle, perhaps no obvious hope of the end. It may be that the best we can hope to see is that struggle getting sharper and bitterer day by day, until it breaks out openly at last into the slaughter of men by actual warfare instead of by the slower and crueller methods of 'peaceful' commerce. If we live to see that, we shall live to see much; for it will mean the rich classes grown conscious of their own wrong and robbery, and consciously defending them by open violence; and then the end will be drawing near.

But in any case, and whatever the nature of our strife for peace may be, if we only aim at it steadily and with singleness of heart, and even keep it in view, a reflection from that peace of the future will illumine the turmoil and trouble of our lives, whether the trouble be seemingly petty, or obviously tragic; and we shall, in our hopes at least, live the lives of men: nor can the present times give us any reward greater than that.

FATHER DAMIEN

This pamphlet may be considered somewhat 'out of series' in so far as it is concerned with a personal matter, and not with the social and political problems discussed by our other pamphleteers. As we observed, even *Non Mi Ricordo* had a political as well as a personal objective.

We have here, however, one of the best examples in the late nineteenth century of the pamphlet as the only possible vehicle for expressing a point of view. Stevenson, who could (normally speaking) have commanded the willing attention of any editor or publisher, had something to say which was urgent; yet there was every reason to doubt whether any periodical would accept it, because, on the author's own admission, it was libellous. Similar reasons would have weighed against publication in book form—but that was out of the question, anyway, on grounds of length. And Stevenson had no intention of losing time while a collection of essays could be prepared for the press, in which this vital challenge to Dr. Hyde would obviously have been lost. Every circumstance indicated the imperative need for immediate publication in pamphlet form—and the reason for this urgency can best be understood by reading the pamphlet itself, which fully explains its own occasion.

The fact that *Father Damien* was frequently republished later in no way conflicts with these statements. It was only when Stevenson had met with impunity after the first publication, in pamphlet form, that the daring libel was allowed to take its place among the more respectable works of R. L. S. How well Stevenson knew the explosive contents of his attack on Dr. Hyde, and the possible consequences to himself and his family, is clearly brought out in his own account of the decision to publish: 'I thought he would bring an action; I made sure I should be ruined; I asked leave of my gallant family, and the sense that I was signing away all I possessed kept me up to high-water mark, and made me feel every insult heroic'. (Letter quoted in Balfour's *Life of Robert Louis Stevenson*.)

Accordingly the 'Open Letter' was privately published at Sydney in March 1890. Among subsequent reprints, one will be found in the collection of essays entitled *Lay Morals*, but we knew no edition of this pamphlet in print since 1937 when we were making our selection, which seemed an additional reason for including it. In later years Stevenson, a kindly man by nature, felt that in his defence of Father Damien he had struck too hard at Damien's traducer. Whatever may be the truth about that, the generous source of his anger would have made it impossible for anyone but Stevenson himself to condemn the pamphlet on those grounds. And apart from all other considerations, this 'Open Letter' deserves a place in any selection of nineteenth century pamphlets for its literary merit alone.

J. V. Farrow, in *Damien the Leper*, has some interesting comments on this pamphlet and on the one small error of fact which is contained in it.

FATHER DAMIEN: AN OPEN LETTER TO THE REVEREND DR. HYDE OF HONOLULU

By Robert Louis Stevenson

Sydney,
February 25, 1890.

Sir,

IT may probably occur to you that we have met, and visited, and conversed; on my side, with interest. You may remember that you have done me several courtesies, for which I was prepared to be grateful. But there are duties which come before gratitude, and offences which justly divide friends, far more acquaintances. Your letter to the Reverend H. B. Gage is a document which, in my sight, if you had filled me with bread when I was starving, if you had sat up to nurse my father when he lay a-dying, would yet absolve me from the bonds of gratitude. You know enough, doubtless, of the process of canonisation to be aware that, a hundred years after the death of Damien, there will appear a man charged with the painful office of the *devil's advocate*. After that noble brother of mine, and of all frail clay, shall have lain a century at rest, one shall accuse, one defend him. The circumstance is unusual that the devil's advocate should be a volunteer, should be a member of a sect immediately rival, and should make haste to take upon himself his ugly office ere the bones are cold; unusual, and of a taste which I shall leave my readers free to qualify; unusual, and to me inspiring. If I have at all learned the trade of using words to convey truth and to arouse emotion, you have at last furnished me with a subject. For it is in the interest of all mankind, and the cause of public decency in every quarter of the world, not only that Damien should be righted, but that you and your letter should be displayed at length, in their true colours, to the public eye.

To do this properly, I must begin by quoting you at large: I shall then proceed to criticise your utterance from several points of view, divine and human, in the course of which I shall attempt to draw again, and with more specification, the character of the dead saint whom it has pleased you to vilify: so much being done, I shall say farewell to you for ever.

'Honolulu,
'*August* 2, 1889.

'Rev. H. B. GAGE.

'DEAR BROTHER,—In answer to your inquiries about Father Damien, I can only reply that we who knew the man are surprised at the extravagant newspaper laudations, as if he was a most saintly philanthropist. The simple truth is, he was a coarse, dirty man, headstrong and bigoted. He was not sent to Molokai, but went there without orders; did not stay at the leper settlement (before he became one himself), but circulated freely over the whole island (less than half the island is devoted to the lepers), and he came often to Honolulu. He had no hand in the reforms and improvements inaugurated, which were the work of our Board of Health, as occasion required and means were provided. He was not a pure man in his relations with women, and the leprosy of which he died should be attributed to his vices and carelessness. Others have done much for the lepers, our own ministers, the government physicians, and so forth, but never with the Catholic idea of meriting eternal life.—Yours, etc.,

'C. M. HYDE.'[1]

To deal fitly with a letter so extraordinary, I must draw at the outset on my private knowledge of the signatory and his sect. It may offend others; scarcely you, who have been so busy to collect, so bold to publish, gossip on your rivals. And this is perhaps the moment when I may best explain to you the character of what you are to read: I conceive you as a man quite beyond and below the reticences of civility: with what measure you mete, with that shall it be measured you again; with you, at last, I rejoice to feel the button off the foil and to plunge home. And if in aught that I shall say I should offend others, your colleagues, whom I respect and remember with affection, I can but offer them my regret; I am not free, I am inspired by the consideration of interests far more large; and such pain as can be inflicted by anything from me must be indeed trifling when compared with the pain with

---

[1] From the Sydney *Presbyterian*, October 26, 1889.

which they read your letter. It is not the hangman, but the criminal, that brings dishonour on the house.

You belong, sir, to a sect—I believe my sect, and that in which my ancestors laboured—which has enjoyed, and partly failed to utilise, an exceptional advantage in the islands of Hawaii. The first missionaries came; they found the land already self-purged of its old and bloody faith; they were embraced, almost on their arrival, with enthusiasm; what troubles they supported came far more from whites than from Hawaiians; and to these last they stood (in a rough figure) in the shoes of God. This is not the place to enter into the degree or causes of their failure, such as it is. One element alone is pertinent, and must here be plainly dealt with. In the course of their evangelical calling, they—or too many of them—grew rich. It may be news to you that the houses of missionaries are a cause of mocking on the streets of Honolulu. It will at least be news to you, that when I returned your civil visit, the driver of my cab commented on the size, the taste, and the comfort of your home. It would have been news certainly to myself, had any one told me that afternoon that I should live to drag such matter into print. But you see, sir, how you degrade better men to your own level; and it is needful that those who are to judge betwixt you and me, betwixt Damien and the devil's advocate, should understand your letter to have been penned in a house which could raise, and that very justly, the envy and the comments of the passers-by. I think (to employ a phrase of yours which I admire) it 'should be attributed' to you that you have never visited the scene of Damien's life and death. If you had, and had recalled it, and looked about your pleasant rooms, even your pen perhaps would have been stayed.

Your sect (and remember, as far as any sect avows me, it is mine) has not done ill in a worldly sense in the Hawaiian Kingdom. When calamity befell their innocent parishioners, when leprosy descended and took root in the Eight Islands, a *quid pro quo* was to be looked for. To that prosperous mission, and to you, as one of its adornments, God had sent at last an opportunity. I know I am touching here upon a nerve acutely sensitive. I know that others of your colleagues look back on the inertia of your Church, and the intrusive and decisive heroism of Damien, with something almost to be called remorse. I am sure it is so with yourself; I am persuaded your letter was inspired by a certain envy, not essentially ignoble, and the one human trait to be espied in that performance. You were thinking of the lost chance, the past day; of that which should have been conceived and was not; of the service due and not rendered. *Time was*, said the voice in your ear, in your pleasant room, as you sat raging and writing; and if the words written were base beyond parallel, the rage, I am happy to repeat—it is the only compliment I shall pay you—the rage was almost virtuous. But, sir, when we have failed, and another has succeeded; when we have stood by, and another has stepped in; when we sit and grow bulky in our charming mansions, and a plain, uncouth peasant steps into the battle, under the eyes of God, and succours the afflicted, and consoles the dying, and is himself afflicted in his turn, and dies upon the field of honour—the battle cannot be retrieved as your unhappy irritation has suggested. It is a lost battle, and lost for ever. One thing remained to you in your defeat—some rags of common honour; and these you have made haste to cast away.

Common honour; not the honour of having done anything right, but the honour of not having done aught conspicuously foul; the honour of the inert: that was what remained to you. We are not all expected to be Damiens; a man may conceive his duty more narrowly, he may love his comforts better; and none will cast a stone at him for that. But will a gentleman of your reverend profession allow me an example from the fields of gallantry? When two gentlemen compete for the favour of a lady, and the one succeeds and the other is rejected, and (as will sometimes happen) matter damaging to the successful rival's credit reaches the ear of the defeated, it is held by plain men of no pretensions that his mouth is, in the circumstance, almost necessarily closed. Your Church and Damien's were in Hawaii upon a rivalry to do well: to help, to edify, to set divine examples. You having (in one huge instance) failed, and Damien succeeded, I marvel it should not have occurred to you that you were doomed to silence; that when you had been outstripped in that high rivalry, and sat inglorious in the midst of your well-being, in your pleasant room—and Damien, crowned with glories and horrors, toiled and rotted in that pigsty of his under the cliffs of Kalawao—you, the elect who would not, were the last man on earth to collect and propagate gossip on the volunteer who would and did.

I think I see you—for I try to see you in the flesh as I write these sentences—I think I see you leap at the word pigsty, a hyperbolical expression at the best. 'He had no hand in the reforms,' he was 'a coarse, dirty man'; these were your own words; and you may think it possible that I am come to support you with fresh evidence. In a sense, it is even so. Damien has been too much depicted with a conventional halo and conventional features; so drawn by men who perhaps had not the eye to remark or the pen to express the individual; or who perhaps were only blinded and silenced by generous admiration, such as I partly envy for myself—such as you, if your soul were enlightened, would envy on your bended knees. It is the least defect of such a method of portraiture that it makes the path easy for the devil's advocate, and leaves for the misuse of the slanderer a considerable field of truth. For the truth that is suppressed by friends is the readiest weapon of the enemy. The world, in your despite, may perhaps owe you something, if your letter be the means of substituting once for all a credible likeness for a wax abstraction. For, if that world at all remembers you, on the day when Damien of Molokai shall be named Saint, it will be in virtue of one work: your letter to the Reverend H. B. Gage.

You may ask on what authority I speak. It was my inclement destiny to become acquainted, not with Damien, but with Dr. Hyde. When I visited the lazaretto, Damien was already in his resting grave. But such information as I have, I gathered on the spot in conversation with those who knew him well and long: some indeed who revered his memory but others who had sparred and wrangled with him, who beheld him with no halo, who perhaps regarded him with small respect, and through whose unprepared and scarcely partial communications the plain, human features of the man shone on me convincingly. These gave me what knowledge I possess; and I learnt it in that scene where it could be most completely and sensitively understood—Kalawao, which you have never visited, about which you have never so much as endeavoured to inform yourself; for, brief as your letter is, you have found the means to stumble into that confession. '*Less than one-half* of the island,' you say, 'is devoted to the lepers.' Molokai—'*Molokai ahina*,' the 'grey', lofty, and most desolate island—along all its northern side plunges a front of precipice into a sea of unusual profundity. This range of cliff is, from east to west, the true end and frontier of the island. Only in one spot there projects into the ocean a certain triangular and rugged down, grassy, stony, windy, and rising in the midst into a hill with a dead crater: the whole bearing to the cliff that overhangs it somewhat the same relation as a bracket to a wall. With this hint you will now be able to pick out the leper station on a map; you will be able to judge how much of Molokai is thus cut off between the surf and precipice, whether less than a half, or less than a quarter, or a fifth, or a tenth—or, say, a twentieth; and the next time you burst into print you will be in a position to share with us the issue of your calculations.

I imagine you to be one of those persons who talk with cheerfulness of that place which oxen and wain-ropes could not drag you to behold. You, who do not even know its situation on the map, probably denounce sensational descriptions, stretching your limbs the while in your pleasant parlour on Beretania Street. When I was pulled ashore there one early morning, there sat with me in the boat two sisters, bidding farewell (in humble imitation of Damien) to the lights and joys of human life. One of these wept silently; I could not withhold myself from joining her. Had you been there, it is my belief that nature would have triumphed even in you, and as the boat drew but a little nearer, and you beheld the stairs crowded with abominable deformations of our common manhood, and saw yourself landing in the midst of such a population as only now and then surrounds us in the horror of a nightmare—what a haggard eye you would have rolled over your reluctant shoulder towards the house on Beretania Street. Had you gone on; had you found every fourth face a blot upon the landscape; had you visited the hospital and seen the butt-ends of human beings lying there almost unrecognisable, but still breathing, still thinking, still remembering; you would have understood that life in the lazaretto is an ordeal from which the nerves of a man's spirit shrink, even as his eye quails under the brightness of the sun; you would have felt it was (even today) a pitiful place to visit and a hell to dwell in. It is not the fear of possible infection. That seems a little thing when compared with the pain, the pity, and the disgust of the visitor's surroundings, and the atmosphere of affliction, disease, and physical disgrace in which he breathes. I do not think I am a man more than usually timid; but I never recall the days and nights I spent upon that island promontory (eight days and seven nights), without heartfelt thankfulness that I am somewhere else. I find in my diary that I speak of my stay as a 'grinding experience'; I have once jotted in the margin, '*Harrowing* is the word'; and when the *Mokolii* bore me at last towards the outer world, I kept repeating to myself, with a new conception of their pregnancy, those simple words of the song—

' 'Tis the most distressful country that ever yet was seen.'

And observe; that which I saw and suffered from was a settlement purged, bettered, beautified; the new village built, the hospital and the Bishop-Home excellently arranged; the sisters, the doctor, and the missionaries, all indefatigable in their noble tasks. It was a different place when Damien came there and made his great renunciation, and slept that first night under a tree amidst his rotting brethren: alone with pestilence; and looking forward (with what courage, with what pitiful sinkings of dread, God only knows) to a lifetime of dressing sores and stumps.

You will say, perhaps, I am too sensitive, that sights as painful abound in cancer hospitals, and are confronted daily by doctors and nurses. I have long learned to admire and envy the doctors and the nurses. But there is no cancer hospital so large and populous as Kalawao and Kalaupapa; and in such a matter every fresh case, like every inch of length in the pipe of an organ, deepens the note of the impression; for what daunts the onlooker is that monstrous sum of human suffering by which he stands surrounded. Lastly, no doctor or nurse is called upon to enter once for all the doors of that gehenna; they do not say farewell, they need not abandon hope, on its sad threshold; they but go for a time to their high calling, and can look forward as they go to relief, to recreation, and to rest. But Damien shut-to with his own hand the doors of his own sepulchre.

I shall now extract three passages from my diary at Kalawao.

A. 'Damien is dead and already somewhat ungratefully remembered in the field of his labours and sufferings. "He was a good man, but very officious," says one. Another tells me he had fallen (as other priests so easily do) into something of the way and habits of thought of a Kanaka; but he had the wit to recognise the fact, and the good sense to laugh at, [over] it. A plain man it seems he was; I cannot find he was a popular.'

B. 'After Ragsdale's death' [Ragsdale was a famous Luna, or over-seer, of the unruly settlement] 'there followed a brief term of office by Father Damien which served only to publish the weakness of that noble man. He was rough in his ways, and he had no control. Authority was relaxed; Damien's life was threatened, and he was soon eager to resign.'

C. 'Of Damien I begin to have an idea. He seems to have been a man of the peasant class, certainly of the peasant type: shrewd, ignorant and bigoted, yet with an open mind, and capable of receiving and digesting a reproof if it were bluntly administered; superbly generous in the least thing as well as in the greatest, and as ready to give his last shirt (although not without human grumbling) as he had been to sacrifice his life; essentially indiscreet and officious, which made him a troublesome colleague; domineering in all his ways, which made him incurably unpopular with the Kanakas, but yet destitute of real authority, so that his boys laughed at him and he must carry out his wishes by the means of bribes. He learned to have a mania for doctoring; and set up the Kanakas against the remedies of his regular rivals: perhaps (if anything matter at all in the treatment of such a disease) the worst thing that he did, and certainly the easiest. The best and worst of the man appear very plainly in his dealings with Mr. Chapman's money; he had originally laid it out' [intended to lay it out] 'entirely for the benefit of

Catholics, and even so not wisely; but after a long, plain talk, he admitted his error fully and revised the list. The sad state of the boys' home is in part the result of his lack of control; in part, of his own slovenly ways and false ideas of hygiene. Brother officials used to call it "Damien's Chinatown". "Well," they would say, "your Chinatown keeps growing". And he would laugh with perfect good-nature, and adhere to his errors with perfect obstinacy. So much I have gathered of truth about this plain, noble human brother and father of ours; his imperfections are the traits of his face, by which we know him for our fellow; his martyrdom and his example nothing can lessen or annul; and only a person here on the spot can properly appreciate their greatness.'

I have set down these private passages, as you perceive, without correction; thanks to you, the public has them in their bluntness. They are almost a list of the man's faults, for it is rather these that I was seeking: with his virtues, with the heroic profile of his life, I and the world were already sufficiently acquainted. I was besides a little suspicious of Catholic testimony; in no ill sense, but merely because Damien's admirers and disciples were the least likely to be critical. I know you will be more suspicious still; and the facts set down above were one and all collected from the lips of Protestants who had opposed the father in his life. Yet I am strangely deceived, or they build up the image of a man, with all his weaknesses, essentially heroic, and alive with rugged honesty, generosity, and mirth.

Take it for what it is, rough private jottings of the worst sides of Damien's character, collected from the lips of those who had laboured with and (in your own phrase) 'knew the man';—though I question whether Damien would have said that he knew you. Take it, and observe with wonder how well you were served by your gossips, how ill by your intelligence and sympathy; in how many points of fact we are at one, and how widely our appreciations vary. There is something wrong here; either with you or me. It is possible, for instance, that you, who seem to have so many ears in Kalawao, had heard of the affair of Mr Chapman's money, and were singly struck by Damien's intended wrong-doing. I was struck with that also, and set it fairly down; but I was struck much more by the fact that he had the honesty of mind to be convinced. I may here tell you that it was a long business; that one of his colleagues sat with him late into the night, multiplying arguments and accusations; that the father listened as usual with 'perfect good-nature and perfect obstinacy'; but at the last, when he was persuaded— 'Yes,' said he, 'I am very much obliged to you; you have done me a service; it would have been a theft.' There are many (not Catholics merely) who require their heroes and saints to be infallible; to these the story will be painful; not to the true lovers, patrons, and servants of mankind.

And I take it, this is a type of our division; that you are one of those who have an eye for faults and failures; that you take a pleasure to find and publish them; and that, having found them, you make haste to forget the overvailing virtues and the real success which had alone introduced them to your knowledge. It is a dangerous frame of mind. That you may understand how dangerous, and into what a situation it has already brought you, we will (if you please) go hand-in-hand through the different phrases of your letter, and candidly examine each from the point of view of its truth, its appositeness, and its charity.

Damien was *coarse*.

It is very possible. You make us sorry for the lepers, who had only a coarse old peasant for their friend and father. But you, who were so refined, why were you not there, to cheer them with the lights of culture? Or may I remind you that we have some reason to doubt if John the Baptist were genteel; and in the case of Peter, on whose career you doubtless dwell approvingly in the pulpit, no doubt at all he was a 'coarse, headstrong' fisherman! Yet even in our Protestant Bibles Peter is called Saint.

Damien was *dirty*.

He was. Think of the poor lepers annoyed with this dirty comrade! But the clean Dr. Hyde was at his food in a fine house.

Damien was *headstrong*.

I believe you are right again; and I thank God for his strong head and heart.

Damien was *bigoted*.

I am not fond of bigots myself, because they are not fond of me. But what is meant by bigotry, that we should regard it as a blemish in a priest? Damien believed his own religion with the simplicity of a peasant or a child; as I would I could suppose that you do. For this, I wonder at him some way off; and had that been his only character, should have avoided him in life. But the point of interest in Damien, which has caused him to be so much talked about and made him at last the subject of your pen and mine, was that, in him, his bigotry, his intense and narrow faith, wrought potently for good, and strengthened him to be one of the world's heroes and exemplars.

Damien *was not sent to Molokai, but went there without orders.*

Is this a misreading? or do you really mean the words for blame? I have heard Christ, in the pulpits of our Church, held up for imitation on the ground that His sacrifice was voluntary. Does Dr. Hyde think otherwise?

Damien *did not stay at the settlement, etc.*

It is true he was allowed many indulgences. Am I to understand that you blame the father for profiting by these, or the officers for granting them? In either case, it is a mighty Spartan standard to issue from the house on Beretania Street; and I am convinced you will find yourself with few supporters.

Damien *had no hand in the reforms, etc.*

I think even you will admit that I have already been frank in my description of the man I am defending; but before I take you up upon this head, I will be franker still, and tell you that perhaps nowhere in the world can a man taste a more pleasurable sense of contrast than when he passes from Damien's 'Chinatown' at Kalawao to the beautiful Bishop-Home at Kalaupapa. At this point, in my desire to make all fair for you, I will break my rule and adduce Catholic testimony. Here is a passage from my diary about my visit to the Chinatown, from which you will see how it is (even now) regarded by its own officials: 'We went round all the dormitories, refectories, etc.—dark and dingy enough, with a superficial cleanliness, which he' [Mr Dutton, the lay-brother] 'did not seek to defend. "It is almost decent," said he; "the sisters will make that all right when we get them here".' And yet I gathered it was already better since Damien was dead, and far better than when he was there alone and had his own (not always excellent) way. I have now come far enough to meet you on a common ground of fact; and I tell you that, to a mind not prejudiced by jealousy, all the reforms of the lazaretto, and even those which he most vigorously opposed, are properly the work of Damien. They are the evidence of his success; they are what his heroism provoked from the reluctant and the careless. Many were before him in the field; Mr. Meyer, for instance, of whose faithful work we hear too little: there have been many since; and some had more worldly wisdom, though none had more devotion, than our saint. Before his day, even you will confess, they had effected little. It was his part, by one striking act of martyrdom, to direct all men's eyes on that distressful country. At a blow, and with the price of his life, he made the place illustrious and public. And that, if you will consider largely, was the one reform needful; pregnant of all that should succeed. It brought money; it brought (best individual addition of them all) the sisters; it brought supervision, for public opinion and public interest landed with the man at Kalawao. If ever any man brought reforms, and died to bring them, it was he. There is not a clean cup or towel in the Bishop-Home, but dirty Damien washed it.

Damien *was not a pure man in his relations with women, etc.*

How do you know that? Is this the nature of the conversation in that house on Beretania Street which the cabman envied, driving past? —racy details of the misconduct of the poor peasant priest, toiling under the cliffs of Molokai?

Many have visited the station before me; they seem not to have heard the rumour. When I was there I heard many shocking tales, for my informants were men speaking with the plainness of the laity; and I heard plenty of complaints of Damien. Why was this never mentioned? and how came it to you in the retirement of your clerical parlour?

But I must not even seem to deceive you. This scandal, when I read it in your letter, was not new to me. I had heard it once before; and I must tell you how. There came to Samoa a man from Honolulu; he, in a public-house on the beach, volunteered the statement that Damien had 'contracted the disease from having connection with the female lepers'; and I find a joy in telling you how the report was welcomed in a public-house. A man sprang to his feet; I am not at liberty to give his name, but from what I heard I doubt if you would care to have him to dinner in Beretania Street. 'You miserable little ——' (here is a word I dare not print, it would so shock your ears). 'You miserable little——,' he cried, 'if the story were a thousand times true, can't you see you are a million times a lower —— for daring to repeat it?' I wish it could be told of you that when the report reached you in your house, perhaps after family worship, you had found in your soul enough holy anger to receive it with the same expressions; ay, even with that one which I dare not print; it would not need to have been blotted away, like Uncle Toby's oath, by the tears of the recording angel; it would have been counted to you for your brightest righteousness. But you have deliberately chosen the part of the man from Honolulu, and you have played it with improvements of your own. The man from Honolulu— miserable, leering creature—communicated the tale to a rude knot of beach-combing drinkers in a public-house, where (I will so far agree with your temperance opinions) man is not always at his noblest; and the man from Honolulu had himself been drinking—drinking, we may charitably fancy, to excess. It was to your 'Dear Brother, the Reverend H. B. Gage', that you chose to communicate the sickening story; and the blue ribbon which adorns your portly bosom forbids me to allow you the extenuating plea that you were drunk when it was done. Your 'dear brother'—a brother indeed—made haste to deliver up your letter (as a means of grace, perhaps) to the religious papers; where, after many months, I found and read and wondered at it; and whence I have now reproduced it for the wonder of others. And you and your dear brother have, by this cycle of operations, built up a contrast very edifying to examine in detail. The man whom you would not care to have to dinner, on the one side; on the other, the Reverend Dr. Hyde and the Reverend H. B. Gage: the Apia bar-room, the Honolulu manse.

But I fear you scarce appreciate how you appear to your fellow-men; and to bring it home to you, I will suppose your story to be true. I will suppose—and God forgive me for supposing it—that Damien faltered and stumbled in his narrow path of duty; I will suppose that, in the horror of his isolation, perhaps in the fever of incipient disease, he, who was doing so much more than he had sworn, failed in the letter of his priestly oath—he, who was so much a better man than either you or me, who did what we have never dreamed of daring—he too tasted of our common frailty. 'O, Iago, the pity of it!' The least tender should be moved to tears; the most incredulous to prayer. And all that you could do was to pen your letter to the Reverend H. B. Gage!

Is it growing at all clear to you what a picture you have drawn of your own heart? I will try yet once again to make it clearer. You had a father: suppose this tale were about him, and some informant brought it to you, proof in hand: I am not making too high an estimate of your emotional nature when I suppose you would regret the circumstance? that you would feel the tale of frailty the more keenly since it shamed the author of your days? and that the last thing you would do would be to publish it in the religious press? the man who tried to do what Damien did, is my father, and the father of the man in the Apia bar, and the father of all who love goodness and he was your father too, if God had given you grace to see it.

LABOUR, NATIONALITY AND RELIGION

JAMES CONNOLLY only barely qualifies for inclusion in this series, on the grounds that when he wrote he was still—much against his will—a British subject in law, and the 'Irish Problem' was still a perennial British headache; the latter fact being due entirely to our own obstinacy and not to any wish of the Irish people.

The name of James Connolly, so well known in Ireland, is insufficiently familiar in other countries, for he was not only the greatest and most far-sighted of the Irish leaders in the Easter Week Rising of 1916, but he was a man with a message for the whole world. Superficially he appeared paradoxical—a revolutionary socialist who was also a Catholic, a nationalist who was at the same time a prophet of internationalism. But on analysis of the man and his ideas one finds no contradictions. His Catholicism, as will be seen in the foreword to *Labour, Nationality and Religion*, did not imply an acceptance of any of the reactionary attitudes observable so often in his Church, when it intervened in temporal affairs. On the other hand, his socialist theories were not tied to the blind materialist formulæ of Marxism. As R.M. Fox said of him in his book, *James Connolly, the Forerunner*, 'Connolly believed in the human spirit'—and again: 'He refused to accept any explanation of world affairs that treated men and women as undifferentiated masses'. Like William Morris, and so many of our own early socialists, Connolly based his socialism on a respect for human personality, which is very far from being antagonistic to religion. In Connolly's case this meant that, though he was more than once engaged in controversy with Catholic priests, he never renounced his Catholicism. Indeed, he frequently affirmed it.

Even more clearly, in the case of nationalism and internationalism, Connolly was able to expose the fraud of those 'internationalists' who proposed that a world commonwealth should be built up while imperialism remained. Many 'socialists' in the great imperialist countries —such as Britain—have long been given to deprecating the nationalism of their colonies and semi-colonies as 'reactionary'. Those who shake their heads at colonial nationalist movements are almost invariably keen imperialists themselves, who have not sufficient imagination to see that other peoples may reasonably object to being treated as inferior breeds, and that until equality is established between nations no international community can exist, any more than a community of individuals can exist where some are masters and some slaves.

As distinct from the French, who are perhaps more cynical in their colonial policy, or the Germans, who may have been, in their time, more brutal, the English probably excel in hypocrisy; for (generally speaking) they have always deplored the progressive form of nationalism, which is an expression of the desire of a subject people to be free, and been quite complacent about the worst perversion of nationalism, the domination of other nations, of which our own colonial empire is still an example, completely accepted even by the British Labour Party. Yet it is this very perversion of nationalism (empire) which makes progressive nationalism (colonial revolt) necessary and inevitable. Connolly's teachings on this subject are of vital importance. The Irish, it is true, enjoyed in Connolly's time a great many advantages denied to the subject peoples of the British Empire; but they were conscious of their own distinctive nationality and still suffered economically from the ruthless policy of their English conquerors, which had made them almost a landless nation in their own land. A Catholic people, by a vast majority, they could see in every village the former possessions of their Church in the hands of a few Protestants, while Protestant landlords, of English or Scottish origin, in all parts of the country held lands that had formerly belonged to the Catholic Irish. Indeed, even the landlord system itself had been imported by the conquerors; and here, more than anywhere, the social and national conflicts seemed to find a single point of focus.

Connolly's task was to weld together the social and national—and the religious—forces of revolt. But his socialist doctrines immediately upset the Catholic hierarchy. It is necessary to remember that the position of the Church in Ireland was unusual. Over the greater part of Europe, and in Latin America, it was associated, generally speaking, with reactionary politics; whilst Socialists, on the other hand, had been driven into a position that was at least anti-clerical, even where it was not frankly anti-religious, as was the case in most countries. (Britain was in this matter an interesting exception.) In Ireland, on the other hand, over four-fifths of the people, including the great majority of the poor and landless, were Catholics, and their interests conflicted directly with those of the Protestant Government and a host of Protestant landlords—many of them absentees whose only interest in the country was to extract money from it, as rent for lands that had been stolen in the time of Elizabeth, Cromwell or William of Orange.

In such circumstances the Catholic cause could not help being involved with that of Irish nationalism and—to some extent—with the cause of the tenant versus the landlord. In spite of this the failings of the Church in both matters were remarkable, as Connolly's indictment makes clear. But when it came to considering Socialism, it is only fair to the Catholic Church to point out that the opposition Connolly received was conditioned by events in a much larger theatre. A Church which was at war with socialism in almost every country in Europe could hardly be expected to regard even 'Catholic' Socialism in Ireland without profound suspicion.

Labour, Nationality and Religion was published in 1910. We republish here the foreword only, a startling exposure of the way in which the high dignitaries of the Church and the Catholic gentry so often betrayed the interests of Catholic Ireland. It is a story little known even now, in Ireland, where the Church has benefited very fully from the revolution it did so much to discourage, whilst the social cause for which Connolly lived and died has so far reaped no results—a strange paradox indeed. In Britain the story is equally unfamiliar, Protestant prejudice having been unwilling to admit how much British imperialism in Ireland owed to unpatriotic Catholics, who worked with us almost to the very end to keep down their own countrymen.

The occasion for this pamphlet was that a certain Jesuit, Father Kane, had delivered a series of lectures attacking socialism; and the main body of *Labour, Nationality and Religion* consists of a detailed reply to Father Kane. Able as this was, merely as a piece of controversial writing and an exposition of socialism, quite the most original and devastating part of the pamphlet is the foreword, with its astonishing commentary on the rôle of the Church in Ireland's long struggle for freedom.

When Connolly was executed, after the failure of the insurrection in 1916, not only did Ireland lose her greatest son, but the world lost one of its most profound thinkers in the realm of social philosophy—a self-educated working man who understood history better than any of the professional historians, and could explain its meaning with a lucidity which most literary men might reasonably envy.

LABOUR, NATIONALITY AND RELIGION

FOREWORD

By James Connolly

NOTHING is more conducive to the spread of a movement than the discussions arising out of the efforts of a capable opponent to refute its principles. Out of such discussions arise clearness of thought, and the consequent realisation on the part of both sides to the controversy of the necessity of considering the movement under discussion in the light of its **essential principles** rather than of its accidental accompaniments—the basic ideas of the movement itself rather than the ideas of the men or women who may for the moment be its principal exponents or representatives. Men perish, but principles live. Hence the recent effort of ecclesiastics to put the Socialist movement under the ban of the Catholic Church, despite the wild and reckless nature of the statements by which the end was sought to be attained, has had a good effect in compelling Catholics to examine more earnestly their position as laymen, and the status of the clergy as such, as well as their relative duties toward each other within the Church and toward the world in general. One point of Catholic doctrine brought out as a result of such examination is the almost forgotten and sedulously suppressed one, that the Catholic Church is theoretically a community in which the clergy are but the officers serving the laity in a common worship and service of God, and that should the clergy at any time profess or teach doctrines not in conformity with the true teachings of Catholicity it is not only the right, but it is the absolute duty of the laity to refuse such doctrines and to disobey such teaching. Indeed, it is this saving clause in Catholic doctrine which has again and again operated to protect the Church from the result of the mistaken attempts of the clergy to control the secular activities of the laity. It seems to be unavoidable, but it is entirely regrettable, that clergymen consecrated to the worship of God, and supposed to be patterned after a Redeemer who was the embodiment of service and humility, should in their relation to the laity insist upon service and humility being rendered to them instead of by them. Their Master served all Mankind in patience and suffering; they insist upon all Mankind serving them, and in all questions of the social and political relations of men they require the common laity to bow the neck in a meekness, humility, and submission which the clergy scornfully reject. They have often insisted that the Church is greater than the secular authority, and acted therefore in flat defiance of the secular powers, but they have forgotten or ignored the fact that the laity are a part of the Church, and that therefore the right of rebellion against injustice so freely claimed by the Papacy and the Hierarchy is also the inalienable right of the laity. And history proves that in almost every case in which the political or social aspirations of the laity came into opposition to the will of the clergy the laity represented the best interests of the Church as a whole and of Mankind in general. Whenever the clergy succeeded in conquering political power in any country the result has been disastrous to the interests of religion and inimical to the progress of humanity. From whence we arrive at the conclusion that he serves religion best who insists upon the clergy of the Catholic Church taking their proper position as servants to the laity, and abandoning their attempt to dominate the public, as they have long dominated the private life of their fellow-Catholics.

The 1910 Lenten Discourses[1] of Father Kane, S.J., in Gardiner Street Church, Dublin, serve to illustrate these, our contentions. The Socialists of Ireland are grateful to those who induced such a learned and eloquent orator in their capital city to attempt combating Socialism. Had it been an antagonist less worthy their satisfaction would not have been so great. But they now feel confident that when an opponent so capable, so wide in his reading, so skilled in his presentation, so admirable in his method of attack, and so eloquent in his language, has said his final word upon the question, they may rest satisfied that the best case against their cause has been presented which can ever be forthcoming under similar auspices. In presenting their arguments against the position of the reverend lecturer—as against his reverend co-workers who all over the world are engaged in the same unworthy task of combating this movement for the uplifting of humanity—we desire, in the spirit of our preceding remarks, to place before our readers a

[1] *Socialism*, by Robert Kane, S.J. Catholic Truth Society of Ireland.

brief statement of some of the many instances in which the Catholic laity have been compelled to take political action contrary to the express commands of the Pope and the Catholic Hierarchy, and in which subsequent events or the more enlightened conscience of subsequent ages have fully justified the action of the laity and condemned the action of the clergy:

Most of our readers are aware that the first Anglo-Norman invasion of Ireland, in 1169, an invasion characterised by every kind of treachery, outrage, and indiscriminate massacre of the Irish, took place under the authority of a Bull issued by his Holiness, Pope Adrian IV. Doubt has been cast upon the authenticity of the Bull, but it is certain that neither Adrian nor any of his successors in the Papal chair ever repudiated it.[1]

Every Irish man and woman, most enlightened Englishmen, and practically every foreign nation to-day wish that the Irish had succeeded in preserving their independence against the English king, Henry II., but at a Synod of the Catholic Church, held in Dublin in 1177, according to Rev. P. J. Carew, Professor of Divinity in Maynooth, in his 'Ecclesiastical History of Ireland', the Legate of Pope Alexander III, 'set forth Henry's right to the sovereignty of Ireland in virtue of the Pope's authority, and inculcated the necessity of obeying him **under pain of excommunication**'. The English were not yet eight years in Ireland, the greater part of the country was still closed to them, but already the Irish were being excommunicated for refusing to become slaves.

In Ireland, as in all Catholic countries, a church was a sanctuary in which even the greatest criminal could take refuge and be free from arrest, as the civil authority could not follow upon the consecrated ground. At the Synod of 1177 the Pope, in order to help the English monarch against the Irish, abolished the right of sanctuary in Ireland, and empowered the English to strip the Irish churches, and to hunt the Irish refugees who sought shelter there. The greatest criminals of Europe were safe once they reached the walls of the church, but not an Irish patriot.

In the year 1319, Edward Bruce, brother of Robert the Bruce of Scotland, was invited into Ireland by the Irish chiefs and people to help them in their patriotic war for independence. He accepted the invitation, was joined by vast numbers of the people in arms, and together the Irish and Scotch forces swept the English out of Ulster and Connacht. The English king appealed for help to Pope John XXII,

---

[1] This Pope was an Englishman. Even in the nineteenth century a leading English Catholic (Cardinal Newman) defended his action. [ED.]

and **that Pontiff responded by at once excommunicating all the Irish who were in arms against the English.**

The Battle of the Boyne, fought July 1st, 1690, is generally regarded in Ireland as a disaster for the Irish cause—a disaster which made possible the infliction of two centuries of unspeakable degradation upon the Irish people. Yet that battle was the result of an alliance formed by Pope Innocent XI with William, Prince of Orange, against Louis, King of France. King James of England joined with King Louis to obtain help to save his own throne, and the Pope joined in the League with William to curb the power of France. When the news of the defeat of the Irish at the Boyne reached Rome the Vatican was illuminated by order of the new Pope, Alexander VIII, and special masses offered up in thanksgiving. See Von Ranke's 'History of the Popes', and Murray's 'Irish Revolutionary History'.

Judge Maguire, of San Francisco, California, writing of this period before the Reformation, says truly: 'Under all their Catholic majesties, from Henry II to Henry VIII (nearly 400 years) the Irish people, with the exception of five families, were outlaws. They were murdered at will, like dogs, by their English Catholic neighbours in Ireland, and there was no law to punish the murderers. Yet during all of this unparalleled reign of terror, history fails to show a single instance in which the power of the Catholic Church was ever exerted or suggested by the Pope for the protection of her faithful Irish children'.

The Irish people, as a whole, are proud of the fact that, according to the reported testimony of General Lee of the American army, more than half of the Continental soldiers during the War of the Revolution were from Ireland, yet during that War of Independence, Bishop Troy, the Catholic Bishop of Ossory, ordered the Catholics of his diocese to 'observe a day's fast and to humble himself in prayer that they might avert the **divine wrath provoked by their American fellow-subjects who, seduced by the specious notions of liberty** and other illusive expectations of sovereignty, disclaim any dependence upon Great Britain and endeavour by force of arms to distress their mother country'. Quite recently, in 1909, Professor Monaghan, speaking before the Federation of Catholic Societies in America, declared with the approval of the bishop and clergy that the Catholic Hierarchy of the United States would, if need be, sell the sacred vessels off the altar in defence of the American Republic. **Thus the enlightened opinion of the Catholics of our day condemns the Pastoral of the Catholic bishop of the Revolutionary period; and endorses the action of the Catholics who disregarded it.**

In 1798 an insurrection in favour of an Irish Republic took place in Ireland, assuming most formidable proportions in County Wexford. The insurrection had been planned by the Society of United Irishmen, many of whose leaders were Protestants and Freethinkers. The Catholic Hierarchy and most of the priesthood denounced the society and inculcated loyalty to the Government. The more intelligent of the Catholic masses disregarded these clerical denunciations. In the Memoirs of his life, Miles Byrne, a staunch Catholic patriot and revolutionist, who took part in the insurrection, says: 'The priests did everything in their power to stop the progress of the Association of United Irishmen, particularly poor Father John Redmond, who refused to hear the confession of any of the United Irish, and turned them away from his knees'. Speaking of Father John Murphy, he says he 'was a worthy, simple, pious man, and one of those Roman Catholic priests who used the greatest exertions and exhortations to oblige the people to give up their pikes and fire-arms of every description'. The wisdom of the people and the foolish-ness of the clergy were amply demonstrated by the fact that the soldiers burned Father Murphy's house over his head, and compelled him to take the field as an insurgent. A heroic fight and a glorious martyrdom atoned for his mistake, but the soldierlike qualities he showed in the field were rendered nugatory by the fact that as a priest he had been instrumental in disarming many hundreds of the men whom he after-wards commanded. As an insurgent officer he discovered that his greatest hope lay in the men who had disregarded his commands as a priest, and retained the arms with which to fight for freedom.

Dr. Troy, when Catholic Archbishop of Dublin, was, according to an incident related in the 'Viceroy's Post-Bag' by Mr. Michael MacDonagh, interrogated by the British authorities as to the duty of a priest who discovered in the confessional a plot against the Govern-ment, and answered that, 'If in confession any plot against the existing Government was disclosed to the priest, he (the priest) would be bound to give information to the Government that such plot was in agitation, taking care that nothing could in any way lead to a suspicion of the person from whom, or the means in which, the information had been obtained'. Chief Secretary Wickham, who reports this conversation with the archibshop, goes on to say, 'I then asked him whether such confession so made to the priest, particularly in the case of a crime against the State, was considered as a full atonement so as to entitle the penitent to absolution without a disclosure of such crime being first made to the police or to the Government of the country. To this the Doctor answered very distinctly that he did not consider the confession to the priest alone, under such circumstances, a sufficient atonement, **and that either the priest ought to insist on such confession to the State or to the police being made,** or to enjoin the making of such disclosure subsequent to absolution in like manner as penance is enjoined under similar circumstances'.

There is little doubt in our mind but that Dr. Troy misrepresented Catholic doctrine, but it is noteworthy that a parish priest at Mallow, Co. Cork, ordered a member of the United Irishmen, who had sought him in the confessional, to give information to the authorities of a plot of the Royal Meath Militia to seize the artillery at that point and turn it over to the revolutionists. This priest, Father Thomas Barry, afterwards drew a pension of £100 per year from the Government for his information; his action was, and is, abhorred by the vast mass of the Irish Catholics, but was in strict accord with his duty as laid down by Archbishop Troy.

All impartial historians recognise that the Legislative Act of Union between Great Britain and Ireland was passed

> By perjury and fraud—
> By slaves who sold
> For place or gold
> Their country and their God.

Yet we are informed by Mr. Plowden, a Cathloic historian, that 'a very great preponderance in favour of the Union existed in the Catholic Body, **particularly in their nobility; gentry; and clergy'.** On March 1st, 1800, no less than 32 Orange lodges protested against the Act of Union, but the Catholic Hierarchy endorsed it.

Every year the members of the Irish race scattered throughout the earth celebrate the memory of Robert Emmet, and cherish him in their hearts as the highest ideal of patriot and martyr; but on the occasion of his martyrdom the Catholic Archbishops of Dublin and Armagh presented an address to the Lord Lieutenant, representative of the British Government in Ireland, denouncing Emmet in the strongest possible terms. That this action was in conformity with the position of the whole Catholic Hierarchy was evidenced in 1808, when all the Catholic bishops of Ireland met in Synod on September 14th, and passed the following resolution, as reported in Haverty's 'History of Ireland': 'That the Roman Catholic prelates pledge themselves to adhere to the rules by which they have been **hitherto uniformly guided;** viz., to recommend to his Holiness (for appointment as Irish Roman Catholic bishops) **only such persons as are of unimpeachable loyalty'.**

After Daniel O'Connell and the Catholics of Ireland had wrested

Catholic Emancipation from the British Government they initiated a demand for a Repeal of the Union. Their service to Catholic Emancipation was a proof positive of their Catholic orthodoxy, but at the urgent request of the British Government, Pope Gregory XVI issued a Rescript commanding the priests to abstain from attending the Repeal meetings. O'Connell said this was an illegal interference with the liberties of the clergy, declared he would 'take his religion from Rome, but not his politics', and the Catholic opinion of our day emphatically endorses his attitude and condemns the action of the Pope.

In 1847 the Catholics among the Young Irelanders prepared a memorial to be presented to the Annual Assembly of the Bishops, defending themselves from the charge of infidelity. The Archbishop of Tuam declared he would retire if they were admitted. **They were not admitted.** To-day the memory of the Young Irelanders is held close to the heart of every intelligent Irish man or woman.

During the great Irish famine of 1845-6-7-8-9, the Irish people died in hundreds of thousands of hunger, whilst there was food enough in the country to feed three times the population. When the starving peasantry was called upon to refuse to pay rent to idle landlords, and to rise in revolt against the system which was murdering them, the clergy commanded them to pay their rents, instructed them that they would lose their immortal souls should they refuse to do so, and threw all the weight of their position against the revolutionary movement for the freedom of Ireland. Mr. A. M. Sullivan, an extremely ardent Catholic, writing in 'New Ireland', says of this attitude of the clergy during that crises that 'Their antagonism was fatal to the movement—more surely and infallibly fatal to it than all the powers of the British Crown'.

The Irish revolutionary movement known popularly as the Fenian Brotherhood was denounced by all the Catholic Hierarchy and most of the clergy, Bishop Moriarty of County Kerry saying that 'Hell was not hot enough nor eternity long enough to punish such miscreants'. The Fenians were represented as being enemies of religion and of morality, yet the three representatives of their cause who died upon the scaffold died with a prayer upon their lips, and Irish men and women the world over to-day make the anniversary of their martyrdom the occasion for a glorification and endorsement of the principles for which they died—a glorification and endorsement in which many of our clergymen participate.

In January, 1871, the Catholic Bishop of Derry denounced the Home Rule movement of Isaac Butt. To-day priests and people agree that the movement led by Isaac Butt was the mildest, most inoffensive movement ever known in Ireland.

The Irish Land League, which averted in 1879 a repetition of the famine horrors of 1847, which broke the back of Irish landlordism, and abolished the worst evils of British rule, was denounced by Archbishop M'Cabe in September, 1879, October, 1880, and October, 1881.

In 1882 the Ladies' Land League, an association of Irish ladies organised for the patriotic and benevolent purpose of raising funds for the relief of distress, of inquiring into cases of eviction, and affording relief to evicted tenants, was denounced by Archbishop M'Cabe as 'immodest and wicked'. After this attack upon the character of patriotic Irish womanhood, Archbishop M'Cabe was created a Cardinal.

On May 11th, 1883, in the midst of the fight of the Irish peasantry to save themselves from landlord tyranny, his Holiness the Pope issued a Rescript **condemning disaffection to the English Government,** and also condemning the testimonial to Charles Stewart Parnell. The Irish people answered by more than doubling the subscription to the testimonial. The leader of that fight of the Irish against their ancient tyrants was Michael Davitt, to whose efforts much of the comparative security of peasant life in Ireland is due. Davitt was denied an audience by the Pope, but at his death priests and people alike united to do tribute to his character and genius.

In 1883, Dr. M'Glynn, a Catholic priest in America, was invited to deliver a lecture for the purpose of raising funds to save from starvation the starving people of the West of Ireland. The Vatican sent a telegram to Cardinal M'Closkey ordering him to 'suspend this priest M'Glynn for preaching in favour of the Irish revolution'. The telegram was signed by Cardinal Simeoni. Afterwards Father M'Glynn was subjected to the sentence of complete excommunication for preaching revolutionary doctrines upon the land question, but after some years the Vatican acknowledged its error and revoked the sentence without requiring the victim to change his principles.

In all the examples covered by this brief and very incomplete retrospective glance into history the instincts of the reformers and revolutionists have been right, the political theories of the Vatican and the clergy unquestionably wrong. The verdict of history as unquestionably endorses the former as it condemns the latter. And intelligent Catholics everywhere accept that verdict. In so far as true religion has triumphed in the hearts of men it has triumphed in spite of not because of, the political activities of the priesthood. That political activity in the past, like the clerical opposition to Socialism at present, was, and is, an attempt to serve God and Mammon—an attempt to combine the service of Him who in His humbleness rode upon an ass, with the service of those who rode roughshod over the hearts and souls and hopes of suffering humanity.

The Capitalist Class rose upon the ruins of Feudal Catholicism; in the countries where it gained power its first act was to decree the confiscation of the estates of the Church. Yet to-day that robber class, conceived in sin and begotten in iniquity, asks the Church to defend it, and from the Vatican downwards the clergy respond to the call. Just as the British Government in Ireland on January 21st, 1623, published a Royal Proclamation banishing all priests from Ireland, and in 1765 [1] established a College at Maynooth, for the education of priests, and found the latter course safer for British rule than the former, so the capitalist class has also learned its lesson and in the hour of danger enlists as its lieutenants and champions the priesthood it persecuted and despised in the hour of its strength. Can we not imagine some cynical supporter of the capitalist class addressing it to-day as the great Catholic orator, Richard Lalor Shiel, addressed the British Government on the occasion of the Maynooth Grant of 1845, and saying in his words:

'You are taking a step in the right direction. You must not take the Catholic clergy into your pay, but you can take the Catholic clergy under your care. . . . Are not lectures at Maynooth cheaper than State prosecutions? Are not professors less costly than Crown Solicitors? Is not a large standing army and a great constabulary force more expensive than the moral police with which by the priesthood of Ireland you can be thriftily and efficaciously supplied?'

[1] Evidently a misprint. The date was 1795. [ED.]

NON-GOVERNMENTAL SOCIETY

IN a previous note we observed the satisfaction which William Morris found in the society of Edward Carpenter, whose way of living seemed to Morris to be so essentially sound.

Edward Carpenter had been curate at one time to Frederick Maurice, a Church of England clergyman who had himself been associated with Kingsley in the Christian Socialist Movement. But the curacy had proved uncongenial to Carpenter, who gave it up in favour of lecturing under the University Extension system. However, it was not until he was able to buy a few acres of land and set up as a market gardener that Carpenter really found what he was looking for—work that gave him health, pleasure, a sense of usefulness and self-fulfilment.

This was in 1882, when Carpenter was a man of thirty-eight. He had already felt the influence of Walt Whitman, and in 1883 was profoundly impressed by reading Thoreau's *Walden* and Hyndman's *England for All*. From that time onwards he developed a connection with the various branches of the socialist movement and with the small anarchist group which was growing up, under the leadership of Kropotkin. He kept aloof, however, from the wrangling among the various sects, and concentrated his attention on practical ways of furthering the co-operative idea, as (for example) by producers' co-operation. Carpenter's conception of Socialism, like that of Morris, was not limited to the communal ownership of the means of production. He too desired much more for humanity than a mere re-organisation and redistribution of material wealth and of leisure. It was culture in the broadest sense that he wanted to be shared by all, and the 'Good Society' for which he worked was to be one where fellowship and loving one's neighbour replaced selfishness and competition as the motives of human action.

In 1911 Carpenter's *Prisons, Police and Punishment* was published. It marked a renewal of the campaign which had been waged, ever since the time of John Howard and Elizabeth Fry, against the English penal system—a campaign which gained new impetus from the imprisonment of the suffragettes and later of the 'Conscientious Objectors' in the first World War. In each case a body of educated people, many of them writers or journalists, was given an opportunity of seeing what happened behind prison walls. In the slow progress of humanity the experience of such prisoners, like that of Edward Gibbon Wakefield before them, helped to bring some small amelioration of the conditions in which delinquents are turned into criminals and criminals are hardened for further enterprise on their release.

Carpenter's contribution struck deeper than most criticisms of the penal system. In its most revolutionary chapter it queried not merely the methods used in the prison, but the prison itself—and not merely the prison but our conception of 'law', a conception of which force is the sanction and the prison system an inseparable part. It was this interesting chapter, entitled *Non-Governmental Society*, which attracted so much interest that it was almost immediately re-issued separately as a pamphlet; and we are fortunate in being able to republish almost the whole of it in this selection, with the kind permission of Edward Carpenter's executors.

William Morris always declared that he was not an anarchist; but his conception of the Socialist Society was much closer to anarchism than he seemed to realise, for his emphasis was always upon right human relationships, and he showed an instinctive distrust of all coercive authority. In Carpenter the anarchist conception was carried still further, and the pages which follow will show how far he had moved in that direction by the year 1911.

NON-GOVERNMENTAL SOCIETY

By Edward Carpenter

P RACTICALLY, every one does admit that Law is an evil; but the defence usually is that it is a necessary evil, that we cannot dispense with it, and that without it disorder, violence and social disruption would ensue.

And yet curiously enough the history of nations and peoples is, on the whole, to contrary effect. Not only have all the early tribes of the world got on and cohered together in order and social amity without any rigid and ponderous system of laws; but even among the peasant peoples of to-day—like the Irish or the Swedes or the Swiss—where they are still living in moderately primitive conditions, we find the same thing. Law and its operations and institutions occupy but small part in their lives. It is true that Custom is strong among all primitive folk, no doubt as a very necessary backbone or framework to their society; but Custom is a very different thing from Law. It is law in its inception—when it is yet in a tentative, rudimentary condition; and however harsh, rigid, or senseless the customs of many savage tribes may be, they are yet easier to alter than when they have become ossified into written Law, with its huge weight of age and ceremony, and the authority of armed men to enforce it.[1]

That human societies can subsist without a considerable amount of Custom we may well doubt; but that they can subsist and maintain themselves in good order and vitality without written law and its institutions there is no reason at all to doubt. And when Custom,

[1] *See* below, p. 19. Spencer and Gillen, in their late book, *The Northern Tribes of Australia*, say that there are no chiefs even or headmen among these people; but the old men constitute an informal council, which punishes 'crime' and the breaking of marriage rules, organizes the ceremonies, and from time to time inaugurates reforms.

among a reasonable and moderately advanced people, leaving behind the barbarities of the savage age, takes on a gentler form, and while exercising considerable pressure on individuals is itself fairly plastic and adaptable to the general movements of society—we seem to see in such pressure a force as far superior to Law as life itself is superior to mere mechanism. A vast amount of our social life to-day in all departments of its activity is ruled by Custom, and some of these customs, like those of 'society' and fashion, have a very powerful sway. There is no *law* for the recovery of betting debts, yet their non-payment is extremely rare.

Of course, accustomed as we are to 'call the policeman' on every emergency, we find it hard to imagine life without this institution; and our life being largely founded on it, it *is* so far necessary, and its removal would cause dislocation. That is, since without the police the present spoliation of the poor would not be possible, and the enormous existing inequalities of wealth and poverty could never have been heaped up—without them the society founded on these artificial inequalities could not well be maintained.[1] But to say that because a certain institution is necessary to build up and retain society in a certain abnormal and unnatural form, therefore society cannot exist without that institution, is the same as to say that because to a Chinese woman of rank foot-bandages are necessary, therefore women generally cannot exist without foot-bandages. We have to realise that our present social forms are as ugly and inhuman as a club foot; and then we shall begin to realise how little necessary are these institutions, like law and police, whose chief concern and office is to retain and defend these forms.

The chief difficulty, then, which arises in people's minds at the thought of a free non-governmental society does not concern its desirability—they are agreed as a rule that it would be desirable—but concerns its practicability. And much of this difficulty is derived from the society of the present. People see, in fact, that an internecine competition for subsistence is the ruling force of life to-day, and the chief incentive to production, and they infer that without government society would dissolve into a mere chaos of plunder on the one hand, and of laziness on the other.[2] It is this difficulty which has first to be removed.

Though it seems a hard thing to say, the outer life of society to-day is

[1] Though, as all more primitive society shows us, small inequalities and such as arise from natural differences of human industry and capacity will always be welcome.

[2] Though it must, to be strictly impartial, be pointed out that this difficulty is chiefly felt by those classes who themselves live on interest and in ornamental idleness.

animated first and foremost by Fear. From the wretched wage-slave, who rises before the break of day, hurries through squalid streets to the dismal sound of the 'hummer', engages for nine, ten, or twelve hours, and for a pittance wage, in monotonous work which affords him no interest, no pleasure; who returns home to find his children gone to bed, has his supper, and, worn out and weary, soon retires himself, only to rise again in the morning and pursue the same deadly round, and who leads a life thus monotonous, inhuman, and devoid of all dignity and reality, simply because he is hounded to it by the dread of starvation;—to the big commercial man, who, knowing that his wealth has come to him through speculation and the turns and twists of the market, fears that it may at any moment take to itself wings by the same means; who feels that the more wealth he has, the more ways there are in which he may lose it, the more cares and anxieties belonging to it; and who to continually make his position secure is, or thinks himself, forced to stoop to all sorts of mean and dirty tricks;—over the great mass of people the same demon spreads its dusky wings. Feverish anxiety is the keynote of their lives. There is no room for natural glad-ness or buoyancy of spirits. You may walk the streets of our great cities, but you will hear no one singing—except for coppers; hardly a ploughboy to-day whistles in the furrow, and in almost every factory (this is a fact) if a workman sang at his work he would be 'sacked'. We are like shipwrecked folk clambering up a cliff. The waves are raging below. Each one clings by handhold or foothold where he may, and in the panic if he push his neighbour from a point of vantage, it is to be regretted certainly, but it cannot be helped.

But such a state of affairs is not normal. Allowing that the struggle for existence in some degree or form is unavoidable, history still, except for rare crises, presents us with no such spectacle of widespread anxiety; the study of native races—whom *we* might consider in a state of destitution—reveals no such dominion of dread. I want the reader to imagine for a moment this burden of fear lifted off the hearts of a whole people; and the result.

Let us imagine for a moment that some good fairy—some trans-cendental Chancellor of the Exchequer—with a stroke of his wand, has assured to us all not only an old age pension, but a decent provision for all our days of the actual necessaries of life (to go no further than that); so that for the future no man could feel any serious or grinding anxiety for his own material safety, or that of his family. What would be the result on our actions?

Perhaps, as many would maintain, nine-tenths of the population would say, 'I'm blessed if I'll ever do another stroke of work'. Like the organ-grinder who came into a little fortune, and who forthwith picked up an axe and fell upon his organ, shouting as he hacked it to pieces, 'You shall neffer play dat tam *Alabama Coon* any more,' we should feel so sick of our present jobs that we should want to turn our backs on them for ever. Very likely, I should say—and rightly enough too; for 'work' in the present day is done under such degrading and miserable conditions by the vast majority of the population that the very best and the most manly thing would be to refuse to continue doing it.

But let us suppose, since a bare living has been assured to us, and we are in no danger of actual starvation, that we all take a good long holiday, and abstain religiously from doing anything. Suppose that we simply twirl our thumbs in idleness for two, three, four, or six months. Still, is it not obvious that at the end of that time nine-tenths of the population would find sheer idleness appallingly dreary, and that they would *set themselves* to work at some thing or other—to produce comforts or conveniences rising above the level of sheer necessity— objects of use or beauty, either for themselves, or for their families and neighbours, or even conceivably for society at large; that, in fact, a spontaneous and free production of goods would spring up, followed of course by a spontaneous and free exchange—a self-supporting society, based not on individual dread and anxiety, but on the common fulness of life and energy?

That people relieved from care do spontaneously set themselves to work is sufficiently shown by the case of the well-to-do classes to-day. For these people, though having *everything* provided for them, and not merely the bare necessities which we have supposed, exhibit the most extraordinary and feverish energy in seeking employment. A few decades of years have been quite sufficient to make them feel the utter failure of picnics as an object in life; and now we are flooded with philanthropic and benevolent societies, leagues, charity organizations, art missions to the poor, vigilance crusades, and other activities, which are simply the expression of the natural energies of the human being seeking an outlet in social usefulness. It is, of course, to be regretted that owing to the very imperfect education of this class their ideas and their capacities of social usefulness should be so limited. However, this is a defect which will no doubt be remedied in the future. All that concerns us here is to see that since the rich, though in many ways ill-adapted by training and circumstance, do spontaneously take up a life of this kind, there is nothing extravagant in supposing that the average man, surrounded by so many unfulfilled needs, might do the same.

And if any one still doubts let him consider the thousands in our large towns to-day who would give their ears to be able to get out and work on the land—not so much from any prospect of making a fortune that way, as from mere love of the life; or who in their spare time cultivate gardens or plots or allotments as a hobby; or the thousands who when the regular day's work is over start some fresh little occupation of their own—some cabinet-making, wood-turning, ornamental iron-work or whatnot; the scores of thousands, in fact, that there are of *natural* gardeners, cabinet-makers, iron-workers, and so forth; and then think how if they were free these folk would sort themselves spontaneously to the work they delighted in.

Thus it appears to be at least *conceivable* that a people not hounded on by compulsion nor kept in subjection by sheer authority, would set itself spontaneously to produce the things which it prized. It does not, of course, at once follow that the result would be perfect order and harmony. But there are a few considerations in the positive direction which I may introduce here.

In the first place, each person would be guided in the selection of his occupation by his own taste and skill, or at any rate would be guided by these to a greater extent than he is to-day; and on the whole would be more likely to find the work for which he was fitted than he is now. The increase in effective output and vitality from this cause alone would be great. While the immense *variety* of taste and skill in human beings would lead to a corresponding variety of spontaneous products.

In the second place, the work done would be useful. It is certain that no man would freely set himself to dig a hole, only to fill it up again— though it is equally certain that a vast amount of the work done to-day is no more useful than that. If a man were a cabinet-maker and made a chest of drawers, either for himself or a neighbour, he would make it so that the drawers would open and shut; but nine-tenths of the chests made on commercial principles are such that the drawers will neither open nor shut. They are not meant to be useful; they are meant to have the semblance of being useful; but they are really made to *sell*. To sell, and by selling yield a profit. And for that purpose they are better adapted if, appearing useful, they turn out really useless, for then the buyer must come again, and so yield another profit to the manufacturer and the merchant. The waste to the community to-day arising from causes of this kind is enormous; but it is of no moment as long as there is profit to a certain class.

Work in a free society would be done because it was useful. It is curious, when you come to think of it, that there is no other conceivable reason why work should be done. And of course I here include what is beautiful under the term useful,—as there is no reason why one should separate what satisfies one human need, like the need of beauty, from another human need, like the need of food. I say the idea of work implies that it is undertaken because the product itself satisfies some human need. But strangely enough in Commerce that is not so. The work is undertaken in order that the product may *sell*, and so yield a profit; that is all. It is of no moment *what* the product is, or whether bad or good, as long as it fulfils this one condition. And so the whole spirit of life and industry in the other society would be so utterly different from that of the present, that it is really difficult for us to compare the results. But it is not difficult to see that if on the principles of freedom there was not so *much* produced in mere quantity, and folk did not (as may indeed be hoped) work so many hours a day as now, still, the goods turned out being sincere and genuine, there would really be far more value shown in a year than on the strictly commercial system.

In the third place, it follows—as William Morris so constantly maintained—that 'work' in the new sense would be a pleasure—one of the greatest pleasures undoubtedly of life; and this one fact would transform its whole character. We cannot say that now. How many are there who take real pleasure and satisfaction in their daily labour? Are they, in each township, to be counted on the fingers? But what is the good of life if its chief element, and that which must always be its chief element, is odious? No, the only true economy is to arrange so that your daily labour shall be itself a joy. Then, and then only, are you on the safe side of life. And, your work being such, its product is sure to become beautiful; that painful distinction between the beautiful and the useful dies out, and everything made is an artistic product. Art becomes conterminous with life.

Thus it will be observed that whereas the present society is founded on a law-enforced system of Private Property, in which, almost necessarily, the covetous hard type of man becomes the large proprietor, and (supported by law and government) is enabled to prey upon the small one; and whereas the result of this arrangement is a bitter and continuous struggle for possession, in which the motive to activity is mainly Fear; we, on the contrary, are disentangling a conception of a society in which Private Property is supported by no apparatus of armed authority, but as far as it exists is a perfectly spontaneous arrangement, in which the main motives to activity are neither Fear nor greed of Gain, but rather Community of life and Interest in life—in which, in fact, you undertake work because you *like* the work, because you feel that you can do it, and because you know that the product will be useful, either to yourself or some one else!

How Utopian it all sounds! How absurdly simple and simple-minded to work because you like the work and desire the product. How delightful if it could be realized, but, of course, how 'unpractical' and impossible.

Yet is it really impossible? From Solomon to Dr. Watts we have been advised to go to the Ant and the Bee for instruction, and lo! they are unpractical and Utopian too. Can anything be more foolish than the conduct of these little creatures, any one of whom will at any moment face death in defence of his tribe? while the Bee is absolutely so ignorant and senseless, that instead of storing up the honey that it has gathered in a little cell of its own, with a nice lock and key, it positively puts it in the common cells, and cannot distinguish it from the stores of the others. Foolish little Bee, the day will surely come when you will bitterly rue your 'unthrifty' conduct, and you will find yourself starving while your fellow-tribesmen are consuming the fruits of your labour.

And the human body itself, that marvellous epitome and mirror of the universe, how about that? Is it not Utopian too? It is composed of a myriad cells, members, organs, compacted into a living unity. A healthy body is the most perfect society conceivable. What does the hand say when a piece of work is demanded of it? Does it bargain first for what reward it is to receive, and refuse to move until it has secured satisfactory terms, or the foot decline to take us on a journey till it knows what special gain is to accrue to *it* thereby? Not so; but each limb and cell does the work which is before it to do, and (such is the Utopian law) the *fact of its doing the work* causes the circulation to flow to it, and it is nourished and fed in proportion to its service. And we have to ask whether the same may not be the law of a healthy human society? Whether the fact of a member doing service (however humble) to the community would not be quite sufficient to ensure his provision by the rest with all that he might need? Whether the community would think of allowing such an one to starve any more than a man would think of allowing his least finger to pine away and die? Whether it is not possible that men would cease to feel any anxiety about the 'reward of their labour'; that they would think first of their work and the pleasure they had in doing it, and would not doubt that the reward would follow?

For indeed the instinct to do anything which is obviously before you to do, which is wanted, and which you *can* do, is very strong in human nature. Even children, those rudimentary savages, are often extremely proud to be 'useful', and it is conceivable that we might be sensible enough, instead of urging them as we do now to 'get on', to make money, to beat their fellows in the race of life, and by climbing on other folk's heads to ultimately reach a position where they would have to work no longer,—that we might teach them how when they grew up they would find themselves members of a self-respecting society which, while it provided them *gratis* with all they might need, would naturally expect them in honour to render some service in return. Even small children could understand that. Is it quite inconceivable that a society of grown men and women might act up to it?

But it is really absurd to argue about the possibility of these things in human society, when we have so many actual examples of them before our eyes. Herman Melville, in that charming book *Typee*, describes the Marquesas Islanders of the Pacific, among whom he lived for some time during the year 1846. He says: 'During the time I lived among the Typees no one was ever put upon his trial for any offence against the public. To all appearances there were no courts of law or equity. There was no municipal police for the purposes of apprehending vagrants or disorderly characters. In short, there were no legal provisions whatever for the well-being and conservation of society, the enlightened end of civilized legislation'. Nevertheless, the whole book is a eulogy of the social arrangements he met with, and with almost a fervour of romance in its tone; and yet, like all his description of the natives of the Pacific Islands, undoubtedly accurate, and well corroborated by the travellers of the period. An easy communism prevailed. When a good haul of fish was made, those who took part in it did not keep the booty to themselves, but parcelled it out, and sent it throughout the tribe, retaining only their proportionate share. When one family required a new cabin, the others would come and help to build it. He describes such an occasion, when, 'at least a hundred of the natives were bringing materials to the ground, some carrying in their hands one or two of the canes which were to form the sides, others slender rods of hibiscus, strung with palmetto leaves, for the roof. Every one contributed something to the work; and by the united but easy labours of all the entire work was completed before sunset.'

Similar communistic habits prevail, of course, through a vast number of savage tribes, and indeed almost anywhere that the distinctively commercial civilization has not set its mark. They may be found close at home, as in the little primitive island of St. Kilda, in the Hebrides, where exactly the same customs of sharing the hauls of fish or the labours of housebuilding exist to-day,[1] which Melville describes in *Typee:* and they may be found all along the edges of our civilization in the harvesting and housewarming 'bees' of the backwoods and out-lying farm-populations. And we may fairly ask, not whether such social habits are possible, but whether they are not in the end the only possible form; for surely it is useless and absurd to call these modern hordes of people, struggling with each other for the means of sub-sistence, and jammed down by violent and barbaric penal codes into conditions which enforce the struggle, *societies:* as it would be absurd to call the wretched folk in the Black Hole of Calcutta a society. If anyone will only think for a minute of his own inner nature he will see that the only society which would ever really satisfy him would be one in which he was perfectly free, and yet bound by ties of deepest trust to the other members; and if he will think for another minute he will see that the only conditions on which he could be perfectly free (to do as he liked) would be that he *should* trust and care for his neighbour as well as himself. The conditions are perfectly simple; and since they have been more or less realized by countless primitive tribes of animals and men, it is surely not impossible for civilized man to realize them. If it be argued (which is perfectly true) that modern societies are so much more complex than the primitive ones, we may reply that if modern man, with his science and his school-boards, and his brain cultivated through all these centuries, is not competent to solve a more complex problem than the savage, he had better return to savagery.

But it is getting time to be practical.

Of the *possibility* of a free communal society there can really, I take it, be no doubt. The question that more definitely presses on us now is one of transition—by what steps shall we, or can we pass to that land of freedom?

We have supposed a whole people started on its journey by the lifting off of a burden of Fear and anxiety; but in the long, slow ascent of evolution sudden miraculous changes are not to be expected; and for this reason alone it is obvious that we can look for no very swift transformation to the communal form. Peoples that have learnt the lesson of 'trade' and competition so thoroughly as the modern nations have—each man fighting for his own hand—must take some time to unlearn it. The sentiment of the common life, so long nipped and blighted, must have leisure to grow and expand again; and we

---

[1] See Chapter XI of *Poverty and the State,* by H. V. Mills.

acknowledge that—in order to foster new ideas and new habits—an inter-
mediate stage of definite industrial organization will be quite necessary.
Formulæ like the 'nationalization of the land and the instruments of
production', though they be vague and indeed impossible of *rigorous*
application, will serve as centres for the growth of the sentiment. The
partial application of these formulæ will put folk through a lot of useful
drilling in the effort to work together and for common ends.

When one looks sometimes at the awful residue and dregs which are
being left as a legacy to the future by our present commercial system—
the hopeless, helpless, drunken, incapable men and women who drift
through London and the country districts from workhouse to workhouse, or the equally incapable and more futile idlers in high places,
one feels that possibly only a rather stringent industrial organization
will enable the coming society to cope with these burdens.

If I might venture (taking only the agencies which we see already
around us at work) to sketch out how possibly the transitions to the
new society will be effected it would be somewhat as follows:—

In the first place the immense growth of the unemployed—which is
so marked a feature of the day, and which is due to the monopoly of
land and machinery in the control of the few[1]—is already forcing the

---

[1] A moment's thought shows that as machinery perfects and perfects itself there
is a tendency for fewer workers to produce more goods or wealth. The balance of
increased wealth goes to the profit-receiving classes; and so there is a double result,
namely, the increase of the wealthy unemployed, and the increase of the unemployed
workers. The increase of these two classes may not go on simultaneously, and there
may and must be fluctuations on both sides; but the general tendency is clear. It
might, of course, be counteracted by shorter hours of labour and increased wage,
which by bringing a greater number of workers in under better conditions would
immensely improve their lot, and at the same time by reducing profits would clean
up and improve the lives of the wealthy; but as the entire tendency of the present
system is the other way (in order to keep *up* profits), this double shrinkage of
employment must go on—as long, in fact, as the system goes on, and until the
unemployed problem *forces* a solution.
  The unemployed (at the lower end of the scale) break roughly into three classes.
(1) The Poor. These are the genuine workers who *cannot get employment;* and they
form a large class, though their numbers, of course, fluctuate greatly with the
fluctuations of trade. In general they suffer more, both mentally and physically—in
their terrible struggle for a livelihood—than any other class in the nation. (2) The
Pauper and the Vagrant. These are they who, having *given up the struggle for work,*
being constitutionally averse or incapable, resign themselves to a life of dependence
and parasitism. When a worker falls from class one into class two, it is usually a
period of great agony with him—the surrender of his home, his *status,* his independence, etc.—but having once fairly passed into class two, he rarely returns. (3) The
Criminal. These are they who also having passed out of class one, instead of becoming passive parasites, take to a life of deliberate attack and warfare on society.
  When we consider that Mr Charles Booth in 1891 found that about thirty per cent.
of the entire population of London were unable to obtain the necessaries for a sound
livelihood; and that Mr B. S. Rowntree some ten years later gave about twenty-nine

hand of the nation to the development of farm-colonies, land-reclamations, and other big industrial schemes. These, partly carried on by voluntary contribution and enterprise, and partly by municipal and State authority, are already leading to a socialization (in some degree) of land and machinery. At the same time the rolling up of companies into huge and huger trusts is making the transference of industries to public control and to public uses, daily more obviously necessary and, in a sense, more easy to effect.

On the other hand, the Trade Unions and Co-operative Societies by the development of productive as well as distributive industries, and by the interchange of goods with each other on an ever-growing scale, are bringing about a similar result. They are creating a society in which enormous wealth is produced and handled not for the profit of the few, but for the use of the many; a *voluntary* collectivism working within and parallel with the official collectivism of the State.

As this double collectivism grows and spreads, profit-grinding will more and more cease to be a lucrative profession. Though no doubt great efforts will be made in the commercial world to discountenance the public organization of the unemployed (because this will cut away the ground of cheap labour on which commercialism is built), yet as we have seen, the necessity of this organization has reached such a point that it can no longer be denied. And as it comes in more and more, it will more and more react on the conditions of the employed, causing them also to be improved. Besides we are fain to hope that something else of which we see growing signs on every hand, will also come in—namely a new sense of social responsibility, a new reading of religion—which will help on and give genuine life to the changes of which we speak. If so, it might not be so very long before the spread of employment, and the growing security of decent wages, combined with the continual improvement of productive processes and conditions, would bring about a kind of general affluence—or at least absence of poverty. The unworthy fear which haunts the hearts of nine-tenths of the population, the anxiety for the beggarly elements of subsistence, would pass away or fade in the background, and with it the mad nightmarish competition and bitter struggle of men with each other. Even the sense of Property itself would be alleviated. To-day the

per cent. for the corresponding figures in the city of York, we realize what a terrible problem this of unemployment is becoming, and how it must inevitably force modern society into great new organizations and transformations. At present the obvious thing to do is simply to organize a graduated and continuous scheme of farm-colonies and industrial production for (1) prisoners, (2) paupers, and (3) the ordinary unemployed.

institution of Property is like a cast-iron railing against which a human being may be crushed, but which still is retained because it saves us from falling into the gulf. But to-morrow, when the gulf of poverty is practically gone, the indicating line between one person and another need run no harsher than an elastic band.[1]

It is possible that some good general rise in well-being, due to a few years of wise and generous organization of labour, may play the part of the good fairy in the transformation-scene of modern society. With the dying-out of fear and grinding anxiety and the undoing of the frightful tension which to-day characterizes all our lives, Society will spring back nearer to its normal form of mutual help. People will wake up with surprise, and rub their eyes to find that they are under no necessity of being other than human.[2]

Simultaneously (i.e. with the lessening of the power of money as an engine of interest and profit-grinding) the huge nightmare which weighs on us to-day, the monstrous incubus of 'business'—with its endless Sisyphus labours, its searchings for markets, its displacement and destructions of rivals, its travellers, its advertisements, its armies of clerks, its banking and broking, its accounts and checking of accounts—will fade and lessen in importance; till some day perchance it will collapse, and roll off like a great burden to the ground! Freed from the great strain and waste which all this system creates, the body politic will recover like a man from a disease, and spring to unexpected powers of health.

Meanwhile in the great industrial associations, voluntary and other, folk will have been learning the sentiment of the Common Life—the habit of acting together for common ends, the habit of feeling together for common interests—and once this has been learnt, the rest will follow of its own accord. We need not fear that State-organization will run to the bitter end so often prophesied—nor is there any danger of poetry and ginger-beer being converted into government monopolies.

[1] This alleviation indeed is already in some curious ways visible. Forty years ago the few dressed in broad-cloth, the masses in fustian; but now that silk is made out of wood-pulp, and everybody can dress and does dress in the latest fashion, it is no distinction to have fine clothes. Similarly with books, travel, and a hundred other things. What is the good of being a millionaire when the man with three pounds a week can make almost as good a show as you?

[2] At the same time it must not be blinked that in the growth of the modern millionaire we are face to face with a serious evil. Now that any man endowed with a little low cunning, and tempted by self-conceit and love of power, has a good chance of making himself enormously rich, society is in danger of being ruled by as mean a set of scoundrels as ever before in history. And nothing less than a great transformation of our moral and social standards will enable us to cope with this danger.

But it may perhaps be hoped that it will go far enough to form the nucleus of immense growths of *voluntary* Socialism, and to give (as government action does) a very distinct direction to the current of public opinion.

In the course of these changes, moving always towards a non-governmental and perfectly voluntary society in the end, it is probable that some Property-founded institutions, like the payment of labour by wages, though not exactly ideal in their character, will continue for a long period. It has to be remembered that there is not the smallest chance of any 'ideal', pure and simple, of society being at any time absolutely realized. Besides, an ideal is at best an awkward thing. For while it is obviously either Smith's ideal or Brown's ideal, it is pretty certain that Brown's ideal would not suit Smith, nor Smith's ideal suit Brown. So that while we can see plainly enough the more communal direction in which society is trending we may both hope and fairly expect that the resulting form will not be the exact ideal of any party; but will be broad enough and large enough to include an immense diversity of institutions and habits, as well as a considerable survival of the social forms of to-day. It may perhaps be said that in some ways a generous wage-payment convention (as for instance sketched in the last chaper of Carruthers' *Commercial and Communal Economy*) on a thoroughly democratic basis, gives more freedom than a formless Anarchism in which each one takes 'according to his needs',—simply because under the first system A could work two hours a day and live on the wage of two, and B could work eight and live on the wage of eight, each with perfect moral freedom—whereas if there was no wage system, A (however much he might wish to loaf) would feel that he was cheating the community—and the community would think so too—unless he gave his eight hours like everybody else.[1]

The great point however to bear in mind in all this matter is that though the Cash nexus may and no doubt will linger on for a long time in various forms of Wages, Purchase, Sale, and so forth, it must inevitably with the changing sentiment and conditions of life lose its cast-iron stringent character, and gradually be converted into the elastic cord, which while it may indicate a line of social custom will yield to pressure when the need arises. Private Property will thus lose its present virulent character, and subside into a matter of mere use or

[1] It is difficult also to see how things like railways and the immense modern industries (if these survive) could be carried on without some such system of wage-payment and the definite engagement to fulfil certain work which it carries with it.

convenience; monetary reckonings and transfers, as time goes on, will seem little more than formalities—as to-day between friends.

Finally, Custom alone will remain. The subsidence of the Property feeling will mean the subsidence of brute-force Law, for whose existence Property is mainly responsible. The peoples accustomed to the varied activities of a complex industrial organism, will still—though not suffering from the compulsion either of hunger or of brute authority—continue through custom to carry on those activities, their Reason in the main approving.

Custom will remain—slowly changing. And the form of the Societies of the future will be more vital and organic, and far more truly human, than they have been or could be under the rigid domination of Law.

[*Extract*]

THE BAWLING BROTHERHOOD

NOT only were socialism and anarchism being freely discussed by the more intelligent section of the public before the First World War, but the question of Women's Suffrage was rapidly coming to the fore and causing embarrassment to the Liberal Government of Mr. Asquith.

The protagonists of 'Votes for Women' were a mixed crowd, drawn from all parties and from those who were free of party allegiance. In the main a women's movement, this growing force could count on the support of many men, including a number of eminent writers, such as Zangwill, Nevinson and the younger Housman, whose pamphlet we reproduce here. In our view the best 'suffragist' literature of the period was, in fact, the work of men—though this may be merely male prejudice. But few of the many pamphlets published on this subject would have much interest today for anyone but a social historian, and we are fortunate in this exception, the wit and irony of which can still be appreciated after the lapse of so many years.

Laurence Housman's method is a skilful turning of every argument used against the enfranchisement of women into an argument for women alone being allowed to vote. On the other hand, the stock arguments used to justify male domination are twisted round and urged as a complete disqualification of men from having any political power whatsoever. This *reductio ad absurdum* takes the form of a story about a country where women rule; and those who demand 'votes for men' are derided as the 'Bawling Brotherhood'—a suitable counterpart to the 'Shrieking Sisterhood', as some had called the British Suffragists. It should be noted that the term 'suffragette' was used chiefly for and by the militants, who formed a relatively small section of the movement and specialised in forms of Direct Action not always approved by other advocates of Women's Suffrage.

Laurence Housman's pamphlet was published in 1913, and is now republished for the first time with Mr. Housman's kind permission.

THE BAWLING BROTHERHOOD

By Laurence Housman

IN the country of Happy Parallel the administration of law and justice had lain from time immemorial in the hands of the women. The men laboured in the field, in the fisheries, and the mines; they filled the inferior departments of the great trades and industries—those, that is to say, which required nothing for their performance except mere muscular strength and endurance; all the lowest and worst paid forms of employment were open to them, and there was not a single industry that secured to its employees less than a living wage from which the law excluded them.

The women, on the other hand, occupied—as was considered only natural—all those higher branches of industry and of the more skilled and highly paid professions which involved delicacy of manipulation, sense of proportion, grasp of detail, and an organising or administrative capacity. For as the State was but the home writ large, and as the woman's sphere was the home, it had naturally come to be the especial and exclusive function of the women to make and to administer all laws which had as their aim the extension of the refining influence and discipline of the home life from the individual to the community. For the same reason the economics of industry remained, with very few exceptions, under the control of the women; for, as all industries existed solely for the supply or the protection of the home, it was evident that those who decided the conditions of the home must also have the directing voice in all matters contributory thereto, or necessary for its defence and preservation.

Different Spheres of Activity

Now all this seemed so logical and obvious to the right-minded people who made up the bulk of the community, that for centuries it had gone unquestioned; and as a consequence the men and the women had occupied their respective places in the body politic without seeking to encroach upon each other's domain. The women made no attempt to crowd into the sweated industries or to take up the harder and coarser forms of labour to which the mental limitations of the men confined them, or to which their insatiable longing for hard work impelled them. The men, on their part, made no ridiculous attempts to wrest from the women that control of education, of medicine, of the fine arts, of the courts of justice and the great administrative offices of State which were theirs by right as the supreme representatives of the home. And this acquiescence of the men in their exclusion from those highly paid forms of labour, for which they were by nature unsuited, was made more easy for them by the fact that for centuries they had been given practically no education at all, and had been taught to confine their interests to mere manual labour, or, in the case of the wealthier classes, to field sports and to fighting. The arts of war and the destruction of life were conceded to man as his speciality—his sphere was the field; and to die fighting for his country was recognised and accepted by every man worthy of the name as the crown of his manhood and the main reason for his existence as a member of the community. It was to men as motherhood was to the women, the ultimate expression of their sex-value to the State. But, of course, this pre-eminence in the arts of war carried, on the very face of it, an argument against their suitability for the arts of peace. It was impossible for one sex to do the work of the other; and if men were to remain efficient fighters, efficient sportsmen, and efficient manual labourers, they could not be allowed to mix themselves up with those fine arts and skilled industries, those intellectual but quiet and sedentary occupations, those minute and complex affairs of internal government, which, as belonging to the domestic side of the State, fell naturally under the control of the women. If they were to remain manly, men must be kept simple; for them the open-air life—their bodies showed it, their great longing for physical exercise proved it—was the only right and proper one; if they were allowed to use their minds too much they would cease to use their hands; their physical prowess would deteriorate, their fighting instincts would gradually disappear; with the result that in any conflict with a State which had kept its men properly disciplined, the country would fall an easy prey to its enemy.

These arguments may be said to have lain instinctively in the general mind of the community, expressed only by its laws and customs; and they need never have emerged into actual statement, had not the government of that country—in an evil hour, as some thought—

decided on compulsory education, the education not only of its women but of its men. And, as the result of that education the men, finding that their brains, when applied to the same task, were very similar to the women's—that they were able, at all events, to pass and sometimes to come out first in the same examinations—began to demand admission to the higher branches of learning and of skilled industry, and even to those positions of dignity and authority which had hitherto been reserved as the special perquisite of the women. In certain departments the demand could not be resisted; for, by an oversight in the constitution, unmarried men were allowed to hold property; and there was, therefore, nothing to prevent them converting that property to their own devices and starting in business upon their own account. Some, for instance, built schools for the higher education of boys, some started factories in which men were given equal wages with women, some set up places of business independent of women altogether, and many of these pioneers of the 'male movement', as it was called, were most incomprehensibly successful. There were, however, other quarters in which a firm stand was made against them. They were kept out of the colleges and out of the professions, both the legal and medical; and even when, as a concession, in course of time and after a hard struggle, they were admitted to some of the examinations, they were still refused the scholarships and the degrees, and were entirely debarred from professional appointments.

Thus matters stood—as far as they could be made to stand while subject to considerable propulsion from the rear—when a fresh and hitherto almost unheard-of demand was raised—namely, that to men also should be given the parliamentary vote on the same terms as it was or should be hereafter granted to women.

But no sooner had that demand been uttered than there arose throughout the country a most terrible uproar. The men who had dared to make it became known as 'The Bawling Brotherhood'—'effeminate,' 'unmanly,' 'betrayers of their sex,' were some of the epithets which were hurled against them. When they endeavoured to speak in public, anti-suffragists went out and pelted them with rotten eggs, accompanied by the apposite advice to 'go home and make an omelette'—a piece of symbolism intended to suggest what sort of omelettes men would make if they were ever allowed to take a hand in the domestic and economic affairs of the community. And when men-suffragists endeavoured to show how they, too, had to obey the laws affecting the home, and that those laws must in consequence affect them, they were constantly met with the stereotyped cry of 'Be off and clean your rifles!' or 'Get along and make bull's-eyes!' and this, whatever their age or occupation might happen to be.

But when, in spite of this sort of argument, the men-suffragists persisted in their demand, and began gradually to gain supporters, a great number of men and women, many of them highly influential people, banded themselves together to resist it: and all these people, especially those who were themselves in comfortable circumstances, or who held Government appointments, and positions from which men were at present excluded either by law or by custom—the lawyers, the doctors, the Royal Academicians, and such like—all these declared that such a demand was ridiculous, unmanly, and a danger to the State. For it was argued that if men were allowed an equal share in the government, they might before long force through some law which the majority of women would not approve of; and rather than allow such laws to be promulgated women might refuse to become mothers, and where would the State be then? Then again, if men were allowed to administer justice, they would bring to that administration all those ferocious and bloodthirsty instincts which at present found a natural outlet in their addiction to sport and their love of fighting. If allowed to serve on a jury, the same instincts would prevail; while their dislike of sedentary occupation, and their natural hankering for an open-air life would prevent their devoting to each case that time and patience which women naturally gave to it. The law, in consequence, would be administered with undue severity and miscarriage of justice would be frequent. But the main reason given by the opponents for men not being granted the vote was that they could not be mothers of children; and as they could not risk their lives in giving citizens to the State, they must necessarily be regarded and treated as 'the irresponsible sex'.

The Cry of the Men

To that objection the suffragists made what their opponents regarded as a very trivial and inconclusive answer: 'It is true,' they said, 'that we cannot be the mothers of children, but we are the fathers of them; and though we do not risk our lives in bringing them into the world, we contribute our share to the maintenance of the home; for though our wives have a legal right to our wages, and are only bound to give us sufficient maintenance to keep us from being chargeable to the rates, still if we did not work there would often be no wages at all, and what, then, would become of the home? And, furthermore, we have an actual life-and-death interest in the welfare of the State; for though we cannot die in producing citizens, we do risk our lives in defending the home

I

from hostile invasion. We pay rates and taxes just as the women do; we have brains—in many things other than domestic as good as theirs; and we have our own interests and points of view, which are not properly represented in a State which is ruled only by women.'

The answer to that was: 'The men are already represented by the women; for as, by a provision of Nature, they are born and reared of women, so at no time in their lives can that divinely ordained relationship ever be said to cease—a point sufficiently proved by the fact that directly they are ill the men come to the women to be nursed, and are daily dependent upon them for the making of their beds, the cooking of their food, and the mending of their clothes. As for the rest, we quite recognise that men, following their natural instincts, risk their lives in war: that is their nature—they can't help it. If war were not provided as an outlet to their energies, they would fall to fighting among themselves, and illegitimate bloodshed would ensue. To die for his country is a man's highest and noblest function; but that very fact disqualifies him from taking part in the peaceful concerns of the home and the administration of the State; for his military duties take him, often for months at a time, right away from the industrial life of the community; frequently he has to go into savage countries where his character is inevitably affected by the manners and customs of those whom he is sent to conquer; also fighting itself, though noble and necessary, has in certain directions a deteriorating effect upon the mind and character; for when a man's blood is up he cannot be expected to have that cool and domesticated outlook which is necessary for deciding upon matters which concern the internal welfare of the State.'

'But,' answered the men, 'we do not all of us fight, for some are too old and some are prevented by infirmity, and even for those who are physically fit there is not enough fighting to go round, since even your biggest wars only require the services of about one man in twenty. Yet the rest of us who are left at home do not turn to bloodshed and civil warfare, but remain quiet and law-abiding citizens. So, even if you feel it necessary to withhold the vote from the army while it is on active service, just as women are debarred by nature while actually performing the supreme function of maternity—still, there is no reason why you should not extend it to those who are forced to remain non-fighters.'

'That,' replied their opponents, 'would never do at all; for as fighting is man's highest function in the State, it would be clearly unjust to the fighters to grant to the non-fighters a mark of citizenship which was withheld from them. Fighting is man's sphere; and as it is his misfortune if he has to be out of it, it must not be converted into a privilege.'

But the most fundamental objection upon that side of the question was the 'physical force' argument. Men, it was pointed out, were physically stronger than women; they were by nature fighting animals, and if once admitted to legislative power they would inevitably attempt to override justice by physical violence, and the result would be 'red ruin and the breaking up of laws'; for if physical force were allowed to dictate its terms, trust and confidence in the justice of the laws would disappear, and men would tend more and more only to do that which was right in their own eyes. Men suffragists answered that the superior physical power of men had always existed, but had not prevented just laws from being passed and carried into practice, and why should it do so any more when men had an equal share in the responsibility for their enactment?

'Because,' said the other side, 'they would then discover for the first time what power they possessed; with the result that, following their natural instincts, they would before long be declaring that physical force was the ultimate basis of government; and the fighting side of the human race being in the ascendant, highly civilised States would in consequence be driven into spending from one-half to three-quarters of their public revenue on naval and military armaments: so that in the end the only limit to the competition of state against state would be manhood conscription and the entire nation under arms.'

'That,' replied the suffragists, 'might possibly happen in states ruled by men alone; but that is not what we are proposing. What we do propose is that those who do all the fighting and so much of the labour, which you consider necessary for the protection and welfare of the State, should have an equal voice in deciding those political questions which lead either to peace or war.'

'But,' said the anti-suffragists, 'that would be the most dangerous thing of all; to allow the fighting sex a voice in politics would entirely destroy the predominating influence of the home; for if the army happened, at any time, to be tired of fighting it might vote for a peace that would be ruinous to the interest of the nation; or, if, on the other hand, it were spoiling for a fight, it would endeavour to force the State into conflicts for which there was no justification whatever; and as a result the interests and welfare of the home, of morality and of religion would no longer form as at present the pivot of the national policy.'

'As for that,' answered the suffragists, 'though we have not votes, we have always had the power, if we did not like fighting, to turn tail and run away; and you have yourselves admitted that if we wanted to fight we could do it among ourselves just for the joke of it; but neither of these things have happened except on rare occasions and among a disreputable minority. Do you think that the vote is going to alter human nature?'

That is exactly what the anti-suffragists did think, and they proclaimed it with no uncertain voice. They declared that if men once got the vote they would never rest till they had entirely supplanted the women; they would then seize on all the quiet and indoor occupations —the shopkeeping, the higher branches of domestic service, the nursing in hospitals, the weaving, tailoring, dressmaking, the baking, the cooking, the confectionery, the directorships, the civil service, the clerkships, and all those posts of emolument and ease which required for their proper fulfilment the dignity and prestige of woman. On the other hand, they would leave field-labour, dairy-work, and country life in general either to the women or to the lowest and most unintelligent of their own sex, with the result that agricultural industry and prosperity would diminish, and the country would be forced to look for its most necessary food supplies from abroad, entailing danger to the State in time of war which even the meanest mind could appreciate. Moreover, with all the indoor and sedentary careers thrown open to them, men would become soft and effeminate; they would cease to care for sport and would lose that manly bloom and vigour from open-air life which gave them their chief attraction for women. They would grow uncombative and peaceable, and with the loss of their military efficiency would deteriorate into such bad marksmanship that the amount of ammunition expended in war, instead of being as now commensurate with the number of the enemy killed or wounded, would be so vast as to arouse the derision of surrounding nations, and result in wastage so enormous as to constitute a staggering burden for the community.

Many people not unfavourable to male suffrage claims felt that some of these evils might indeed come about if men obtained the entire control of the State, and they were anxious, therefore, to extend the franchise in a form which did not give to the men a superiority or even an equality of numbers. But the objection to that was that once started there would be no stopping them, and that before long, from wanting the vote they would go on to wanting to become Members of Parliament. That, it was agreed, was unthinkable. For men, who were by habit hard swearers and hard drinkers, smokers, spitters, and makers of unclean jokes, to be admitted to the legislature, reeking of the pothouse and the smoking-saloon, was felt to be inconsistent with the dignity of the Mother of Parliaments; how could a sex addicted to such habits be given a voice in the councils of the nation? Moreover, men did not care about politics, and would, therefore, be ready to sell their votes, whether as electors or as Members of Parliament, for a pot of beer. Suffragists said: 'Any man who gets into Parliament must get there by election; and is it reasonable to suppose that candidates who indulge to excess in such proclivities, or who have no interest in politics, will stand any chance of election when women themselves form half of the electorate?' But opponents said: 'Men in standing for Parliament will rely on their sex-charm, and, when they get there, upon their physical strength. They will, in consequence, ignore the authority of the Speaker; when they get hot in argument they will fall to fisticuffs, and Parliament, instead of being a deliberative assembly, will become a bear-garden'. Others said: 'Fancy a man in a pair of trousers, a cut-away coat, and mutton-chop whiskers sitting upon the Woolsack!' And having fancied it to themselves, they laughed consumedly, and considered that they had provided for their own side an absolutely knock-down argument.

A Moderate Demand

But while the more extreme claims of 'the Bawling Brotherhood' were thus providing a whetstone for the wit and satire of their opponents, there were others in the male movement who made milder and more moderate demands. Some, indeed, did not want a vote at all in legislative matters, if in the professions and the industries they might be allowed to stand on the same footing as the women. But when they came to particulars, they were met by just as much opposition and hostility as their more extreme brethren. Some of them wanted to have men doctors, so that men might, if they wished, have the chance of being attended by their own sex. There were some, it was contended, who shrank from submitting themselves to medical treatment from instincts of modesty, and, in consequence, many physical evils, which might be cured if taken in time, went unremedied with much consequent harm to the health of the community. The answer to these was that such a pandering to morbid tastes was undesirable; from their infancy men had been accustomed to be in the hands of women to be bathed, dressed, and attended to; women were the natural nurses of the race, and were, therefore, its natural doctors as well. If men were admitted to the medical profession their sporting and bloodthirsty instincts would get the better of them: vivisection and desperate surgical operations would be indulged in to a dangerous extent, experiment for experiment's sake would become the rule, and men would think far more of making a great reputation by the sensational daring of their operations than of securing the alleviation of suffering by safer and more humdrum methods.

As for those who claimed for men a share in the higher branches of education, they were frankly told that it could do them no possible good. Nature had shown clearly, by giving them big muscles, that they were meant to be hewers of wood and drawers of water; and was it likely that, by any amount of training, they could develop that fineness and subtlety of intellect which was the woman's speciality? 'The Bawling Brotherhood' answered: 'We can but try. How can we discover our limits or our qualifications until you give us the same advantages in education, in administration, and in authority which have belonged to women in this country from time immemorial?'

Thus, in these and other points which have not been touched on, the controversy stood; and gradually, in the various branches of the professions and industries—in spite of the disabling enactments of the Legislature—the men were winning their way to economic independence. But when it came to the granting of the Parliamentary vote the ruling powers were as adamant. They had, they said, so many more important things to attend to, about which they were in more general agreement, and so year after year, and decade after decade, the question when brought before Parliament was defeated with ridicule or shelved with fair and plausible arguments; and meanwhile the 'Men's Movement' went on'.

And at last some of the more advanced and determined spirits among them said: 'What is the use of listening to all this soothing flattery which our rulers are constantly pouring into our ears—this talk about our manliness and our chivalry and the admiration that women feel for us? They have given to these a definition of their own which only serves to bind us to their will; let us show that we feel we have just as much right as they to say what is manly and what is chivalrous; you cannot have true manliness without independence, and there is no chivalry worth having where there is not freedom'.

So the 'Bawling Brotherhood' set to work and began to make things very uncomfortable for the ruling powers; for they began to interrupt at public meetings and to hold meetings of their own, and even to go where they were told not to go—and, as a consequence of that, to go where they were made to go—namely, to prison. And all this they did to show that they had just as much right as women to the vote, and how very real and deep was their need for it. And all the anti-suffragists —especially the sportsmen, and the military men, and those with com-

fortable incomes and comfortable wives who gave them everything
they asked for—lifted up their hands in horror against them and cried,
'Oh, you unmanly creatures! How you make us blush for our sex!'

How Wisdom Came in a Ship

Now what, at that particular moment, would have been the result of
the struggle thus begun, we have no means of knowing, for just then a
very extraordinary thing happened which gave quite a new and unexpected turn to events. For there came to that country, driven by a great
storm, a ship which had on board four or five hundred women with
marks upon their bodies of bruises and of chains. They were all clothed
in purple, or white, or green; and, in spite of their battered condition,
they were all of exceedingly cheerful countenance and of a strangely
uplifted spirit.

As the ship came to land, the five hundred women stood up in the
rigging and cried with one voice: 'Votes for Women!' Everybody who
heard them laughed: the proposition in that country was so self-evident;
and it seemed a strange thing for a ship's crew which had just escaped
from the perils of the deep to cry in the moment of their safe deliverance
something that everybody knew as well as their A B C. So when, a few
moments later, the five hundred women stepped to land, everybody
was very eager to hear who such amusing people might be, and where
they had come from. But before long, as they listened to the story of
these new arrivals, their curiosity and amusement were changed to
wonder and indignation. For the travellers told how in the land they
had come from women were without the vote and were, in consequence,
subject to many indignities and to much injustice, permitted both by
law and custom. And because they had fought for their rights of citizenship they had been subjected to imprisonment and ridicule, and when
that proved of no avail, then a new law was passed under which they
were sentenced to exile and transportation, so that the Government of
that country might no longer be troubled by them or have to listen to
arguments which it could not answer. And so five hundred leaders of
the movement had been taken, and without trial by jury—for in the new
law it had been carefully provided that the trial was to be before
magistrates only—had been sentenced to banishment and immediate
transportation.

Now when the people of Happy Parallel heard how these things
happened in a country where men had the vote, they welcomed the
newcomers as a godsend to the cause for which they themselves were
contending; for here, they cried triumphantly, you have an example of

what men do with the vote when they get it. We have only to bring these women to speak at our meetings and to show their wounds and the marks of their imprisonment, and 'the Bawling Brotherhood' will be routed and put to shame and silence for ever.

When the newcomers heard that, they inquired: 'Who are the "Bawling Brotherhood"? They sound as if they were very important people.'

But the people of Happy Parallel answered confidently: 'Indeed, they are of no importance whatever; they are only a ridiculous set of unmanly and effeminate creatures who, to the disgrace of their sex, think that man ought to have the vote. Some of them are quite unteachable, but to the few who have any sense left in their heads you will be able to tell a story that will convince them for ever of their folly'.

But no sooner had the travellers heard that answer than they cried, to the amazement of all the people: 'But "the Bawling Brotherhood" are right, and you are wrong; and no one can show you why better than we, for we in our own country have been called the "Shrieking Sisterhood", and you in this country have been doing just as the men in our country have been doing, and are no wiser and no juster than they. We knew that men, if they kept power all to themselves, could be stupid; but we never imagined that women could be as stupid as they could be. So when we go back in triumph to our own country—as we mean to do soon—we shall be all the better able to forgive them for what they have done to us; for we see now that under like circumstances women might do very much the same things; and men have very much the same difficulties to get over. And now we know that when the storm carried us to your shores, it was that we might help "the Bawling Brotherhood" to win from you their right to equal citizenship. That we are now prepared to do; and when we have done so, then they and you shall come along and help us to win the same rights which have been denied to us in our own country'.

So the 'Shrieking Sisterhood' went to the help of the 'Bawling Brotherhood', and wherever they went they had only to tell their story for the people of Happy Parallel to realise at once that it was indeed only their own case reversed and made plain; and the result was what anyone who has taken the trouble to follow the argument of my story will be able to guess. For which reason there is no occasion for me to write it.

THE ORIGINS OF THE GREAT WAR

WARS have a habit of being fought for anything on earth but their ostensible motives. The Second World War began with the German invasion of Poland, and the intervention of Britain and France to save the Poles. At the end of the war it appeared that much of this country, to defend which we had taken up arms, was really Russian territory, whilst large pieces of what we had called Germany were really in Poland. The whole country had moved westward, assuming so different a shape and so changed a political complexion (under the heavy persuasion of Russia) that we may reasonably doubt whether the Poland which has survived is the Poland which so many millions died to save.

Similarly, when the First World War broke out, there was a general impression in England that we were fighting primarily to defend Belgium, which was therefore made into a battlefield. It is perhaps significant that among the few who maintained a more objective view of the situation was E. D. Morel, whose book *Red Rubber*, first published in 1906, had startled this country with its gruesome record of Belgian atrocities in the Congo. Public opinion had, in fact, been roused on this point, but not to the point of going to war with King Leopold as an aggressor against helpless Africans. In fact, though Morel's unwelcome limelight had caused the Belgians to behave less abominably in the Congo, they were still there, like the other successful aggressors who had carved themselves empires in other parts of Africa. To some people in 1914 it seemed slightly incongruous that there should be so much excitement, in a civilisation pivoted upon successful aggression, merely because one aggressor attacked another.

Morel, who had better reason than most to see through the pretensions of the contemporary war propaganda, was associated with Ramsay MacDonald, Arthur Ponsonby and others in the work of the 'U.D.C.'—the Union of Democratic Control, which aimed at a democratic peace. One of the first necessities was to provide some real understanding of what the war really was about. This was no easy task, in view of the tangled skeins of diplomacy with which the origins of the war were involved; and much of the vital information was still withheld from the public. When one considers this U.D.C. pamphlet by

Brailsford in conjunction with the information which became public later, it is astonishing how accurate it was and how little it missed. The publication of Czarist documents after the Russian Revolution, and the admissions and indiscretions in various memoirs published after the First World War made it very clear that the German Government was not the only one responsible for the catastrophe.

In another pamphlet (*Belgium and the Scrap of Paper*, 1915) Brailsford discussed the peculiarly unilateral ethics whereby such unique opprobrium was attached to the German infringement of Belgian neutrality. He recalled Canning's action during the Napoleonic wars, when a British fleet was sent to Copenhagen, in order to destroy the fleet of a neutral country on the mere supposition that Napoleon intended to seize these Danish ships and use them against Britain. In the First World War (Brailsford pointed out), as soon as Turkey had joined Germany, the Russians had violated Persian territory in order to attack the Turks on their flank—an action which had passed without any protest from those who were so indignant about the invasion of Belgium, and that in spite of the fact that Britain and Russia had signed a joint guarantee of Persian integrity and independence in 1907. Japan, then our ally, had similarly violated Chinese neutrality, in order to attack the German colony of Kiao-Chow.

At a later stage in the same war the French and the British violated the neutrality of Greece in the Salonika campaign; and the whole ethical basis on which the Allied Cause was supposed to rest must soon have looked very foolish to neutral observers. Such events are now sufficiently remote to be viewed with some measure of objectivity even by ourselves, but they were hard to assess at the time and to interpret rationally to a nation at war. It will be many years before impartial historians will be able to measure the Italian conquest of Abyssinia or Albania against—for example—the quiet annexation of a vast slice of Arabian territory by the British in 1937. The most recent[1] of many such acts (whereby the British Empire was built up), this was carried out by an Order in Council of March, 1937, and followed by twelve months of 'police work' in which Arab villagers in the Hadhramaut were bombed into submission. This annexation of territory larger than Albania, by the same methods that were used by the Italians, was barely even reported and carried out with scarcely a comment in the British press, which had been so indignant with regard to the aggressive imperialism of Mussolini. It will be long before such things can be seen in proper perspective; and it will be even longer before the actions of

[1] Our apologies to the Colonial Office: it has since annexed Sarawak.

the Germans in the Second World War, with respect to the small countries which they over-ran, will be rationally compared with the action of the British, Russians and Americans in occupying Irak, Iran, Iceland and Liberia.

All such violations of neutrality are justified by those who perpetrate them on the same plea of 'necessity'. H. N. Brailsford, in writing the pamphlet mentioned above, and the one reproduced below, did not in any way condone that plea. But he showed that the same faults were to be found on both sides and were equally to be condemned. More than that, he exposed the whole sordid game of power politics from which such crimes inevitably arise; and it was an action of great courage at the time to state plainly such unpleasant truths.

What is today particularly interesting in *The Origins of the Great War* is that so much which Brailsford feared when he wrote this pamphlet, in 1915, has come true—as a result, not of the First World War, but of the Second. The Russian Revolution, which took Russia out of the War, upset one part of Brailsford's calculation, that 'Our fleet in the North Sea, our army in France, may be winning for the Tsar millions of fresh subjects, and for the familiar process of forcible Russification unnumbered victims'. This, by an unexpected turn in history, did not prove true at the time; but if we substitute Stalin for 'the Tsar' and his version of 'communism' for 'Russification' it might be considered as a fairly good prophecy of what happened in the Second World War. Brailsford's theme that people did not really know what they were fighting for was never better demonstrated than it is to-day. And how right Brailsford was in saying that the Allies could destroy German armies, but that only the Germans could destroy German militarism, the future was soon to show. The reader will also notice that Brailsford ironically followed this statement with a list of the steps to be taken (the very steps for which the press was clamouring) in order to ensure that the German people did *not* destroy militarism, but revived it. The steps he described were faultlessly followed by the victors at Versailles —they made, in fact, just such a peace as the Union of Democratic Control had been formed to prevent, if possible, based upon the very conceptions which Brailsford had so ably exposed.

The Origins of the Great War is republished herewith by the kind permission of Mr. Brailsford and of the Union of Democratic Control.

THE ORIGINS OF THE GREAT WAR

By Henry Noel Brailsford

For Englishmen this war is primarily a struggle between Germany and France. For the Germans it is emphatically a Russo-German war. It was our secret naval commitment to France, and our fatal entanglement through ten years in the struggle for a European balance of power, which sent our fleets to sea. It is our sympathy with France which makes the one human link that binds us to the Triple Entente. We have dramatised the struggle (and this clearly was for Sir Edward Grey the dominant consideration) as an attempt to crush France. German thinking followed other lines. Alike for the deputies in the Reichstag and for the mob in the streets of Berlin, the enemy is Russia. It is true, indeed, that if the war should end in the defeat of the Triple Entente, some part of the consequences of defeat would be borne by France. It is clear that German statesmen hoped to acquire some part at least of her extensive and valuable colonial possessions, and on her no doubt would have fallen the financial brunt of the war. She would have paid in money and in colonies for her imprudence in allying herself to Russia. But in spite of this, her place in Germany's imagination was secondary. Her army must indeed be broken before Russia could be dealt with. That was a fatality, a detail in the mechanics of the problem which affected its central political purpose hardly more than the resistance of the Belgians. The politics which made the war, and the sentiment which supported it, had reference exclusively to Russia. Read the speech by which the Chancellor induced the Reichstag to vote the war-credit without a dissentient voice; the only mention of France in it is a reply to the French accusation that German troops had violated the French frontier. The illuminating White Paper (Denkschrift) in which the history of the outbreak of the war is set out from the German official standpoint, contains hardly so much as an incidental reference to France. More significant still is the speech in which Dr. Haase, on behalf of the Social Democrats in the Reichstag, while repudiating the diplomacy which made the war, accepted on behalf of his comrades the duty of patriotic defence. He, too, made no reference to France. 'For our people,' he declared, 'and for the future of its liberties, much, if not everything, depends on a victory over Russian despotism, stained, as it is, with the blood of its noblest subjects.' It is for us in this country of the first importance to follow the direction of German thought. If we are to understand why the war was made at all, if we are to grasp the reasons which will make it on the German side an obstinate and determined struggle, if we are to think out with any hope of success the problem of shortening it, we must realise that it was the fear of Russia which drove German diplomacy into a preventive war, and in the end mobilised even the Social Democrats behind German diplomacy. To the diplomatists and the statesmen the issue was from the first not merely whether Austria or Russia would exert a hegemony in the Balkans, but also whether Russia, using Servia as her vanguard, should succeed in breaking up the Austrian Empire. It is not merely a tie of sentiment or kinship which unites Germany to Austria. Austria is the flying buttress of her own Imperial fabric. Cut the buttress and the fabric itself will fall. To the masses of the German people the fate of Servia and even of Bosnia was a matter of profound indifference. A month before the war broke out, three Germans in four would probably have said that not all the Serbs in Christendom were worth the bones of one Pomeranian grenadier. But the Russian mobilisation and the outbreak of war made even for the German masses a supreme and only too intelligible issue.[1] There is rooted deep in the memory of the German people a recollection of the exploits of the Cossacks during the Seven Years' War. The simplest peasant of the Eastern marches has his traditions of devastated fields, and ruined villages. He knows, moreover, that the intervening generations which have transformed the West have left the Russian steppes still barbarous. Even for the Social Democrat the repugnant

[1] Read, for example, this typical declaration by the *Volkstimme*, one of the German Socialist Party organs: 'All must set aside the aims and purposes of their party, and bear in mind one fact—Germany, and in a larger sense all Europe, is endangered by Russian despotism. At this moment we all feel the duty to fight chiefly and exclusively against Russian despotism. Germany's women and children must not become the prey of Russian bestiality; the German country must not be the spoil of Cossacks; because if the Allies should be victorious, not an English governor or a French republican would rule over Germany, but the Russian Tsar. Therefore we must defend at this moment everything that means German culture and German liberty against a merciless and barbaric enemy.'

thought that he was marching out to shoot down his French and Belgian comrades was overborne by the imperious necessity of arming to defend his soil against the millions which the Russian Tsar had mobilised.

The Military Rivalry

The broad fact about the general war of 1914 is that it is the postponed sequel of the Balkan war of 1912. We all congratulated each other that Sir Edward Grey's diplomacy and the Conference of London had enabled the Eastern peoples to settle the Eastern question without involving the Great Powers in war. The armaments of the Great Powers betrayed their belief that a war averted is only a war postponed. For two years this chaotic struggle, which came in the end with such vertiginous speed, had cast its shadow before it. The first move in the last round of the war of armaments was the direct consequence of the creation of the Balkan League. In justifying the last increase of the peace-effectives of its army the German Government pointed to the new fact of the entry on the European scene of these young and victorious Balkan armies, and spoke bluntly of a possible struggle between the Slav and Teuton worlds. The Balkan League of 1912, formed under Russian guidance, was, in fact, an alliance directed as much against Austria as against Turkey. There followed the reply of France and Russia, the return in the one to Three Years' Service and in the other the imprudently-advertised schemes of military reorganisation, with its vast naval expenditure, its new strategic railways near the German frontier, its rearmament of the artillery, and its gigantic increase in the standing 'peace' army. Russia (so an official memorandum declared) would henceforth be able to assume in case of need not merely a defensive, but an offensive strategy.[1] The early months of this year witnessed the outbreak of a military panic in the German press. The fear inspired by the growth of the Tsar's armies was beginning to tell on German nerves, and a pamphlet to which the German Crown Prince

[1] In an article entitled 'Europe Under Arms' (June 3, 1914), the military correspondent of the *Times* explained how well founded were these German fears of Russian preparations. Russia, he explained, had raised her peace-effectives by 150,000 men, 'making a total peace strength of about 1,700,000, or approximately double that of Germany'.... 'The Russian reply to Germany is next door to a mobilisation in time of peace, and it quite accounts for the embittered outburst of the *Cologne Gazette*, and for the German pot calling the Russian kettle, black.... There are signs that Russia has done with defensive strategy.... The increased number of guns in the Russian Army Corps, the growing efficiency of the Army, and the improvements made or planned in strategic railways are, again, matters which cannot be left out of account. These things are well calculated to make the Germans anxious.'

contributed an approving note, predicted that the Slav world would have completed its armaments by the year 1916, and would then attempt to deal the death-blow to the German peoples. If Germany has by her own act made the general war in 1914, it is chiefly because her military caste was convinced that it would sooner or later have to meet a Russian challenge.

The Servian Menace

The German White Paper explains the political issue which was the obverse of this military rivalry. For a generation we in this country have thought of the Eastern question as an issue between Turkey and the Christian races of the Balkans. With the destruction of the Ottoman empire in Europe the Eastern question became primarily an Austrian question. Russia and Austria, up to the eve of the Young Turkish revolution had been content to divide the hegemony of the Near East. They worked in close association; they presided jointly over the Macedonian reforms; they even recognised a certain division of spheres of influence. Austria was allowed by Russia to exert a predominant pressure upon Servia, while Russia was the leading partner in all that concerned Bulgaria. It was never, at the best, an easy arrangement to maintain. Austria was always detested in Belgrade, and the dominant political party in Servia, the Radicals, were vehemently Russophile. With the murder of King Alexander, and the coming of King Peter, the moral influence of Russia in Servia became supreme, but the little kingdom remained none the less within the Austrian sphere, until the Bosnian crisis shattered the whole conception of an Austro-Russian *condominium* in the Balkans. From the autumn of 1909 onwards, Servia became as absolutely and almost as openly the protégé of Russia, and the tool of Russian policy, as Montenegro had been for generations. It would hardly be an exaggeration to say that the dominant personality in Belgrade was not King Peter, nor yet M. Pachitch, but the brilliant energetic, unscrupulous Russian Minister, the late M. de Hartwig. He formed the Balkan League, and he also encouraged the Servians to tear up the Treaty of Partition, which the Tsar had guaranteed. There were several reasons why Russian policy regarded the Servians as its favoured foster-children, and willingly aggrandised them at the expense of the Bulgarians. The Servians, in the first place, have always been the more pliable, the less independent of the Balkan Slav peoples. But while the Bulgarians were useful as a piece in an anti-Turkish policy, the Servians were doubly valuable, for they were indispensable to any move against Austria. The annexation of Bosnia, so far from being accepted by the

Servians as a final and irrevocable fact, had actually been the starting point of an agitation more conscious, more open, and more reckless than any which had preceded it. The triumph of Servian arms in Macedonia, first over the Turks and then over the Bulgarians, was accepted by most Servians as the presage of a greater victory to come. There was evident a tremendous heightening of the national consciousness. Some of its effects worked uncompensated mischief. It showed itself as brutal intolerance towards the Albanians and the Bulgars in Macedonia. The Servians are an attractive race, imaginative, quick-witted, excitable, and richly endowed with the artistic temperament. But their morals and their politics belong to the Middle Ages. They were judged more harshly than they deserved for the murder of that neurotic despot, King Alexander. But the officers who at the same time murdered his queen, mutilitated her corpse, and flung it naked into the streets of Belgrade, gave the measure of their own social development. Their record in Macedonia reveals their political immaturity. By exile and imprisonment they forced the conquered Bulgarians to sign documents in which they declared themselves not merely loyal Servian subjects, but Servians by race and choice. They totally suppressed the Bulgarian Church, and exiled its bishops. They forbade the public use of the Bulgarian language. They denied the conquered population all political and some civil rights. They have ruled by the harshest form of martial law. This revival of patriotism created a militarism wholly alien to the democratic traditions of the Balkan races. But it also set the nation to the work of organising itself for the future with a new seriousness and a new devotion. Under her two last Obrenovitch Kings, Servia had been nothing but a meaningless and isolated *enclave* in the Balkans, wedged between Austria and Bulgaria, without a future and without a mission. Her national life was stagnant and corrupt. The coming of the new dynasty, and still more the breach between Austria and Russia, opened a brilliant path before her. She believed at last that the re-union of all the Servian peoples was possible, and she resolved that it should come about under her leadership. She saw herself destined to do for the Serbs what Piedmont had done for the Italians. The adventure might seem to sober minds impossible. Servia in isolation could hardly dream of challenging Austria with success, even if she had the moral and material resources which enabled Piedmont to expand into the Kingdom of Italy. But the Servians remembered that Piedmont did not overcome Austria by her own resources. She had Louis Napoleon behind her. If the Servians armed and plotted for the liberation of Bosnia and the other Serb lands under the Austrian yoke, it was with the firm conviction that when the hour of destiny struck, Russia would stand behind them.[1]

Russia Behind Servia

When historians come to deal with the real causes of this general war, it is possible that exact documentary evidence may show how far Russian diplomacy stood behind the Greater Servian propaganda. The general presumption is strong. No one doubts that Russian influence was supreme in Belgrade. The Serbs owed much to their own arms, but on the whole they owed more to Russian diplomacy. But for Russia, the Austrians would have crushed them in 1909; but for Russia, Austria would certainly not have remained neutral during the two Balkan wars. To Russian pressure Servia owed such of her conquests in Albania as she was allowed to retain, and but for Russia, Austria would have torn up the iniquitous Treaty of Bucharest. There were more material bonds between the Great Power and her satellite. The Servian soldiers made the winter campaign of 1912–1913 in Russian greatcoats, and the second Balkan War was financed by the French banks which do nothing in the Balkans that would run counter to Russian policy. When the full tide of Servian aspirations set towards Bosnia, and the National Union (Narodya Odbrana) began to turn against Austria all the criminal 'comitadji' methods of agitation consecrated by long usage in Macedonia, Russia, had she chosen, might have set her veto on a development of Servian policy which threatened European peace. It is this absolute dependence of Servia upon Russian countenance and support, which makes it probable that when Servia openly launched and assisted the Great Servian propaganda, she did this with Russia's approval. This propaganda involved much more than a mental disturbance in the minds of the Servian population of Bosnia and Herzegovina, who were organised in patriotic leagues and clubs with a view to an insurrection in the future. It had begun to smuggle arms, and it had been guilty of a series of assassinations of Austrian officials, to which the murder of the

---

[1] My statement has since been confirmed by a distinguished historian, who writes as a friend and admirer of the Serbs. 'Last year,' writes Mr G. M. Trevelyan in the *Times* of September 18, 'when I was among them, they looked forward to this [a war with Austria] as the grand national object, and they regarded the then impending war with Bulgaria as an unfortunate but necessary prelude to the war of liberation against Austria. . . . The young men in Serbia, many of them, spoke of themselves as belonging to the "Piedmontese Party", and books about Piedmont's part in the Italian *risorgimento* were the commonest "serious literature" in the Belgrade shops, and lay on the table in the waiting-room of their Foreign Office.' I may add that an influential daily newspaper was called *Piemonte*. Can we wonder that Austria first shuddered and then struck out?

Archduke Francis Ferdinand and his Consort came as the climax. The Archduke was singled out for vengenace, not at all because he was the enemy, or oppressor of the Slavs. He was feared by Servians because his aim was to reconcile the Slavs to Austria. The historical memorandum in the German White Paper declares bluntly that this reckless and provocative attitude was possible for Servia 'only because she believed that she had Russian support in her activities'. The memorandum goes on to make an even graver statement. After referring to the original creation of the Balkan League under Russian auspices, it continues:—

'Russian Statesmen planned the rise of a new Balkan League under Russian protection, a league which was aimed not at Turkey—now vanished from the Balkans—but against the Austro-Hungarian monarchy. The idea was that Servia should be compensated for the cession of its Macedonian acquisitions to Bulgaria by receiving Bosnia and Herzegovina at Austro-Hungary's expense.'

There is nothing improbable in this statement. The original Serbo-Bulgarian alliance of 1912, afterwards expanded into the Balkan League, was directed against Austria as well as Turkey. The treaty, as more than one Balkan diplomat has told me, required Bulgaria to put all her forces at Servia's disposal in the event of a war against Austria. These preparations for a united Slav assault upon Austria explain the determination of the German Powers to challenge Russia. Nor should it be forgotten that Pan-Slavism was busy in Galicia as well as in the Serbian lands. An active propaganda, disclosed in some famous State trials, was endeavouring, in Russian interests, to win the Ruthenians for the Orthodox Church. At its head stood the Russian reactionary politician, Count Bobrinsky, who, as Governor of Galicia, is now officially promoting the conversion of the Catholic Ruthenians to Orthodoxy.

It is not easy in the midst of the horrors and resentments of war to view such a situation as this in cold retrospect. The peril in front of Austria was grave, but it was not immediate. Russia had not at the first essay succeeded in restoring the Balkan League. Bulgaria could not forget her resentment, and had become a loosely attached associate of the Triple Alliance. If the Slavs were to choose their own hour, they would wait presumably until the Balkan armies had somewhat recovered from the exhaustion of two campaigns, and until the Russian military re-organisation was completed. But there was good reason to infer that, sooner or later, the blow would be struck. A rising in Bosnia, organised by Servian comitadjis, would bring Servia herself into the field, and behind Servia would be the Balkan League and the Russian Empire. Such conspiracies as this are so remote from Western habits of life and thought, so inconceivable in our own experience, that we are apt to dismiss them as fantastic. They are the stuff of daily life in the Balkans, and we may do Austrian statesmen the justice of supposing that their fears were sincere. 'The country,' wrote Sir Maurice de Bunsen in his final despatch, 'certainly believed that it had before it only the alternative of subduing Servia, or of submitting sooner or later to mutilation at her hands.' An enlightened Power in Austria's place would not have acted as she did. The 'Great Servian' idea is dangerous to Austria, because she lacks the courage to be liberal without reserves. Servia may compare herself to Piedmont, but the parallel is imperfect. Her culture is so backward, her politics so corrupt, her economic life so primitive, that she has little to commend her to the Austrian Serbs save the community of blood. Our fathers sympathised with Italian aspirations, because the Italians were a race with a great past and a living culture, subject to an Empire which was not their superior in civilisation, and which denied them any species of auto-nomy. Austria does not deny Home Rule to their Serbs, though she gives it grudgingly, and she represents an older and maturer civilisa-tion. The Italians, moreover, were a homogeneous people. Of the Austrian Serbs one third are Catholic, who have no reason to hope for equal treatment from an Orthodox State, whose record in Macedonia is a defiance of toleration, and another third are Moslems, who will emigrate *en masse* if the Servians should conquer Bosnia. Even the remaining third, who are Orthodox Serbs, would not have been ready-made material for a Servian propaganda, if Austria had known how to treat them with generosity. Faced by this Great Servian danger, and forced to realise at last that it was serious, a big man in Count Berch-told's place would have resolved to make Austria a home so attractive even to Servian idealists, that the half-civilised kingdom over the bor-der, with its backward culture and Oriental morals, would have lured and beckoned them in vain. He would have made them feel, as the Poles have long felt, that they are Austrians with a share in the fortunes of the Empire. He would have made their autonomy a handsome reality. He would have banished the spies and the policemen, enemies of the Austrian idea more dangerous than all the Servian bomb-throwers and comitadjis. He would have released the Croatians from the Magyar yoke, and bidden Dalmations, Croatians, and Bosnians realise their Great Servia to their heart's content within the Austrian Empire itself. That was the policy which the dead Archduke was supposed to favour. Against such a policy, conceived with some bold-ness of imagination and executed with good faith and tact, the incite-ments and conspiracies of Belgrade would have been powerless. Count

Berchtold is neither a Liberal nor a man of genius. He acted after the Serajevo murder as the average Imperialist bureaucrat commonly does act in such cases. He tightened his police system. He made Austrian rule a little more than usually hateful to men of Servian race. He determined to crush and humiliate Servia, and realising that behind Servia stood Russia, he turned to his ally for aid.

A Preventive War

The policy on which Austria and Germany determined is a matter of history, and the German White Paper describes it with an approach to frankness. This interesting document has not been fairly reproduced by our daily newspapers, and the main passage may be worth translating at length:—

'In these circumstances Austria was driven to the conclusion that the dignity and self-preservation of the Monarchy alike forbade her to watch this movement from across the frontier any longer in passivity. She communicated her view to us and asked our advice. We were able with all our hearts to inform our ally that we shared her opinion of the situation, and we assured her of our approval for any action which she might take to put an end to the movement in Servia directed against the integrity of the Monarchy. We were well aware that any military action by Austria against Servia might bring Russia on the scene, and involve us in war by reason of the obligations of our alliance. Realising, as we did, that the vital interests of Austria-Hungary were at stake, we could neither counsel our ally to a pliability inconsistent with her dignity, nor refuse her our aid in this difficult moment. Nor could we forget that our own interests were nearly threatened by this continual Servian agitation. Had the Servians been allowed, with the help of Russia and France, to endanger the integrity of the neighbouring Monarchy much longer, the consequence must have been the gradual disruption of Austria, and the subjection of the whole Slav world to the Russian sceptre, with the result that the position of the German race in central Europe would have become untenable.'

There lies, in its naked simplicity, the German case for this war. The provocations followed in an alternating series. Russia encouraged the Great Servian movement, which aimed at the break-up of Austria, whereupon Austria struck at Servia, and thereby challenged Russia. The issue now was, in plain words, whether Servia should become an Austrian vassal or remain a Russian tool. While a diplomatic accommodation was still possible, Russia took the menacing step of proclaiming a general mobilisation, and Germany replied with an ultimatum followed in a few hours by war. This war is a co-operative crime. To its making have gone Russian ambitions and German fears. It would be as just to say that the real aggressor was the Power which stood behind Servia, as it would be to say that it was the Power which first lit the conflagration by hurling its shells at Belgrade. On their own showing, the Germans had planned a bold challenging stroke, which might lead them into a preventive war. The last thing which they wanted was a universal war. They tried to buy our neutrality. They even appealed to us to keep France neutral. There is evidence enough in our own White Paper that they did not believe that Russia would fight. They thought that they had defied her in good time before her armaments were ready. They had bullied her with success in the similar crisis of 1909, and with the characteristic clumsiness of Bismarckian psychology, they did not realise that a public act of bullying can never be repeated. It was precisely because Russia had yielded in 1909, that she could not yield again. It is nonsense to say, as M. Sazonoff said, that the prestige of Russia as a Great Power would be gone if Servia became an Austrian vassal. Servia had been an Austrian vassal throughout the lifetime of King Milan, and for many a year after his abdication. But it may be true to say that Russia would have lost in prestige, if Servia had been torn from her orbit by Austrian arms and German threats. It is more to the point that such a humiliation would have ended the dream of a Great Servia for ever. That was the real issue. What Russia dreaded was not so much the humiliation of her little Slav brothers, the Serbs; she had watched the humiliation of her other little brothers in Bulgaria with equanimity, and even with satisfaction. The Servians, however, were more than brothers; they were tools. They were an indispensable price in the game of chess for the Empire of the East.

The Russian Mobilisation

The historian of the future will be in one sense more biassed in his judgment of this moving chapter of history than we are ourselves. He will give his verdict, as historians commonly do, to the side that wins. To us the issue is unknown, and we must divide our wonder and our censures. The Pan-Slavists have brought the whole of European civilisation to a test which may come near submerging it, in order to accomplish their dream of racial unity. The Germans, by rashly precipitating an issue which might never, in fact, have been forced upon them, may well have brought upon themselves the very catastrophe which they dreaded. A preventive war, if it is not a crime as inexcusable as a war of naked aggression, is always a folly. Nothing obliged Austria to fight now. From Servia she might have had ample reparation, with pledges for her future good behaviour. The crime of Serajevo was far from raising Servia's prestige among the Austrian Slavs; it had, on the contrary, lowered and besmirched it. A policy of conciliation might have rendered any insurrection impossible. Nor was Russia's star in the ascendant in the counsels of Europe. Persian affairs had led to a marked cooling in Sir Edward Grey's hitherto uncritical regard for Russia. The Anglo-German friendship was deepening, and something like the 'Utopian' proposal of our White Paper (Sir Edward Grey's conception of a collective guarantee by the Triple Entente that it would allow no aggression against the Triple Alliance) might have isolated Russia in the future, if, in fact, she meditated a war of Slav against Teuton. What is clear to-day is, that Germany, reasoning in cold blood amid profound peace, that Austria's future status was threatened by this Pan-Servian danger, has made a war in which the chief issue may soon be whether Austria can continue to exist. The event will probably show that Germany, when she forced the quarrel to a trial of armed strength, acted with folly. Her violation of Belgian neutrality was certainly as imprudent as it was iniquitous. It cannot be honestly argued that the Russian mobilisation justified her declaration of war. The answer to mobilisation is not war, but a counter mobilisation. But when this overwhelming case against German policy is stated, the fact remains that Germany could fairly plead that Russian policy was provocative. Russia was backing Servia in manœuvres which threatened to break up Germany's ally, Austria. Russia was, moreover, the first of the Great Powers to order a general mobilisation. This capital fact is ignored in nearly all the statements of the British case against Germany. It is slurred over in Sir Maurice de Bunsen's final despatch. It is omitted altogether in the historical preface to the cheap edition of the White Paper. That is not the way to write candid history. The dates are given in the White Paper. Russia, after a partial mobilisation of her Southern provinces against Austria, made her mobilisation general (*i.e.*, called out the reserves in the Northern provinces for use against Germany) on July 31 (No. 113). Austria and Germany ordered their general mobilisations on August 1 (Nos. 127 and 142). Up to the first day of August Austria had only partially mobilised; Germany had not mobilised at all; Austria in this last phase of the negotiations was showing moderation, and had conceded, as Sir Maurice de Bunsen has recognised, the main point at issue. The Kaiser was offering his personal services as mediator, and there can be no doubt that at the last moment, when she realised that the Austro-Serbian War could not be localised, Germany did use her influence with success to induce Austria to be moderate. She now saw in the Russian mobilisation a threat to herself, and she replied to the threat with a defiance. The Tsar's order to mobilise compromised the hope of peace; the Kaiser's ultimatum ruined it. The moral responsibility for the universal war must be shared between Germany and Russia.

The Eastern Melting-Pot

If the Triple Entente should be victorious, and if Russian policy is allowed to dominate the settlement, it is hard to draw a fortunate horoscope for Austria. A Russian proclamation has already snatched from Germany the Polish province of Posen, and from Austria the loyal and contented Poles of Galicia. We may be sure, if Servian arms should meet with any measure of success, that Russia will aim at creating a Greater Servia by amalgamating Croatia, Dalmatia, Bosnia, and Herzegovina with Servia and Montenegro. The *tertius gaudens*, as the Balkan struggle shows, is apt to exact a heavy price for his neutrality. Italy will not forget that Trent is peopled by Italians, and that the miserable Albanians will require some strong hand to restore their wretched country to order and peace. Roumania is a formidable military power, and at the moment when the struggle becomes desperate, her weight might be decisive in one or other of the Eastern scales of power. She has no love for either Empire, though her king is a Hohenzollern. Russia took Bessarabia from her, and Hungary is the mistress of a large Roumanian population in Transylvania. She may elect to move her armies into one or the other of these provinces, but more probably she will sell her neutrality for an assurance that the victor will reward her. Bulgaria is in the same case. An armed neutrality will pay her best. If Russia wins, then Servia, rich in her new acquisitions, can well afford to give up a part at least of Macedonia The whole of the Near East is in the melting-pot, but the central question of all is in what shape Austria will emerge from the tremendous test. A decisive victory would mean for her that Russian hegemony would be ended in Europe. She would have become herself the rival Slavonic power. She anticipated Russia by promising the restoration of Polish unity. She would either annex Servia outright, or reduce her to vassalage, while Roumania, Bulgaria, and Turkey, each aggrandised somewhat by the pursuit of a profitable neutrality, would be attached to her as graceful satellites. She would dominate the Balkans, and in the act she would have solved triumphantly the problem of her own internal cohesion. A beaten Russia would no longer attract the Southern Slavs. The other alternative is, if possible, still more cataclysmic. If Russia wins and has her way, little will be left of Austria save her German provinces, and these might be incorporated at length in a German Empire which had lost Posen and Alsace-Lorraine. Roumania and Servia would emerge as big States, attached by interest to the Russian system. Bulgaria would be reconciled by the gift of Macedonia. The doubtful points would be the future of the

Czechs and Magyars. But whatever their fate might be, the German Powers would have been cut off for ever from the East, and Russia with some millions of Poles and Ruthenians added to her territories and the Southern Slavs enlisted as her allies and vanguard, would dominate the Eastern Mediterranean and overshadow Turkey, as to-day she overshadows Persia.

Defence or Conquest

We are taking a parochial view of Armageddon if we allow ourselves to imagine that it is primarily a struggle for the independence of Belgium and the future of France. The Germans are nearer the truth when they regard it as a Russo-German war. It began in a struggle for the hegemony of the Near East, with its pivotal point at Belgrade. It will end logically, if either side achieves a decisive success, in a melting of all the frontiers of the East, and the settlement by force of arms of the question whether its destinies shall be governed by Germany or by Russia. It is, to my mind, an issue so barbarous, so remote from any real interest or concern of our daily life in these islands, that I can only marvel at the illusions, and curse the fatality which have made us belligerents in this struggle. We are neither Slavs nor Germans. How many of us, high or low, dare form a decided opinion as to whether Bosnia would in the end be happier under the native but intolerant and semi-civilised rule of the Serbs, or the alien but relatively civilised rule of Austria? How many of us would dare to answer one by one the questions whether Poles and Ruthenians and Slovacks would be the happier for passing from Austrian to Russian rule? We have not even debated these questions, yet our arms are helping to settle them. Our fleet in the North Sea, our army in France may be winning for the Tsar millions of fresh subjects, and for the familiar process of forcible Russification unnumbered victims. They will pass from a higher to a lower civilisation, from a system usually tolerant and fitfully Liberal, to one which has not even begun to grasp the idea of toleration, and whose answer to Liberalism is the censorship, the prison, and the 'truly Russian' pogrom. The Russian exiles who ask us to believe in the Liberal Russia of to-morrow can only repeat their pathetic, instinctive hopes. They admit, with a candour which enlists our respect, that nothing is changed as yet. One may hope for some slow evolution in Russian politics. One may dream of a future federal organisation of its many nationalities. But are we so secure in our anticipation of that brighter future that we will back it by our arms? On the lower level of self-interest and Imperial expediency have we reason to desire a world in which the Balance of Power will lurch violently to the side of this unscrupulous and incalculable Empire? Within a year from the breaking of Germany's power (if that is the result of this war), as Russia forces her way through the Dardanelles, dominates Turkey, overruns Persia and bestrides the road to India, our Imperialists will be calling out for a strong Germany to balance a threatening Russia.[1] A mechanical fatality has forced France into this struggle, and a comradeship, translated by secret commitments into a defensive alliance, has brought us into the war in her wake. It is no real concern of hers or of ours. It is a war for the Empire of the East. If our statesmanship is clear-sighted, it will stop the war before it has passed from a struggle for the defence of France and Belgium, into a colossal wrangle for the dominion of the Balkans and the mastery of the Slavs. When the campaign in the West has ended, as we all hope that it soon will end, in the liberation of French and Belgian soil from a deplorable invasion, the moment will have come to pause. To back our Western friends in a war of defence is one thing, to fling ourselves into the further struggle for the Empire of the East quite another. No call of the blood, no imperious calculation of self-interest, no hope for the future of mankind requires us to side with Slav against Teuton. We cannot wish that either Austria or Russia should dominate the Balkans, but if we had to make the choice in cold blood, most of us would prefer the more tolerant and more civilised German influence. Our orators talk of the cause of nationality. Two months ago what man in his senses would have suggested that the best way to serve the cause of nationality was to bring fresh subject races under the Russian yoke? The Poles and Ruthenians are Slavs indeed but they are not Russians. One might as well propose to further the cause of nationality by annexing Holland to the German Empire. If in the heat of battle, we allow ourselves to rush onward without reflection from a war of defence to a war of conquest, we shall find that all the old problems confront us anew. Enthusiasts for this hateful war may applaud it as an effort to 'destroy German militarism'. That is a meaningless phrase. The Allies may indeed destroy the German armies, but no one can destroy German militarism, save the German people itself. Militarism seizes a nation only when the prophets of the gospel of force can preach to ears prepared by fear. We are about to make new fears for the German people. Crush that people, load it with indemnities, lop it of its provinces, encircle it with triumphant allies, and so far from turning to depose its Prussian leaders, it will rally behind

---

[1] Here, once more, Brailsford's prophecy—fulfilled to some extent in the nineteen thirties—applies even more forcibly to the Second World War and its aftermath. (ED.)

them in a national struggle to recover its standing, its integrity, its power of free movement. Not France but Germany will arm to recover lost provinces, and weave new alliances to adjust the ever-shifting balance of power. If once the world begins to play at map-making, it will create unsatisfied appetites; there will be States enough to join with Germany in an effort to upset the settlement. The future will stretch before us, a new phase of the ruinous armed peace, destined to end, after further years of anger and waste, in another war of revenge. It lies with public opinion to limit the duration of this quarrel, and to impose on our diplomacy, when victory in the West is won, a return to its natural *rôle* of moderator in a quarrel no longer its own.

THE PRINCIPLE OF A SETTLEMENT

A Letter reprinted from 'The Nation'

War is like all great tragedies; it is not a simple struggle between evil and good. It is a conflict between two things that are good. To see in this war a mere trial of brute force would be to misunderstand it. Each side is inspired by its own idealism, for no Government can hope to-day to lead any free people into war unless it can convince it that it is fighting under dire necessity for the defence of right. The German popular attitude is, in brief, that this war came about by reason of a Russo-Servian plot against the Austrian ally, and its object is defined as the destruction of 'Tsarism'. What that means in detail, I do not know but in the minds of German Socialists, and of men like Hauptmann, Haeckel, and Eucken, it answers to some honest and liberal thought. Finland is to be liberated; Russian Poland is to be restored to the ranks of the nation; and, in some undefined way, the autocracy is to be broken. We can see with the pitiless insight of enemies how facile and partisan is this idealism.

The Two Idealisms

And what, meantime, of our own idealism? Each side in this war is bent on liberating its enemies. We aim at freeing Germany from 'militarism', and we, too, have our plans, if not for Finland, at least for Poland. There is material in this shock of two idealisms for tragedy, and even for bitter comedy. But there is something else. If we could, for a moment, blot out from our thoughts the various Governments, whose collective bankruptcy in statesmanship made this war; if we could forget the long struggle for the Balance of Power, from the Moroccan affair to the Servian crisis; if we could somehow envisage the various nations fighting amid error, half-knowledge, and anger, should we find in their real purposes a serious disagreement? Each, by some strange sophistry, believes that it is waging a defensive war. Each is persuaded that its triumph will advance European liberty. There is in all the confusion, a general will among the bemused and deceived peoples for ideal ends. The problem for the world is to bring this general will to bear upon the settlement. The secret ends of the Governments are mutually destructive. The avowed ends of the peoples are not incompatible, and if we intend that a united Europe shall emerge from these horrors, we must see to it that the triumph of our arms is also a victory for the general will.

Crushing German Militarism

The other programme is simpler. The Allies are to dictate peace in Berlin. It is also to be a 'fight to a finish', and the beaten Germans are to be crushed until they can resist no demand which the victors care to impose. They will lose by the law of conquest Alsace and Posen; Austria will be dismembered and may cease to exist, and some talk of destroying Essen and the Kiel Canal, and taking what is left of the German navy. A ring of Allied Powers will then surround a prostrate Germany, so that she can move neither in the East nor the West, except at their good pleasure. Then we hope German militarism will be crushed, and an angry people will depose the Hohenzollerns. This programme would cost, not months but years of warfare, for the German Government is no more tied to Berlin than was the French to Paris. It would decimate the whole manhood of Europe. In the effort to destroy the German Empire, it would certainly ruin France. But would it end as its partisans expect? So far from resulting in a German revolution, it would probably unite the German people as it never has been united since the Napoleonic wars, and everything that is virile in the race would rally, first, to resist, and then to wipe out the humiliation. German militarists, simply because they have been defeated, will not burn their copies of Bernhardi, and take to reading Tolstoy. They will merely say that several nations with a total population of over two hundred millions have with much difficulty beaten two nations who number one hundred millions. They will arm and plot and plan to renew the struggle under better conditions. No punishment could prevent the German people from remaining the best-organised, the best-educated, and one of the most prolific of European races. Disarmed and isolated it may be; but arms are quickly forged, and amid the shifting and conscienceless play of diplomacy, alliances are easily contracted. Napoleon was banished in 1815. The Napoleonic idea was once more triumphant in 1848. A settlement which left eighty millions of Germans angry, embittered, and cherishing revenge, might last for five, or ten, or twenty years. But it would perpetuate, even while it lasted, the armed peace, and so far from crushing militarism in Germany, it would impose it also on ourselves. Militarism is, primarily, the child of fear. The Bernhardis do, indeed, cherish a real aggressive ambition. But the masses of the German middle class consented to their naval and military programme, only because they feared the Russian millions and our Dreadnoughts.

The Principle of Reciprocity

Can an alternative programme be drafted, which will make an end, not only of German, but of every other 'militarism'? Armies may destroy armies, but no army ever broke militarism. It is a state of mind, and will vanish with the fears that made it. There is, it seems to me, one test by which a just and durable settlement may be distinguished from a settlement which merely registers the momentary triumph of one force over another. It is that the settlement, in all the changes which it lays down, shall apply a universal principle. A settlement may take two forms. A and B, because they are stronger, may force C to suffer certain things. But, also, A, B, and C, after a tragic struggle, may jointly decide that certain principles shall govern them all for the future, and these principles they may agree to apply to stated cases. One must come back to the elements of morality. The real question is whether we are going to impose by force on Germany principles which we will not apply to ourselves. One must in war strive to do the maximum of harm to the enemy. But the law of peace ought to rule from the moment that negotiations begin, and the law of peace is to seek the good of one's neighbour. If certain principles which are more or less held in common by enlightened men in all nations are applied impartially, then there is a hope that when the first sorrow of defeat is over, the better mind of Germany may feel that what has triumphed is not the arms of an enemy, but a common European idealism.

Armaments

These are vague words. Let me attempt to illustrate them. They apply alike to the question of armaments, to changes of territory, and to alliances: (1) The first point is the simplest, and needs few words. Every democracy in Europe, including that of Germany, desires to make an end of the armed peace. If we *impose* disarmament on Germany by taking her ships, destroying the Kiel Canal, dismantling her fortresses, or by the indirect method of a crushing indemnity, we must not expect even her Socialists to welcome the change. Let us take neither money nor colonies for ourselves—to Belgium, however, a special indemnity by way of fine and compensation must certainly be paid. One-sided disarmament would come not as deliverance, but as humiliation. The disarmament in form as well as effect must be general. All the Powers, without exception, must bind themselves either to reduce their future military and naval expenditure to some fraction of the figure that it had reached before the war, or else to accept a militia system with six or twelve months' service. Such a provision would be a triumph for German as well as for French democracy.

Nationality and the Plebiscite

(2) The difficult question is that of territory. No 'warproof map' of Europe can be constructed which rests upon the right of conquest. We are told that the principle of nationality will govern the settlement. To take bits of Poland from one Empire and give them to another is not an honest application of the principle of nationality. That principle might be satisfied if all the Powers pledged themselves in the treaty of peace to accept federalism. The benefit would fall in that case to Ireland, Finland, and the Caucasus, as well as to Alsace and Poland. But, probably, territorial changes are inevitable. There is one way by which such changes may receive a national and democratic sanction. In the last resort, the fate of provinces must be decided not only by the fortunes of alien armies, but by the votes of their own inhabitants. Then, and then only, will the principle of nationality be satisfied. Let Alsace and Posen, Galicia, and the Servian and Italian lands of Austria settle their own fate by a *plebiscite*. It must be, moreover, an honest *plebiscite*, conducted with full liberty for discussion, and by neutral commissioners. Is this an idle formality? I do not think so. In the first place, it would compel Russia to define clearly what sort of autonomy she offers to the Poles. In the second place, it would enable the democratic parties of the defeated Powers to acquiesce, without loss of honour, in the sacrifice of territory. They would be yielding not to the brute force of the allied armies, but to the expressed will of the population concerned. No honest German Radical or Socialist, however much he might regret such a settlement, could regard it as the mere triumph of violence, or scheme to upset it by a future war of re-conquest. But if it is to mean anything, the *plebiscite* must be honest. Alsace, for example, must be free to choose between full Home Rule within the German Empire, neutralisation, or annexation to France.

Alliances

(3) The last point is not the least important. The future of Europe will be no brighter if it relapses once more into two armed camps, knit by military alliances. There will be no rest while the Allies 'pen' Germany in, and she hunts for associates among dissatisfied and ambitious Powers. I am not among the optimists who imagine that a true Concert is going to emerge by miracle from the hatreds of this war. One cannot call the Germans 'Goths, Vandals, and Huns' to-day and embrace them cordially in a Concert to-morrow. But we can at least avoid the mistake which the Allies made a century ago, when they isolated and ostracised France. The first step is that each and all the Powers should, at the peace, renounce their existing alliances. The next step is to erect some barrier against aggression, by a general defensive understanding among all the Great Powers, by which each should agree to defend another if menaced by an enemy who, in any quarrel had rejected the arbitrament of neutrals. This may seem a Utopian programme. The war has taught us that we must choose between Utopia and Hell.

When to Make Peace

Any settlement will be good which legislates for Europe in a sense which the general will for freedom, speaking to-day in the sundered and hostile idealisms of the warring nations, can uphold and defend. Any settlement is bad which will have against it the whole force of the united German race. If our aim is a one-sided disarmament, a tearing away by violence of conquered provinces, and, to crown all, a coalition against the vanquished, then, indeed, we must fight to the bitter end, and dictate peace over burned villages to a nation of refugees. A peace that rests on principles common to all democracies may be reached the sooner and will last the longer. It would be intolerable that this war should end in a half-peace. Worse even than bloodshed would be the shedding of blood to no purpose. We must fight till our end is attained. But what is our central end? If at any point in the struggle Germany is ready to consider a general disarmament, then German militarism has been broken. That, and not the splendour of our victories or the arrival of the Allied Armies in Berlin, is the test by which we may distinguish a durable peace from a half-peace. The moment will have come to think of such a peace, and to welcome it through the mediation of neutrals, when the German invasion is hurled back from France and Belgium, and the German armies are fighting no longer to overwhelm their rivals, but to defend their own homes.

September 17th, 1914.

WHY WE BURNT THE BOMBING SCHOOL

OUR final item in this volume is from the pen of a Welsh Nationalist. It is remarkable for the circumstances by which it was occasioned, for the admirable way in which Mr Saunders Lewis presented his case, and for the fact that it is very much more than what it might appear to be at first sight—a defence of Welsh Nationalism or of 'militant pacifism'. It is, in fact, a powerful plea for those cultural values which are in danger of complete destruction, as much in Capitalist America as in Stalin's Russia, and equally so in our own island.

The story of the Bombing Range of Penrhos is told in Saunders Lewis's *apologia*—the efforts that were made to prevent what leading Welshmen regarded as a desecration of their country and the final, desperate remedy to which Mr Saunders Lewis, the Rev Lewis Valentine and Mr D. J. Williams resorted in setting fire to the Bombing School. All were respected citizens—the first a lecturer on Welsh litera-ture at Univerity College, Swansea, the second a minister of religion, and the third a schoolmaster. The pamphlet, *Why We Burnt the Bombing School*, consists of the speeches made by two of the defendants at the Caernarvon assizes, on October 13, 1936, when the jury failed to agree on a verdict. This was interesting, as it will be observed that the defendants openly and proudly admitted what they had done. Alarmed, the Government arranged for the second trial to take place at the Old Bailey—an action for which they had no doubt some musty old legal precedent (as they had in the trial of Sir Roger Casement), though in equity, as distinct from legal chicanery, it was indefensible.

At the Old Bailey the prisoners refused to plead and were each sentenced to nine months' imprisonment. Saunders Lewis, as a result of the case, lost his post at University College, Swansea, and has since lived mainly by his pen, writing plays and contributing to Welsh weekly periodicals.

Of the two speeches which formed the original pamphlet we have only republished here that of Mr Saunders Lewis (without any intentional disrespect to his courageous colleagues): and we are grateful for

Mr Lewis's kind permission to use his work for this purpose. We may add that, although the difficulties involved in selecting a suitable pamphlet to represent the past decade have proved insuperable (if there are any really good ones we confess ourselves too near them to assess their true merit), this statement on the Bombing Range may be considered as still topical. Our latest information is that the Government has by no means abandoned the idea of trying out its bombs in North Wales; and the Welsh press is still periodically agitated by the predatory eyes of the Air Ministry and the War Office. The popular resistance movement against the War Office at Trawsfynydd is correct news as this book goes to the press.

WHY WE BURNT THE BOMBING SCHOOL

By Saunders Lewis

THE fact that we set fire to the buildings and building materials at the Penrhos Bombing Range is not in dispute. We ourselves were the first to give the Authorities warning of the fire, and we proclaimed to them our responsibility. Yet we hold the conviction that our action was in no wise criminal, and that it was an act forced upon us, that it was done in obedience to conscience and to the moral law, and that the responsibility for any loss due to our act is the responsibility of the English Government.

We are professional men who hold positions of trust, of honour, and of security. I must speak now with reluctance for myself. I profess the literature of Wales in the University College of Wales at Swansea. That is my professional duty. It is also my pride and my delight. Welsh literature is one of the great literatures of Europe. It is the direct heir in the British Isles of the literary discipline of classical Greece and Rome. And it is a living, growing literature, and draws its sustenance from a living language and a traditional social life. It was my sense of the inestimable value of this tremendous heirloom of the Welsh Nation that first led me from purely literary work to public affairs, and to the establishment of the Welsh Nationalist Party. It was the terrible knowledge that the English Government's Bombing Range, once it were established in Llŷn, would endanger and in all likelihood destroy an essential focus of this Welsh culture, the most aristocratic spiritual heritage of Wales, that made me think my own career, the security even of my family, things that must be sacrificed in order to prevent so appalling a calamity. For in the University lecture rooms I have not professed a dead literature of antiquarian interest. I have professed the living literature of this Nation. So that this literature has claims on me as a man as well as a teacher. I hold that my action at Penrhos aerodrome on September 8th saves the honour of the University of Wales, for the language and literature of Wales are the very *raison d'être* of this University.

And now for my part in Welsh public life. I speak briefly about it. I have been for ten years President of the Welsh Nationalist Party, and Editor of its organ *Y Ddraig Goch*. I've been a member of the Advisory Committee of the University of Wales on Broadcasting, the chairman of which has been the Pro-Chancellor of the University, the Bishop of Monmouth. I have made a special study of the economic problems of Welsh unemployment and reconstruction, and was the originator of the Welsh National Industrial Development Council.

In South Wales I have been in constant touch with my unemployed fellow-countrymen and have successfully founded a Club, the membership of which is growing and spreading over Wales, whereby on Thursday of every week a man whose position in life is comfortable gives up his dinner and sends the price of it to provide a three-course dinner for an unemployed fellow-Welshman whose larder on Thursday is empty.

Now, if you examine these activities and if you examine the record of the Welsh Nationalist Party during the past ten years, you will find that our works, our programme, our propaganda have been entirely constructive and peaceful. There has never been any appeal to mob instincts. In fact, our leadership has been accused of being too high-brow and academic. I have repeatedly and publicly declared that the Welsh nation must gain its political freedom without resort to violence or to physical force. It is a point I wish to re-affirm today. And I submit to you that our action in burning the Penrhos Aerodrome proves the sincerity of this affirmation. Had we wished to follow the methods of violence with which national minority movements are sometimes taunted, and into which they are often driven, nothing could have been easier for us than to ask some of the generous and spirited young men of the Welsh Nationalist Party to set fire to the Aerodrome and get away undiscovered. It would be the beginning of methods of sabotage and guerilla turmoil. The Rev. Lewis Valentine and I determined to prevent any such development. When all democratic and peaceful methods of persuasion had failed to obtain even a hearing for our case against the Bombing Range, and when we saw clearly the whole future of Welsh tradition threatened as never before in history, we determined that even then we would invoke only the process of law, and that a jury from the Welsh people should pronounce on the right and wrong of our behaviour. We ourselves public men in Wales, and leaders of the Welsh Nationalist Party, fired these buildings and timbers. We ourselves reported the fire to the police. We have given the police all the help we could to prepare the case against us. Is that the conduct of men acting 'feloniously and maliciously?' I submit that we are in this dock of our own will, not only for the sake of Wales, but also for the sake of peace and unviolent, charitable relations now and in the future between Wales and England.

It is charged against us that our action was 'unlawful'. I propose to meet that charge by developing an argument in four stages. First, I shall show with what horror the building of a Bombing Range in Llŷn was regarded by us and by a great number of Welsh people in every part of Wales. Secondly, how patiently and with what labour and at what sacrifice we tried and exhausted every possible way of legitimate persuasion to prevent the building of the Bombing Range. Thirdly, how differently the protests and remonstrances of Wales and Welsh public men were treated by the English Government, compared with similar protests, though less seriously grounded protests, made in England in the same period. Fourthly, I shall try to put before you the dilemma and the conflict of obedience in which the Government's cruelty placed the leaders of the crusade against the Bombing Range, and the limits of the rights of the English State when it transgresses the moral law and acts in violation of the rights of the Welsh Nation.

In an English pamphlet stating the case against the Bombing School in Llŷn, Professor Daniel has expressed with pregnant brevity the heart-felt fear of all thoughtful Welshmen. He says:

'It is the plain historical fact that, from the fifth century on, Llŷn has been Welsh of the Welsh, and that so long as Llŷn remained unanglicised, Welsh life and culture were secure. If once the forces of Anglicisation are securely established behind as well as in front of the mountains of Snowdonia, the day when Welsh language and culture will be crushed between the iron jaws of these pincers cannot be long delayed. For Wales, the preservation of the Llŷn Peninsula from this Anglicisation is a matter of life and death.'

That, we are convinced, is the simple truth. So that the preservation of the harmonious continuity of the rural Welsh tradition of Llŷn, unbroken for fourteen hundred years, is for us 'a matter of life and death'. I have said that my professional duty is the teaching of Welsh literature. My maternal grandfather was a minister of religion and a Welsh scholar and man of letters. He began his ministerial career in

Pwllheli. He wrote the greatest Welsh prose work of the 19th century, *Cofiant John Jones Talsarn*. One of the most brilliant chapters in that book is the seventh chapter, which is a description of the religious leaders of Llŷn and Eifionydd in the middle of the 19th century. It is impossible for one who has blood in his veins not to care passionately when he sees this terrible vandal bombing range in this very home of Welsh Culture. I have here in my hand an anthology of the works of the Welsh poets of Llŷn, *Cynfeirdd Llŷn*, 1500-1800, by Myrddin Fardd. On page 176 of this book there is a poem, a Cywydd, written in Penyberth Farmhouse in the middle of the 16th century. That house was one of the most historic in Llŷn. It was a resting-place for the Welsh pilgrims of the Isle of Saints, Ynys Enlli, in the Middle Ages. It had associations with Owen Glyndŵr. It belonged to the story of Welsh literature. It was a thing of hallowed and secular majesty. It was taken down and utterly destroyed a week before we burnt on its fields the timbers of the vandals who destroyed it. And I claim that the people who ought to be in this dock are the people responsible for the destruction of Penyberth Farmhouse. Moreover, that destruction of Penyberth House is, in the view of most competent Welsh observers, typical and symbolic. The development of the Bombing Range at Llŷn into the inevitable arsenal it will become will destroy this essential home of Welsh Culture, idiom and literature. It will shatter the spiritual basis of the Welsh Nation.

It was the knowledge of the catastrophe that the proposed Bombing Range would bring to Welsh culture and tradition in this, one of the few unspoilt homes of that culture, which led us and thousands of Welshmen not normally interested in political affairs to protest vigorously against such an outrage. I have to show now that these protests were on a national scale, that they were representative of the Welsh Nation, that nothing was neglected or left undone to convince English Government of the seriousness of the occasion, and that efforts of peaceful, legitimate persuasion were exhausted in our endeavour to prevent the catastrophe. I shall summarise the story of the protests as briefly as possible.

It was in June, 1935, that the Air Ministry's proposal to establish a Bombing Range in Llŷn was first announced. Immediately the Caernarvonshire branches of the Welsh Nationalist Party held a delegate committee and sent to the Ministry a statement of their unanimous objection to the plan.

In the autumn of 1935 the war in Abyssinia, the general expectation of an Anglo-Italian war and of a general European war, and then the dissolution of the English Parliament and the general election, all threw the Llŷn bombing range proposal into obscurity. But Professor J. E. Daniel made it a special matter of protest and condemnation in his election address in Caernarvonshire.

In January, 1936, the campaign against the Bombing Range was renewed with urgency, and from that time on it ceased to be a matter of local interest. It was taken up throughout Wales and became a national concern. Protest meetings were organised generally in Llŷn and Caernarvonshire. Resolutions of protest were passed by Welsh churches and representative meetings of the religious bodies throughout Wales. It is a tribute I rejoice to pay to the ministers and leaders of the Welsh Nonconformist churches that they gave a lead to the whole country in the matter.

Protests were equally general from all the Welsh secular societies and institutions. The University of Wales Guild of Graduates and the Welsh national youth movement (Urdd Gobaith Cymru), as well as Welsh Cymrodorion Societies in Cardiff, Swansea, Llanelli, Aberystwyth, and representative meetings of Welshmen living outside Wales, in London, in Liverpool, Manchester, Birmingham. Before the first day of May more than 600 Welsh societies and religious bodies had passed unanimous resolutions demanding the withdrawal of the Bombing Range. These resolutions were sent on to the Air Ministry, and the agitation in the Welsh Press was a sign of the widespread approval of the protests.

We kept the Prime Minister and the English Air Ministry fully informed of our opposition. On March 31st I wrote to the Prime Minister begging, in view of the gravity of the affair, for an interview. I said in my letter:

'An important body of Welsh people regard this proposal as one to prevent which even liberty, even life itself, might properly be thrown away.'

The Prime Minister declined to grant an interview, and sent in answer a stereotyped statement exactly similar to that sent to all other protesters.

On May 1st I was invited to broadcast a talk through the national wavelength of the British Broadcasting Corporation on Welsh Nationalism. I took the opportunity to make an urgent appeal for the saving of Llŷn from this bombing range. The talk was later published in The Listener. The Government continued to ignore every appeal.

We organised a plebiscite of the people of Llŷn. It was conducted entirely by voluntary workers giving their spare time to tramping the scattered villages and farmhouses of the peninsula and paying their own expenses in food and 'bus fares. Over 5,000 of the electors of Llŷn signed the petition to Parliament and to the Prime Minister asking for the cessation of the Bombing Range. Our workers were welcomed everywhere. They met with a practically unanimous sympathy, and with time they would have obtained the signatures of almost the entire rural population of Llŷn.

Similar plebiscites were conducted in Llanberis and among the Welsh of Liverpool, where 5,000 adult Welsh men and women also signed petitions. Before the end of May well over one thousand Welsh churches and lay bodies, representing over a quarter of a million Welsh people, had passed resolutions of protest.

On May 23rd we held a final demonstration at Pwllheli. It was attended by seven or eight thousand people and they had come in motor 'buses from all parts of South Wales and central Wales, as well as from Welsh centres outside Wales, such as Liverpool and Birmingham. The meeting received much notice in the English newspapers everywhere because of the attempt of a gang of some 50 drunken roughs in Pwllheli to prevent the speeches from the platform.

The platform represented the whole of Wales, leaders of religion, of scholarship and public life. The chairman was the most eminent literary man in Wales, Professor W. J. Gruffydd. A newspaper report (*Liverpool Daily Post*) says:

'Professor Gruffydd put the resolution calling on the government to withdraw their plans for Llŷn and inviting the Prime Minister to receive a deputation on the subject. A show of hands revealed an overwhelming majority in favour of the resolution. The negative did not exceed fifty.'

On June 4th the request was sent to the Prime Minister to receive a Welsh National deputation. It was sent on behalf of the 5000 petitioners of Llŷn, the thousands of petitioners outside Llŷn and the fifteen hundred bodies representing nearly half a million Welshmen who had resolved to protest against the Llŷn bombing range. The letter, requesting the Prime Minister to receive a deputation, was signed by over twenty eminent Welsh leaders. They included the Principals of Aberystwyth and of Bala and of Bala-Bangor Theological Colleges, the secretary of the Honourable Society of Cymrodorion, the Bishop of

Menevia, Moderators of the Presbyterian Church of Wales and the Chairman of the Congregational Union of Wales, Editors of important Welsh journals and the Professors of Welsh Language and of Welsh Literature at the University College of Bangor and of Aberystwyth.

A secretary to the Prime Minister replied that:

'The Prime Minister does not feel that any useful purpose would be served by his acceding to the request that he should receive a deputation.'

On June 15th the English newspapers circulating in Wales reported thus:

'More than 200 acres at Penyberth Farm have been cleared and levelled for an aerodrome site. The contractors are beginning to erect an aerodrome today.'

Thus ended peaceful persuasion along legitimate democratic lines. There only remained now the way of sacrifice.

But the effect of the English Government's contemptuous rejection of this nation-wide protest from Wales, both on Welsh national sentiment in general and on the Reverend Lewis Valentine and myself as the accepted leaders of the crusade, cannot be properly gauged without considering also the contrast between the Government's treatment of Wales and their treatment of England.

Let me recount briefly the story of three bombing range sites proposed to be set up in England at the same time as the Llŷn establishment. One was at Abbotsbury in Dorsetshire. It is a well-known breeding place for swans. Because of that, and because English writers and poets were allowed space in the *Times* newspaper and generally in the English Press to express their passion for swans and natural beauty of scene, the Dorsetshire site was moved.

Then came Holy Island in English Northumberland. Mr G. M. Trevelyan wrote a letter to the *Times* on January 13th to explain that Holy Island was a sacred region: it was a holiday resort for city workers; it had historical associations with Lindisfarne and St Cuthbert; it was the most important home of wild birds in England. He argued that Northumberland duck were no less sacred than Dorset swans. He was supported by leaders of English scholarship and letters. The Air Ministry summoned a public conference to consider the matter, and the Bombing Range was withdrawn.

Thus again at Friskney on the Wash. Here the local authorities of the area took the lead and protested against the waste of so large an area of excellent agricultural land and the destruction of fishing. The Air Ministry withdrew.

Will you try to understand our feelings when we saw the foremost scholars and literary men of England talking of the 'sacredness' of ducks and swans, and succeeding on that argument in compelling the Air Ministry to withdraw its bombing range, while here in Wales, at the very same time, we were organising a nation-wide protest on behalf of the truly sacred things in Creation—a Nation, its language, its literature, its separate traditions and immemorial ways of Christian life—and we could not get the Government even to receive a deputation to discuss the matter with us? The irony of the contrast is the irony of blasphemy.

On June 22nd the Union of the Congregational Churches of Wales met at Bangor. The chairman was one of the foremost divines in Welsh Nonconformity and he was also newly appointed Archdruid of Wales— the Reverend J. J. Williams. Speaking to a resolution condemning the Llŷn bombing range, he said:

'It is our intention to prevent the establishment of this bombing school by every legitimate means possible. But if legitimate means finally fail, I believe there is enough resolution in the Welsh Nation to remove the bombing camp by other means.'

The Rev. J. J. Williams spoke for Wales. But—and I come now to a crucial point in my argument—he spoke also for the universal moral law which is an essential part of Christian tradition and is recognised by moral theologians to be binding on all men.

'Remember that the God Who created men ordained nations,'

said Emrys ap Iwan, and the moral law recognises the family and the nation to be Moral Persons. They have the qualities and the natural rights of Persons. And by the law of God the essential rights of the family and of the nation, and especially their right to live, are prior to the rights of any State. It is part also of the moral law that no State has the right to use any other national entity merely as a means to its own profit, and no State has a right to seek national advantages which would mean genuine harm to any other nation. All that is universal Christian tradition.

It is also universal Christian tradition that men should obey the moral law rather than the law of a State whenever the two should clash. It is universal Christian tradition that it is the duty of members of a family and of a nation to defend the essential rights of the family and of the nation, and especially it is a duty to preserve the life of a nation, or to defend it from any mortal blow, by all means possible short of taking human life unjustly or breaking the moral law.

That is the Christian tradition as Emrys ap Iwan understood it, as the Reverend J. J. Williams understands it today, and as the Universal Christian Church has always maintained it.

It was in the clear light of this fundamental principle of Christendom that Lewis Valentine, D. J. Williams and I resolved to act in Llŷn. The responsibility of leadership was ours. We could not shirk it. We saw the English State preparing mortal danger to the moral person of the Welsh nation. We had exercised the greatest patience in attempting every possible means of persuasion and appeal to prevent the wrong. We had the unanimous voice of all the religious leaders of Wales with us. English government took no heed at all. The bombing range was begun. Building was proceeding.

We resolved to act. We determined on an action that would proclaim our conviction that the building of this bombing range in Llŷn is by all Christian principles wrong and unlawful. We resolved on an act that would compel English government to take action at law against us. We made absolutely sure that no human life would be endangered. You have heard the pitiful story of the night-watchman. The only true statement in all his story is that he suffered no harm at all.

We damaged property. It is valued at some two thousand pounds odd. Exactly by that action we have compelled the English State to put us in this dock. Only by appearing in this dock on a charge sufficiently serious to allow a maximum sentence on us of penal servitude for life could we bring the action of the English State to the bar of conscience and of Christian morality. Every other means had failed. But we have put our lives in the balance against this act of Government iniquity. It was in preparation for this day and this hour, when we should appear before you twelve, our fellow-Christians and fellow-countrymen, and should explain all our action to you and the meaning and significance of that action, and should ask your judgment on us—it was for this and in the belief that we could prove the moral justice, the absolute justice, of our act that we have lived and hoped from the moment that our decision was made.

It is perhaps necessary to say something about the amount of the damage we caused by our fire. It exceeds two thousand pounds, we are told. It is obvious that the damage caused is frivolous compared with the harm that the successful establishment of this Bombing Range in Llŷn will cause. Actually, if it were practicable to estimate in terms of money the cost to us of the efforts we all expended in our crusade to persuade the Government to withdraw the Bombing Range, the cost of the time and labour freely given by all our fellow-workers and by Welsh religious leaders who travelled to and fro addressing protest meetings, it could be shown that the Bombing Range has already cost us very many hundreds of pounds.

But the loss that this Bombing Range, if it be not withdrawn, will cause to Wales is not a loss that can be estimated in thousands of pounds. You cannot calculate in figures the irreparable loss of a language, of purity of idiom, of a home of literature, of a tradition of rural Welsh civilisation stretching back fourteen hundred years. These things have no price. You cannot pay compensation for them. It is only in Eternity that the destruction of these things can be valued. We were compelled, therefore, to do serious damage to the Bombing School buildings. Only serious damage could ensure that we should appear before a jury of our fellow-countrymen in a last desperate and vital effort to bring the immorality of the Government's action before the judgment of Christian Wales.

You, gentlemen of the jury, are our judges in this matter. As you have to give verdict on a case that is not only exceptional but a case that is of momentous importance. I suppose there is no previous example of the leaders of a struggle for the defence of a nation's culture against an alien and heedless State staking their freedom, their livelihood, their reputation and almost their lives, and putting themselves in the dock in order that a jury of their countrymen should judge between them and the brute power of the State. To do this is to show our trust not only in your justice as the jury, but also in your courage. We ask you to have no fear at all. The terminology of the law calls this Bombing Range 'the property of the King'. That means the English Government. It means these bureaucrats in the Air Ministry in London to whom Wales is a region on the map and who know nothing at all of the culture and language of Wales, but will desecrate our sanctuaries like a dog raising its hind leg at an altar.

But there is another aspect to this trial that gives it special importance. We have said from the beginning, and it was the point we emphasised in our letter to the Chief Constable of Caernarvonshire, that our action was a protest against the ruthless refusal of the English State even to discuss the rights of the Welsh nation in Llŷn. Now, everywhere in Europe today we see Governments asserting that they are above the moral law of God, that they recognise no other law but the will of the Government, and that they recognise no other power but the power of the State. These Governments claim absolute powers: they deny the rights of persons and of Moral Persons. They deny that they can be challenged by any code of morals, and they demand the absolute obedience of men. Now that is Atheism. It is the denial of God, of God's Law. It is the repudiation of the entire Christian tradition of Europe, and it is the beginning of the reign of chaos.

English Government's behaviour in the matter of the Llŷn bombing range is exactly the behaviour of this new Anti-Christ throughout Europe. And in this assize-court in Caernarvon today we, the accused in this dock, are challenging Anti-Christ. We deny the absolute power of the State-God. Here in Wales, a land that has no tradition except Christian tradition, a land that has never in all its history been pagan or atheist, we stand for the preservation of that Christian tradition and for the supremacy of the moral law over the power of materialist bureaucracy. So that whether you find us guilty or not guilty is of importance today to the future of Christian civilisation and Christian liberty and Christian justice in Europe.

If you find us guilty the World will understand that here also in Wales an English Government may destroy the moral person of a nation, may shatter the spiritual basis of that nation's life, may refuse to consider or give heed to any appeal even from the united religious leaders of the whole country, and then may use the law to punish with imprisonment the men who put those monstrous claims of Anti-Christ to the test. If you find us guilty you proclaim that the law of the English State is superior to the moral law of Christian tradition, that the will of the Government may not be challenged by any person whatsoever, and that there is no appeal possible to morality as Christians have always understood it.

If you find us guilty you proclaim the effective end of Christian principles governing the life of Wales.

On the other hand, if you find us not guilty you declare your conviction as judges in this matter that the moral law is supreme; you declare that the moral law is binding on Governments just as it is on private citizens.

You declare that 'Necessity of State' gives no right to set morality aside, and you declare that justice, not material force, must rule in the affairs of nations.

We hold with unshakeable conviction that the burning of the monstrous Bombing Range in Llŷn was an act forced on us for the defence of Welsh civilisation, for the defence of Christian principles, for the maintenance of the Law of God in Wales. Nothing else was possible for us. It was the Government itself that created the situation in which we were placed, so that we had to choose either the way of cowards, and slink out of the defence of Christian tradition and morality, or we had to act as we have acted, and trust to a jury of our countrymen to declare that the Law of God is superior to every other law, and that by that law our act is just.

We ask you to be fearless. We ask you to bring in a verdict that will restore Christian principles in the realm of law, and open a new period in the history of nations and governments. We ask you to say that we are Not Guilty.

APPENDIX

A Peep into the Cave of Jacobinism—frontispiece

This cartoon by James Gillray, first published in the *Anti-Jacobin Review* of September 7, 1798, is typical of the anti-Jacobin propaganda of the period: it is the pictorial equivalent of Burke's writings. Thelwall, in spite of a verbosity equal to that of Burke himself, provides an admirable commentary on all such representations of the political situation at the time of the French Revolution.

Gillray provided an almost classic example of the connection between genius and madness. Having made savage attacks on everything from the English Court to the French Revolution, he was with difficulty prevented from taking his own life in the period of insanity which preceded his premature death.

The Contrast—p. 38

This is another typical anti-Jacobin cartoon, by an unknown hand. It is reproduced here from a broadside of 1792.

Three Illustrations to 'Non Mi Ricordo!'—pp. 83, 91, 95

Cruikshank's cartoons need no explanation. His target, in each case, is the king.

George Cruikshank was at this time closely associated with Hone. He was an ardent political reformer and also deserves particular credit for his part in forcing the abolition of the death penalty for forgery (see notes on Wakefield's pamphlet).

The Game Laws—p. 111

This cartoon by John Leech appeared in 1845, in *Punch*—at that time a mildly Liberal journal. In spite of strenuous efforts to reform the penal laws (e.g. Wakefield's attack on capital punishment) and a slow progress during the early part of the century, much remained to be done.

The Game Laws afforded a spectacular instance of legislation designed by propertied classes in the interest of property. In the very year of the Reform Act (1832) an Act of Parliament had reaffirmed that night poaching was punishable, on a third conviction, by transportation; and this long remained the law of the land, in spite of the fact that many poor countrymen could not live at that time unless they supplemented their wages by poaching.

'Not so very Unreasonable'—p. 133

This is another of Leech's *Punch* cartoons (1848) and deals with the Chartist agitation. The Whigs, having forced through the Reform Act of 1832, were determined to make it the last word in constitutional reform. In opposition to both Whigs and Tories, the Chartists demanded voting by ballot (see Sydney Smith's pamphlet), the abolition of a property qualification for membership of Parliament, payment of M.P.'s, manhood suffrage, electoral reform and annual elections. All these demands (except the last) were later recognised as reasonable, and implemented. Whilst military and police precautions were taken to prevent a procession from presenting the Charter to Parliament, Leech represented the Government as not unfriendly and willing to consider Chartist demands impartially.

Great Autumn Manœuvre—p. 177

This cartoon by Sir John Tenniel (*Punch*, August 9, 1873) is really a comment on the whole period of rivalry between Gladstone and Disraeli. Both Liberals and Conservatives sought, by cautious and well-timed popular reforms, to win support among the people; and most of the reformist measures of the late nineteenth century can be traced to this necessity for outbidding the other party. In this case the issue is the extension of the franchise to the agricultural labourer. For the reaction of the privileged classes to extension of the franchise, see Sir George Chesney's comments in *The Battle of Dorking*.